ID0878904

ENGLISH
FOR EVERYONE

COURSE BOOK

LEVEL ❸ INTERMEDIATE

🔊 **FREE AUDIO**
website and app
www.dkefe.com

Author

Gill Johnson is an experienced English-language teacher, author, teacher-trainer, and conference speaker. She currently runs a large modern languages department at an international school in Sussex, UK, and spends her holidays training teachers worldwide.

Course consultant

Tim Bowen has taught English and trained teachers in more than 30 countries worldwide. He is the co-author of works on pronunciation teaching and language-teaching methodology, and author of numerous books for English-language teachers. He is currently a freelance materials writer, editor, and translator. He is a member of the Chartered Institute of Linguists.

Language consultant

Professor Susan Barduhn is an experienced English-language teacher, teacher trainer, and author, who has contributed to numerous publications. In addition to directing English-language courses in at least four different continents, she has been President of the International Association of Teachers of English as a Foreign Language, and an adviser to the British Council and the US State Department. She is currently a Professor at the School of International Training in Vermont, USA.

ENGLISH
FOR EVERYONE

COURSE BOOK

LEVEL 3 INTERMEDIATE

Penguin Random House

US Editors Allison Singer, Jenny Siklos
Editors Hayley Maher, Laura Sandford
Art Editors Rachel Aloof, Dominic Clifford
Senior Art Editor Sharon Spencer
Editorial Assistants Jessica Cawthra, Sarah Edwards
Illustrators Edwood Burn, Denise Joos, Michael Parkin, Jemma Westing
Audio Producer Liz Hammond
Managing Editor Daniel Mills
Managing Art Editor Anna Hall
Project Manager Christine Stroyan
Jacket Designer Natalie Godwin
Jacket Editor Claire Gell
Jacket Design Development Manager Sophia MTT
Producer, Pre-Production Luca Frassinetti
Producer Mary Slater
Publisher Andrew Macintyre
Art Director Karen Self
Publishing Director Jonathan Metcalf

DK India
Jacket Designer Surabhi Wadhwa
Managing Jackets Editor Saloni Singh
Senior DTP Designer Harish Aggarwal

First American Edition, 2016
Published in the United States by DK Publishing
345 Hudson Street, New York, New York 10014

Copyright © 2016 Dorling Kindersley Limited
DK, a Division of Penguin Random House LLC
16 17 18 19 20 10 9 8 7 6 5 4 3 2 1
001–284202–Jun/2016

All rights reserved.
Without limiting the rights under the copyright reserved above, no part of
this publication may be reproduced, stored in or introduced into a retrieval
system, or transmitted, in any form, or by any means (electronic,
mechanical, photocopying, recording, or otherwise), without the prior
written permission of the copyright owner.
Published in Great Britain by Dorling Kindersley Limited.

A catalog record for this book
is available from the Library of Congress.
ISBN 978-1-4654-4763-0

DK books are available at special discounts when purchased
in bulk for sales promotions, premiums, fund-raising, or educational use.
For details, contact: DK Publishing Special Markets, 345 Hudson Street,
New York, New York 10014
SpecialSales@dk.com

Printed and bound in China

All images © Dorling Kindersley Limited
For further information see: www.dkimages.com

A WORLD OF IDEAS:
SEE ALL THERE IS TO KNOW

www.dk.com

Contents

How the course works

English for Everyone is designed for people who want to teach themselves the English language. Like all language courses, it covers the core skills: grammar, vocabulary, pronunciation, listening, speaking, reading, and writing. Unlike in other courses, the skills are taught and practiced as visually as possible, using images and graphics to help you understand and remember. The best way to learn is to work through the book in order, making full use of the audio available on the website and app. Turn to the practice book at the end of each unit to reinforce your learning with additional exercises.

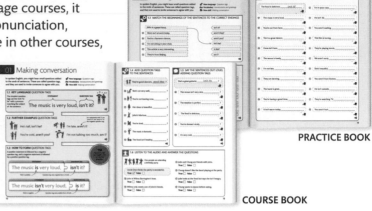

PRACTICE BOOK

COURSE BOOK

Unit number The book is divided into units. The unit number helps you keep track of your progress.

Learning points Every unit begins with a summary of the key learning points.

Modules Each unit is broken down into modules, which should be done in order. You can take a break from learning after completing any module.

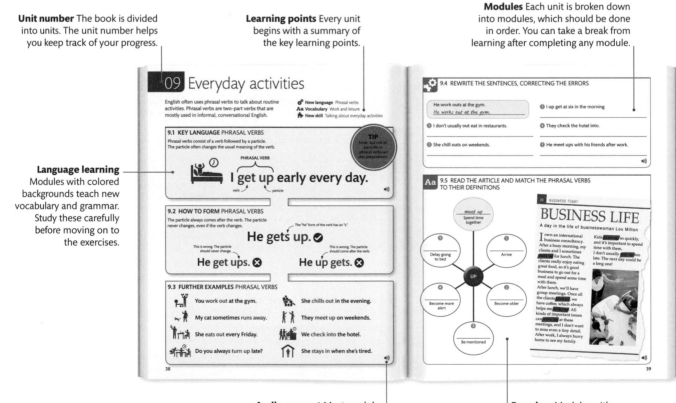

Language learning Modules with colored backgrounds teach new vocabulary and grammar. Study these carefully before moving on to the exercises.

Audio support Most modules have supporting audio recordings of native English speakers to help you improve your speaking and listening skills.

Exercises Modules with white backgrounds contain exercises that help you practice your new skills to reinforce learning.

FREE AUDIO
website and app
www.dkefe.com

Language modules

New language points are taught in carefully graded stages, starting with a simple explanation of when they are used, then offering further examples of common usage, and a detailed breakdown of how key constructions are formed.

Module number Every module is identified with a unique number, so you can track your progress and easily locate any related audio.

Module heading The teaching topic appears here, along with a brief introduction.

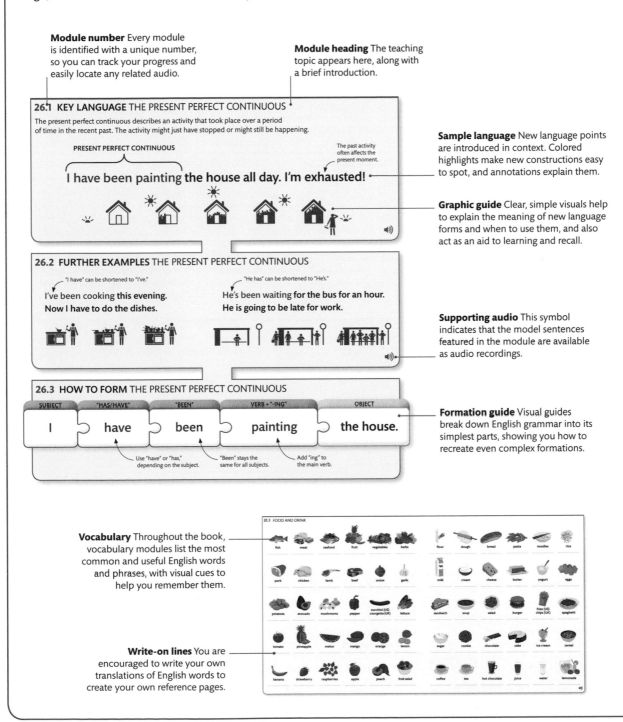

26.1 KEY LANGUAGE THE PRESENT PERFECT CONTINUOUS

The present perfect continuous describes an activity that took place over a period of time in the recent past. The activity might just have stopped or might still be happening.

PRESENT PERFECT CONTINUOUS

The past activity often affects the present moment.

I have been painting the house all day. I'm exhausted!

Sample language New language points are introduced in context. Colored highlights make new constructions easy to spot, and annotations explain them.

Graphic guide Clear, simple visuals help to explain the meaning of new language forms and when to use them, and also act as an aid to learning and recall.

26.2 FURTHER EXAMPLES THE PRESENT PERFECT CONTINUOUS

"I have" can be shortened to "I've."

I've been cooking this evening.
Now I have to do the dishes.

"He has" can be shortened to "He's."

He's been waiting for the bus for an hour.
He is going to be late for work.

Supporting audio This symbol indicates that the model sentences featured in the module are available as audio recordings.

26.3 HOW TO FORM THE PRESENT PERFECT CONTINUOUS

SUBJECT	"HAS/HAVE"	"BEEN"	VERB + "-ING"	OBJECT
I	have	been	painting	the house.

Use "have" or "has," depending on the subject.

"Been" stays the same for all subjects.

Add "ing" to the main verb.

Formation guide Visual guides break down English grammar into its simplest parts, showing you how to recreate even complex formations.

Vocabulary Throughout the book, vocabulary modules list the most common and useful English words and phrases, with visual cues to help you remember them.

Write-on lines You are encouraged to write your own translations of English words to create your own reference pages.

9

Practice modules

Each exercise is carefully graded to drill and test the language taught in the corresponding course book units. Working through the exercises alongside the course book will help you remember what you have learned and become more fluent. Every exercise is introduced with a symbol to indicate which skill is being practiced.

 GRAMMAR
Apply new language rules in different contexts.

 READING
Examine target language in real-life English contexts.

 LISTENING
Test your understanding of spoken English.

 VOCABULARY
Cement your understanding of key vocabulary.

 WRITING
Practice producing written passages of English text.

 SPEAKING
Compare your spoken English to model audio recordings.

Module number Every module is identified with a unique number, so you can easily locate answers and related audio.

Sample answer The first question of each exercise is answered for you, to help make the task easy to understand.

Supporting graphics Visual cues are given to help you understand the exercises.

Exercise instruction Every exercise is introduced with a brief instruction, telling you what you need to do.

Space for writing You are encouraged to write your answers in the book for future reference.

Supporting audio This symbol shows that the answers to the exercise are available as audio tracks. Listen to them after completing the exercise.

Speaking exercise This symbol indicates that you should say your answers out loud, then compare them to model recordings included in your audio files.

Listening exercise This symbol indicates that you should listen to an audio track in order to answer the questions in the exercise.

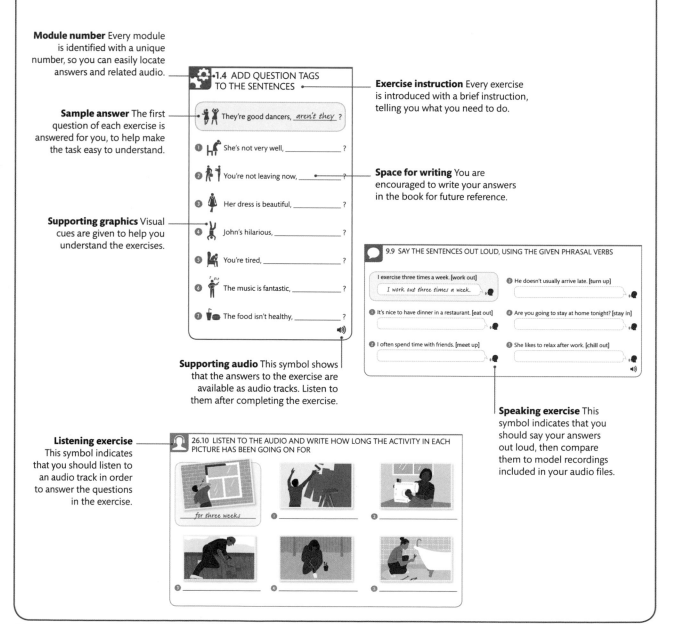

1.4 ADD QUESTION TAGS TO THE SENTENCES

They're good dancers, *aren't they* ?

❶ She's not very well, _____ ?

❷ You're not leaving now, _____ ?

❸ Her dress is beautiful, _____ ?

❹ John's hilarious, _____ ?

❺ You're tired, _____ ?

❻ The music is fantastic, _____ ?

❼ The food isn't healthy, _____ ?

9.9 SAY THE SENTENCES OUT LOUD, USING THE GIVEN PHRASAL VERBS

I exercise three times a week. [work out]
I work out three times a week.

❶ It's nice to have dinner in a restaurant. [eat out]

❷ I often spend time with friends. [meet up]

❸ He doesn't usually arrive late. [turn up]

❹ Are you going to stay at home tonight? [stay in]

❺ She likes to relax after work. [chill out]

26.10 LISTEN TO THE AUDIO AND WRITE HOW LONG THE ACTIVITY IN EACH PICTURE HAS BEEN GOING ON FOR

for three weeks

❶ _____
❷ _____
❸ _____
❹ _____
❺ _____

Audio

English for Everyone features extensive supporting audio materials. You are encouraged to use them as much as you can, to improve your understanding of spoken English, and to make your own accent and pronunciation more natural. Each file can be played, paused, and repeated as often as you like, until you are confident you understand what has been said.

LISTENING EXERCISES
This symbol indicates that you should listen to an audio track in order to answer the questions in the exercise.

SUPPORTING AUDIO
This symbol indicates that extra audio material is available for you to listen to after completing the module.

FREE AUDIO
website and app
www.dkefe.com

Track your progress

The course is designed to make it easy to monitor your progress, with regular summary and review modules. Answers are provided for every exercise, so you can see how well you have understood each teaching point.

Checklists Every unit ends with a checklist, where you can check off the new skills you have learned.

06 ✓ CHECKLIST
🔤 Letters and numbers ☐   **Aa** Contact details ☐   🧩 Exchanging personal information ☐

Review modules At the end of a group of units, you will find a more detailed review module, summarizing the language you have learned.

Check boxes Use these boxes to mark the skills you feel comfortable with. Go back and review anything you feel you need to practice further.

⚙ REVIEW THE ENGLISH YOU HAVE LEARNED IN UNITS 1–6

NEW LANGUAGE	SAMPLE SENTENCE	☑	UNIT
QUESTION TAGS	The music is very loud, isn't it? The music isn't very loud, is it?	☐	1.1, 1.3
PREPOSITIONS OF PLACE	I live on an island off the coast of Australia.	☐	3.1
FRACTIONS	The stadium was only ¾ full.	☐	4.1
DECIMALS AND PERCENTAGES	According to our survey, 55.5% of people exercise more than twice a week.	☐	4.2, 4.3
TIMES AND DATES	The meeting took place at half past two on Monday, April 6.	☐	5.1, 5.3
CONTACT DETAILS	My email address is rob@webmail.net.	☐	6.1

Answers Find the answers to every exercise printed at the back of the book.

Exercise numbers Match these numbers to the unique identifier at the top-left corner of each exercise.

Audio This symbol indicates that the answers can also be listened to.

01

1.4 ◀))
1 She's not very well, **is she**?
2 You're not leaving now, **are you**?
3 Her dress is beautiful, **isn't it**?
4 John's hilarious, **isn't he**?
5 You're tired, **aren't you**?
6 The music is fantastic, **isn't it**?
7 The food isn't healthy, **is it**?

1.5 ◀))
1 This venue isn't very nice, **is it**?
2 The weather is perfect, **isn't it**?
3 The food is delicious, **isn't it**?
4 You're dressed nicely, **aren't you**?
5 It's very cold, **isn't it**?

1.6 ◀))
1 False 2 False 3 True 4 False
5 False 6 True

1.8 ◀))
1 Great **to meet you**, too.
2 This **is Tess**.
3 I'm **delighted to meet** you, Mrs. MacIntosh.
4 Hi Cameron. **How are you doing**?
5 May **I introduce** Dev Chandera?

1.9 ◀))
1 I'm very well, thank you.
2 I'm delighted to meet you, Ms. Tate.
3 I'm very pleased to meet you, too.
4 Great to meet you.
5 Pete! Great to see you, too!

1.10 ◀))
1 Fine, thanks.
2 You, too!
3 I'm delighted to meet you, too.
4 Great to meet you.
5 I'm very well, thank you.
6 I'm very pleased to meet you.
7 Great to meet you.

01 Making conversation

In spoken English, you might hear small questions added to the ends of sentences. These are called question tags, and they are used to invite someone to agree with you.

⚙ **New language** Question tags
Aa Vocabulary Introductions and greetings
🧩 **New skill** Making conversation

1.1 KEY LANGUAGE QUESTION TAGS

The simplest question tags use the verb "to be" with a pronoun matching the subject of the sentence.

STATEMENT   QUESTION TAG

The music is very loud, isn't it?

1.2 FURTHER EXAMPLES QUESTION TAGS

 He's tall, isn't he?

You're cold, aren't you?

I'm late, aren't I?

I'm not talking too much, am I?

For statements with "I" use "aren't I?" not "amn't I?" in the negative question tag.

1.3 HOW TO FORM QUESTION TAGS

A positive statement is followed by a negative question tag, and a negative statement is followed by a positive question tag.

TIP
Question tags are mostly used in informal situations.

STATEMENT	QUESTION TAG
The music **is** very loud,	**isn't** it?

Verb is positive.   Question tag uses negative form of verb.

STATEMENT	QUESTION TAG
The music **isn't** very loud,	**is** it?

Verb is negative.   Question tag uses positive form of verb.

1.4 ADD QUESTION TAGS TO THE SENTENCES

They're good dancers, _aren't they_ ?

1. She's not very well, _____ ?

2. You're not leaving now, _____ ?

3. Her dress is beautiful, _____ ?

4. John's hilarious, _____ ?

5. You're tired, _____ ?

6. The music is fantastic, _____ ?

7. The food isn't healthy, _____ ?

1.5 SAY THE SENTENCES OUT LOUD, ADDING QUESTION TAGS

She's a great guitarist, _isn't she_ ?

1. This venue isn't very nice, _____ ?

2. The weather is perfect, _____ ?

3. The food is delicious, _____ ?

4. You're dressed nicely, _____ ?

5. It's very cold, _____ ?

1.6 LISTEN TO THE AUDIO AND ANSWER THE QUESTIONS

Five people are attending a birthday party.

Uncle Don thinks the party is wonderful.
True ☑ False ☐

1. John is Wilma Barrington's boss.
True ☐ False ☐

2. Wilma only meets one of John's friends.
True ☐ False ☐

3. Julie and Chung are friends with John.
True ☐ False ☐

4. Chung doesn't like the band playing at the party.
True ☐ False ☐

5. Julie looks at the food but says she isn't hungry.
True ☐ False ☐

6. Chung wants to dance before eating.
True ☐ False ☐

1.7 KEY LANGUAGE FORMAL AND INFORMAL CONVERSATIONS

Chatting to friends uses informal language, while greeting people at work may use formal language.

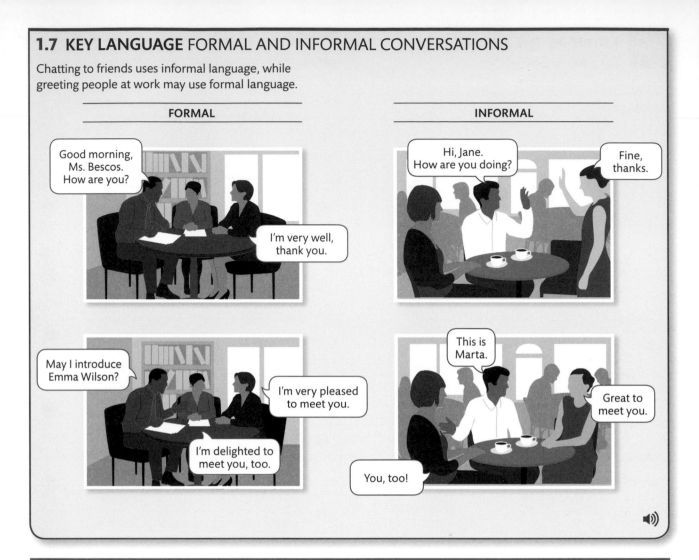

FORMAL

Good morning, Ms. Bescos. How are you?

I'm very well, thank you.

May I introduce Emma Wilson?

I'm very pleased to meet you.

I'm delighted to meet you, too.

INFORMAL

Hi, Jane. How are you doing?

Fine, thanks.

This is Marta.

Great to meet you.

You, too!

Aa 1.8 FILL IN THE GAPS USING THE PHRASES IN THE PANEL

Good evening, Mr. Fisher. _____*How are you*_____ ?

1. Great _____ , too.

2. This _____ .

3. I'm _____ you, Mrs. MacIntosh.

4. Hi Cameron. _____ ?

5. May _____ Dev Chandera?

~~How are you~~   I introduce

delighted to meet   is Tess

to meet you

How are you doing

Aa 1.9 MARK THE BEST REPLY TO EACH GREETING

All of these replies are correct, but some are more appropriate for formal or informal situations.

Hi, Jo.

Hi, Mandy. ✓

Good afternoon, Mrs. Sullivan. ☐

① Good evening, Mr. Ri. How are you?

I'm very well, thank you. ☐

Fine, thanks. ☐

② May I introduce Ruth Tate?

Great to meet you, Ruth. ☐

I'm delighted to meet you, Ms. Tate. ☐

③ I'm delighted to meet you.

I'm very pleased to meet you, too. ☐

You, too! ☐

④ This is Vicky.

I'm very pleased to meet you, too. ☐

Great to meet you. ☐

⑤ Kayar! Lovely to see you!

I'm delighted to see you, too. ☐

Pete! Great to see you, too! ☐

🔊

1.10 RESPOND TO THE AUDIO, SPEAKING OUT LOUD

May I introduce Mr. Tom Grant.

I'm delighted to meet you. 🗣

① Hi, Andrew! How are you doing?

🗣

② Great to meet you, Camilla.

🗣

③ I'm very pleased to meet you.

🗣

④ Jatinda, this is my friend, Amy.

🗣

⑤ Good morning, Mr. Watt. How are you?

🗣

⑥ May I introduce Mrs. Girdwood?

🗣

⑦ This is Shahid.

🗣

🔊

01 ✔ CHECKLIST

⚙ Question tags ☐   Aa Introductions and greetings ☐   🧩 Making conversation ☐

02 Vocabulary

2.1 COUNTRIES

Canada

United States of America / US

Mexico

Cuba

Bolivia

Peru

Chile

Argentina

Venezuela

Paraguay

Uruguay

Brazil

Algeria

Nigeria

Uganda

South Africa

Egypt

Sudan

Kenya

Portugal

Spain

Republic of Ireland / ROI

Netherlands

France

United Kingdom / UK

 **Germany**

 **Italy**

 Slovakia

 **Czech Republic**

 **Poland**

 Greece

 **Romania**

 Turkey

 Russia

 Lebanon

Saudi Arabia

United Arab Emirates / UAE

Pakistan

India

Mongolia

 China

 Thailand

 Singapore

 **Indonesia**

 **Philippines**

 South Korea

 Vietnam

 Japan

 **Australia**

 **New Zealand**

03 Where things are

English uses prepositions to talk about where things are. It is important to learn the correct prepositions for different phrases describing locations and directions.

⚙ **New language** Prepositions of place
Aa Vocabulary Countries and nationalities
🧩 **New skill** Talking about where things are

3.1 KEY LANGUAGE PREPOSITIONS OF PLACE

Many locations must have a particular preposition before them. Using the wrong preposition can change the meaning of a sentence about where things are.

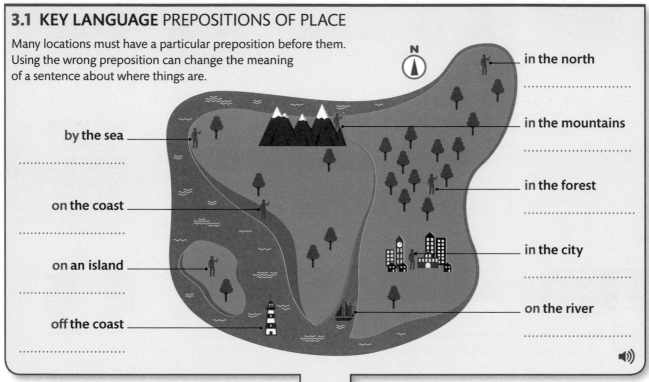

in the north
....

in the mountains
....

in the forest
....

in the city
....

on the river
....

by the sea
....

on the coast
....

on an island
....

off the coast
....

3.2 VOCABULARY COMPASS POINTS AND USEFUL PHRASES

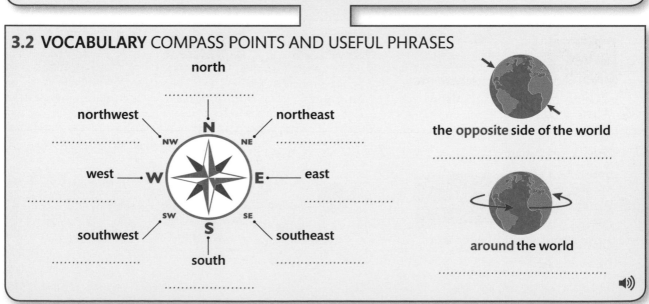

north
....

northwest
....

northeast
....

west
....

east
....

southwest
....

south
....

southeast
....

the opposite side of the world
....

around the world
....

3.3 READ THE POSTCARD AND FILL IN THE GAPS WITH THE CORRECT PREPOSITION OF PLACE

Dear Yasmin,

We're having a nice time ____on____ the island of Tenerife, which is just _____ the African coast. Today we're _____ the city of Santa Cruz. Our hotel is _____ the coast, which is great because I love being _____ the sea.

Love, Hannah

3.4 LISTEN TO THE AUDIO AND ANSWER THE QUESTIONS

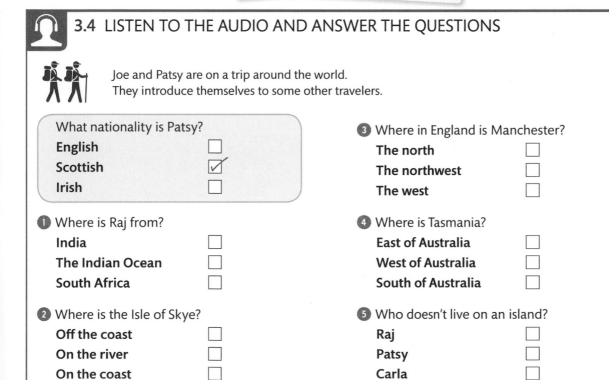

Joe and Patsy are on a trip around the world.
They introduce themselves to some other travelers.

What nationality is Patsy?

English ☐
Scottish ☑
Irish ☐

❶ Where is Raj from?

India ☐
The Indian Ocean ☐
South Africa ☐

❷ Where is the Isle of Skye?

Off the coast ☐
On the river ☐
On the coast ☐

❸ Where in England is Manchester?

The north ☐
The northwest ☐
The west ☐

❹ Where is Tasmania?

East of Australia ☐
West of Australia ☐
South of Australia ☐

❺ Who doesn't live on an island?

Raj ☐
Patsy ☐
Carla ☐

3.5 RESPOND TO THE AUDIO, SPEAKING OUT LOUD

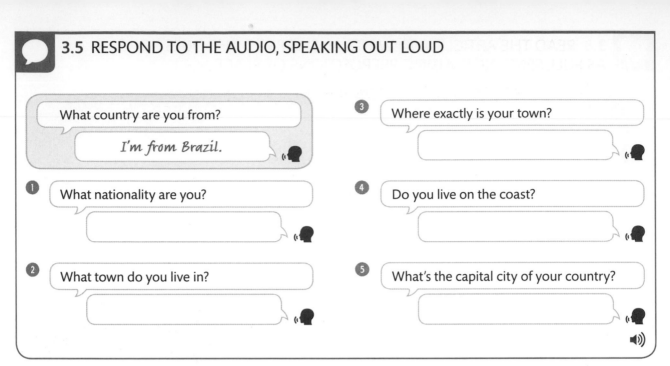

What country are you from?

I'm from Brazil.

1 What nationality are you?

2 What town do you live in?

3 Where exactly is your town?

4 Do you live on the coast?

5 What's the capital city of your country?

3.6 KEY LANGUAGE PRECISE PREPOSITIONAL PHRASES

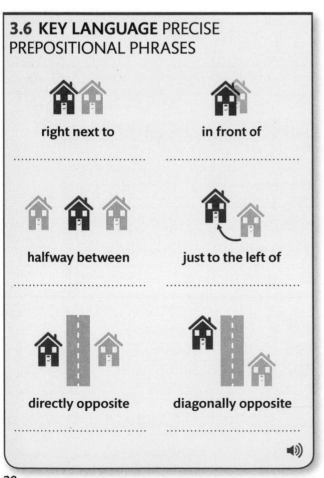

right next to

in front of

halfway between

just to the left of

directly opposite

diagonally opposite

Aa 3.7 MATCH THE PICTURES TO THE CORRECT SENTENCES

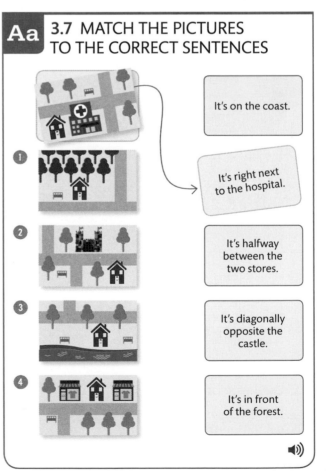

It's on the coast.

It's right next to the hospital.

It's halfway between the two stores.

It's diagonally opposite the castle.

It's in front of the forest.

3.8 READ THE ARTICLE AND WRITE ANSWERS TO THE QUESTIONS AS FULL SENTENCES, USING PREPOSITIONS OF PLACE

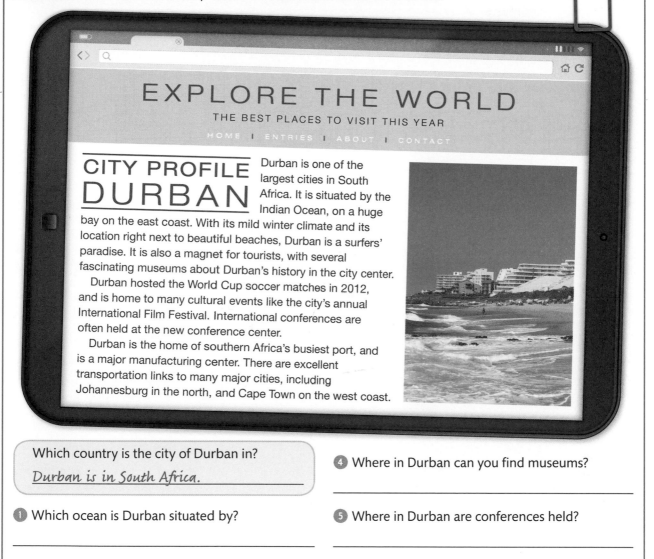

EXPLORE THE WORLD
THE BEST PLACES TO VISIT THIS YEAR
HOME I ENTRIES I ABOUT I CONTACT

CITY PROFILE
DURBAN

Durban is one of the largest cities in South Africa. It is situated by the Indian Ocean, on a huge bay on the east coast. With its mild winter climate and its location right next to beautiful beaches, Durban is a surfers' paradise. It is also a magnet for tourists, with several fascinating museums about Durban's history in the city center.

Durban hosted the World Cup soccer matches in 2012, and is home to many cultural events like the city's annual International Film Festival. International conferences are often held at the new conference center.

Durban is the home of southern Africa's busiest port, and is a major manufacturing center. There are excellent transportation links to many major cities, including Johannesburg in the north, and Cape Town on the west coast.

Which country is the city of Durban in?

Durban is in South Africa.

❶ Which ocean is Durban situated by?

❷ Which coast is Durban on?

❸ How close is the city to beaches?

❹ Where in Durban can you find museums?

❺ Where in Durban are conferences held?

❻ Where in South Africa is Johannesburg?

❼ Which coast is Cape Town on?

---

03 ✔ CHECKLIST

⚙ Prepositions of place ☐   **Aa** Countries and nationalities ☐   🧩 Talking about where things are ☐

Numbers and statistics

Fractions, decimals, and percentages are all pronounced differently in spoken English, following a few simple rules.

⚙ **New language** Numbers in spoken English
Aa Vocabulary Sports events
New skill Using numbers in conversation

4.1 KEY LANGUAGE FRACTIONS

You might see fractions written out as words. Aside from "half" and "quarter," the bottom number of a fraction is written or spoken as an ordinal number.

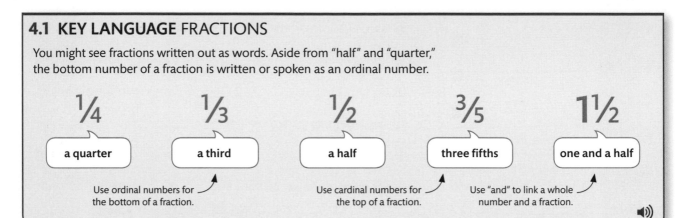

¼ — **a quarter**
⅓ — **a third**
½ — **a half**
⅗ — **three fifths**
1½ — **one and a half**

Use ordinal numbers for the bottom of a fraction.
Use cardinal numbers for the top of a fraction.
Use "and" to link a whole number and a fraction.

4.2 KEY LANGUAGE DECIMALS

Decimals are always written as numbers, not words. The decimal point is pronounced "point," and all numbers after the decimal point are spoken separately.

Decimal points are written in English using a period, or full stop.

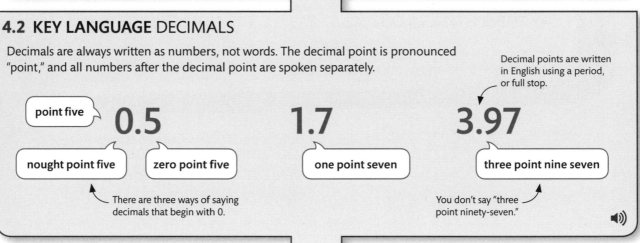

point five
0.5
nought point five **zero point five**

1.7
one point seven

3.97
three point nine seven

There are three ways of saying decimals that begin with 0.

You don't say "three point ninety-seven."

4.3 KEY LANGUAGE PERCENTAGES

The % symbol is written and spoken as "percent." You might also see "per cent" written in UK English. Percentages are normally written as numbers, not words.

The % symbol is pronounced "percent."

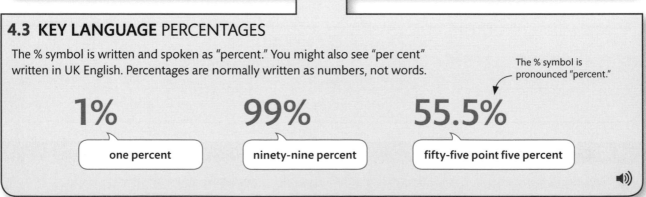

1% — **one percent**
99% — **ninety-nine percent**
55.5% — **fifty-five point five percent**

4.4 SAY THE NUMBERS OUT LOUD

³/₄ [three quarters]

① **30%**

② **0.75**

③ **⅛**

④ **82%**

⑤ **2.9**

⑥ **3½**

4.5 LISTEN TO THE AUDIO AND COMPLETE THE SENTENCES WITH NUMBERS

You will hear a sports report from the Athletics Championship.

Jerry Smith beat the 400m record by _____1.5_____ seconds.

① Kamau Mburu's time in the 400m was _____ seconds.

② Kenya holds _____ of the long-distance medals.

③ Su Chin jumped _____ meters in the high jump.

④ The Millennium Stadium was _____ full.

⑤ Lorna Davis jumped _____ meters in the long jump.

⑥ John Wood won the 800m by _____ seconds.

4.6 SAY THE SENTENCES OUT LOUD, SAYING THE NUMBERS CORRECTLY

Ed Lee jumped 8.96 meters in the long jump.

Ed Lee jumped eight point nine six meters in the long jump.

① Tony Elliot was just 30 centimeters behind Lee.

② Jessie Cope ran the 100 meters in 9.6 seconds.

③ This was 2/3 of a second faster than his last race.

④ Jenny O'Day ran the 100 meters in 10.2 seconds.

⑤ The US currently holds 19% of the medals.

04 ✔ CHECKLIST

⚙ Numbers in spoken English ☐   **Aa** Sports events ☐   🧩 Using numbers in conversation ☐

Times and dates

There are many ways of saying the time and the date in English. American and British English speakers often use different forms.

🔧 **New language** Precise times
Aa Vocabulary Dates in US and UK English
🧩 **New skill** Talking about times and dates

5.1 KEY LANGUAGE SAYING WHAT THE TIME IS

US English and informal spoken UK English use the 12-hour clock.

You might hear the 24-hour clock in public transport announcements.

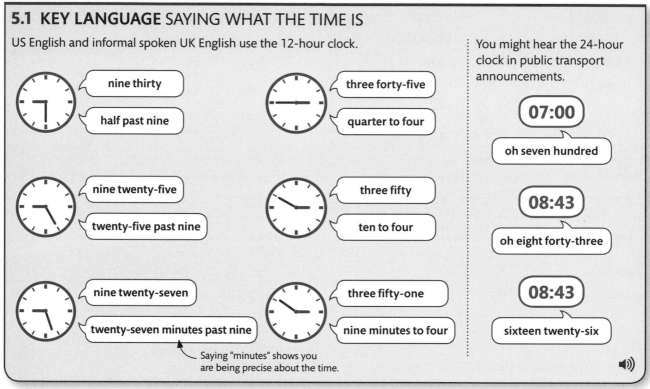

nine thirty
half past nine

nine twenty-five
twenty-five past nine

nine twenty-seven
twenty-seven minutes past nine

three forty-five
quarter to four

three fifty
ten to four

three fifty-one
nine minutes to four

07:00
oh seven hundred

08:43
oh eight forty-three

08:43
sixteen twenty-six

Saying "minutes" shows you are being precise about the time.

5.2 LISTEN TO THE AUDIO AND FILL IN THE GAPS USING THE TIMES IN THE PANEL

Sofia and Dylan are going to see a play. Dylan calls Sofia to say he will be late.

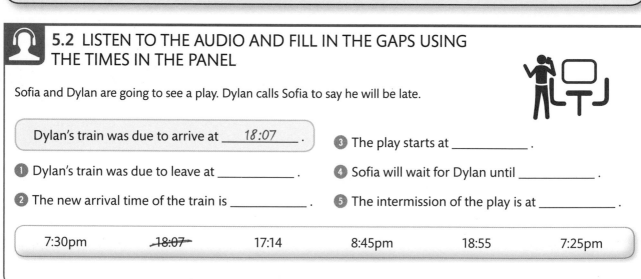

Dylan's train was due to arrive at ___18:07___ .

1 Dylan's train was due to leave at _____ .

2 The new arrival time of the train is _____ .

3 The play starts at _____ .

4 Sofia will wait for Dylan until _____ .

5 The intermission of the play is at _____ .

| 7:30pm | ~~18:07~~ | 17:14 | 8:45pm | 18:55 | 7:25pm |

5.3 KEY LANGUAGE DATES

Dates in American English are usually written with the month first. Dates in British English are usually written with the day first.

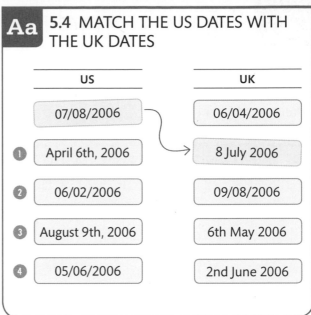

MARCH
10
WEDNESDAY

US	UK
03/10/04	10/03/04
03/10/2004	10/03/2004
March 10, 2004	10 March 2004
March 10th, 2004	10th March 2004

March tenth, two thousand and four

the tenth of March, two thousand and four

🔊

Aa 5.4 MATCH THE US DATES WITH THE UK DATES

US	UK
07/08/2006	06/04/2006
① April 6th, 2006	8 July 2006
② 06/02/2006	09/08/2006
③ August 9th, 2006	6th May 2006
④ 05/06/2006	2nd June 2006

5.5 LOOK AT THE POSTER, THEN RESPOND TO THE AUDIO, SPEAKING OUT LOUD

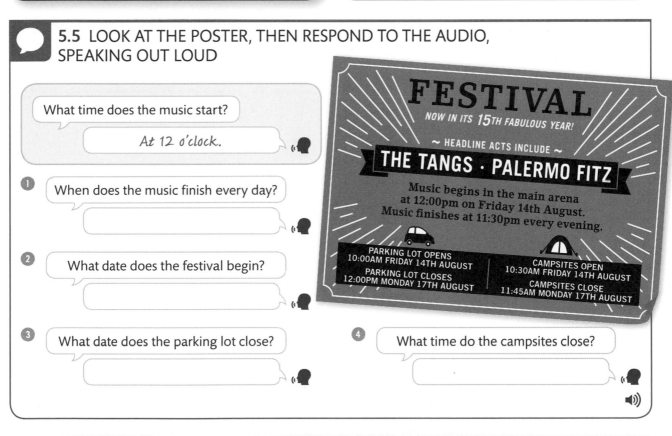

What time does the music start?

At 12 o'clock. 🗣

① When does the music finish every day?

🗣

② What date does the festival begin?

🗣

③ What date does the parking lot close?

🗣

④ What time do the campsites close?

🗣

🔊

FESTIVAL
NOW IN ITS **15**TH FABULOUS YEAR!
~ HEADLINE ACTS INCLUDE ~
THE TANGS · PALERMO FITZ
Music begins in the main arena at 12:00pm on Friday 14th August.
Music finishes at 11:30pm every evening.

PARKING LOT OPENS
10:00AM FRIDAY 14TH AUGUST
PARKING LOT CLOSES
12:00PM MONDAY 17TH AUGUST

CAMPSITES OPEN
10:30AM FRIDAY 14TH AUGUST
CAMPSITES CLOSE
11:45AM MONDAY 17TH AUGUST

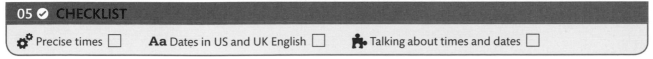

05 ✓ CHECKLIST

⚙ Precise times ☐   Aa Dates in US and UK English ☐   🧩 Talking about times and dates ☐

06 Contact details

Telephone numbers, street addresses, email addresses, and web addresses are expressed in slightly different ways in US and UK English.

⚙ **New language** Letters and numbers
Aa Vocabulary Contact details
🧩 **New skill** Exchanging personal information

6.1 VOCABULARY CONTACT DETAILS

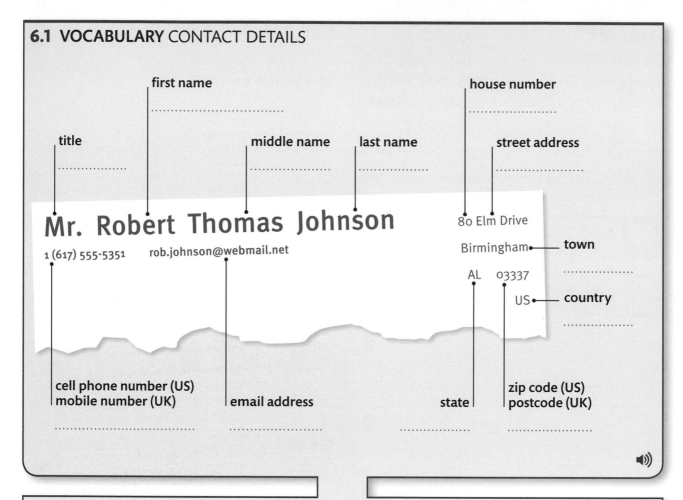

first name

house number

title

middle name   last name

street address

Mr. Robert Thomas Johnson

1 (617) 555-5351   rob.johnson@webmail.net

80 Elm Drive

Birmingham ● ── **town**

AL   03337

US ● ── **country**

cell phone number (US)
mobile number (UK)

email address

state

zip code (US)
postcode (UK)

6.2 PRONUNCIATION WEBSITES AND EMAILS

In spoken English, ".com," "@," and ".co.uk" are pronounced as follows:

www.domain.com   **gill.smith99@domain.com**   **gill.smith99@domain.co.uk**

dot com   at domain dot com   at domain dot co dot UK

6.3 READ THE BUSINESS CARD AND WRITE ANSWERS TO THE QUESTIONS AS FULL SENTENCES

Jonathan William Smith
2629 Gateway Street
Portland, OR
97205

(503) 225-3500
jonny@jonathansmithfilms.com

What is Mr. Smith's first name?

His first name is Jonathan.

1️⃣ What is his middle name?

_____

2️⃣ What is his house number?

_____

3️⃣ What town does he live in?

_____

4️⃣ What is his zip code?

_____

5️⃣ What is his cell phone number?

_____

6.4 LISTEN TO THE AUDIO AND WRITE THE PLACE NAMES THAT ARE SPELLED OUT

Illinois

6 _____

1 _____   7 _____

2 _____   8 _____

3 _____   9 _____

4 _____   10 _____

5 _____   11 _____

6.5 ANSWER THE QUESTIONS BY SPELLING THE PLACE NAMES OUT LOUD

How do you spell "Northville?"

N-O-R-T-H-V-I-L-L-E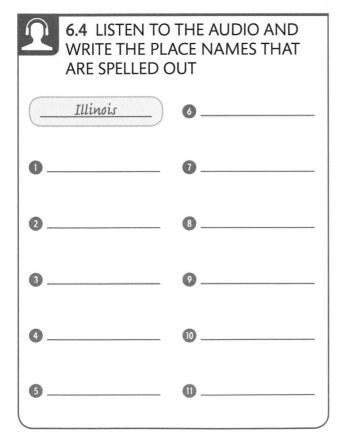

1 How do you spell "Chicago?"

2 How do you spell "Madagascar?"

3 How do you spell "Beijing?"

4 How do you spell "Arkansas?"

6.6 PRONUNCIATION NUMBERS

In American English, the number "0" is pronounced "zero," and repeated numbers are said individually.
In British English, many different pronunciations are possible for 0 and rows of repeated numbers.

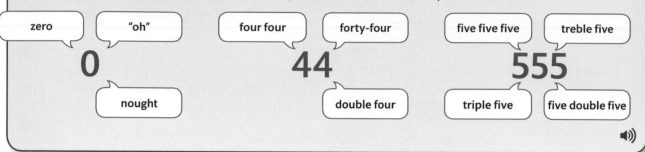

| zero | "oh" | | four four | forty-four | | five five five | treble five |

0   **44**   **555**

| nought | | double four | triple five | five double five |

🔊

6.7 LISTEN TO THE AUDIO AND ANSWER THE QUESTIONS

 Joe is swapping contact details with the new
friends he met on his trip around the world.

What is Steve and Eva's street address?
100a Valley Road

❶ What is Steve and Eva's phone number?
_____

❷ What is Raj's house number?
_____

❸ What is Raj's email address?
_____

❹ What state does Will live in?
_____

❺ What is Will's zip code?
_____

❻ What is Joe's street address?
_____

❼ What is Joe's postcode?
_____

6.8 PRONUNCIATION VOWEL SOUNDS

The names that you heard in the dialogue include
different vowel sounds. Practice saying the
names below, then listen and repeat.

Eva   **Joe**

Steve   **Will**   **Raj**

🔊

6.9 LOOK AT THE LUGGAGE TAG, THEN RESPOND TO THE AUDIO, SPEAKING OUT LOUD

Who does the missing luggage belong to?

Jude Jones

NAME: Jude Jones
ADDRESS: 21 Combe Avenue
Minehead, Somerset TA54 6AY
TELEPHONE: 00 44 1191 278 594
MOBILE: 07700900742
EMAIL: judy219@webmail.net

❶ What is the name of her street?

❷ Spell out the name of her town.

❸ What's her mobile number?

❹ What is her email address?

---

06 ✔ CHECKLIST

⚙ Letters and numbers ☐   **Aa** Contact details ☐   🧩 Exchanging personal information ☐

♻ REVIEW THE ENGLISH YOU HAVE LEARNED IN UNITS 1–6

NEW LANGUAGE	SAMPLE SENTENCE	☑	UNIT
QUESTION TAGS	The music is very loud, isn't it? The music isn't very loud, is it?	☐	1.1, 1.3
PREPOSITIONS OF PLACE	I live on an island off the coast of Australia.	☐	3.1
FRACTIONS	The stadium was only ¾ full.	☐	4.1
DECIMALS AND PERCENTAGES	According to our survey, 55.5% of people exercise more than twice a week.	☐	4.2, 4.3
TIMES AND DATES	The meeting took place at half past two on Monday, April 6.	☐	5.1, 5.3
CONTACT DETAILS	My email address is rob@webmail.net.	☐	6.1

Talking about jobs

English uses the words "job" and "work" in a variety of contexts to talk about different professions, working conditions, and career paths.

⚙ **New language** "Job" and "work"
Aa Vocabulary Jobs and professions
🧩 **New skill** Talking about your career

7.1 VOCABULARY JOBS

architect

electrician

musician

flight attendant

firefighter

travel agent

mechanic

fashion designer

hairdresser

plumber

surgeon

pilot

butcher

journalist

vet

writer

Aa 7.2 READ THE JOB ADVERTISEMENTS AND WRITE THE HIGHLIGHTED WORDS NEXT TO THEIR DEFINITIONS

JOB LISTINGS

URGENTLY WANTED: Trainee hairdresser, 30 hours per week, divided between part-time work in the salon and part-time work at our Hair Academy.

SPORTS JOURNALIST NEEDED: Attractive salary of $40,000 per year, and generous annual vacation. This position is full-time.

PART-TIME BUTCHER NEEDED FOR BUSY LOCAL SHOP! We offer a competitive wage of $15 per hour and the possibility of overtime work for the right candidate.

ARCHITECTURAL PRACTICE is looking for an intern for six months. No salary is offered, but the position may lead to a full-time job.

FIREFIGHTERS REQUIRED URGENTLY. Are you fit and healthy? Happy to work an eight-hour shift? Apply online with your CV now.

Someone who is learning a job.　　=　*trainee*

1　Work in addition to your set hours.　　=　_____

2　Describes a complete working week.　　=　_____

3　Someone who does unpaid work to gain experience.　　=　_____

4　A period of work of a set number of hours.　　=　_____

5　A fixed amount of money paid per year, often monthly.　　=　_____

6　Describes an incomplete working week.　　=　_____

7　A fixed number of days off work per year.　　=　_____

8　A fixed amount of money paid per hour, often weekly.　　=　_____

🔊

Aa 7.3 REWRITE THE HIGHLIGHTED WORDS, CORRECTING THE ERRORS

trainee

1　_____

2　_____

3　_____

4　_____

5　_____

Dear Ms. Cox,

I am very excited to hear that your company needs a traineee architect. I worked as an inten at an architecture firm last year, and believe that I have the skills and experience needed for this job. I am happy to work overhours, and would expect a wage of $30,000 per year. I am ideally looking for fulltime work, but would also be willing to consider a half-time job.

Yours sincerely,

Joshua Adams

7.4 KEY LANGUAGE "JOB" OR "WORK"

The words "job" and "work" are commonly confused in English.

I enjoy my job.

"Job" can only be a noun.
It cannot be a verb.

"Work" can be a noun.

I enjoy my work.
I work in an office.

It can also
be a verb.

I'm looking for a job.

"Job" is used for a specific role.
It is a countable noun.

I have so much work to do.

"Work" is uncountable,
and used for general activities.

I start work at 9 o'clock.

I get to work by bus.

English uses "work" to talk about working hours and travel.

7.5 FILL IN THE GAPS WITH "JOB" OR "WORK"

I am looking for a new ___*job*___ .

1 This is really hard _____ .

2 I can't come as I have to _____ late.

3 It is a difficult _____, but I love it!

4 It took me years to find a _____ I love.

5 I have a lot of _____ to finish.

6 I really want to _____ in marketing.

7 I have a part-time _____ .

8 Do you get to _____ by car or train?

9 What time do you finish _____ ?

10 Tyler wants to leave his _____ .

7.6 LISTEN TO THE AUDIO, THEN NUMBER THE PICTURES IN THE ORDER THEY ARE DESCRIBED

Aa 7.7 READ THE ARTICLE AND MATCH THE HIGHLIGHTED WORDS TO THEIR DEFINITIONS

BUSINESS TODAY

TWO CAREERS

Teacher Selim Hussain and financial consultant Josie MacDonald talk to Joan Riddon about their career paths since finishing their studies.

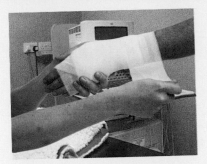

SELIM: After I completed my advanced studies in nursing, I worked in teaching hospitals and enjoyed a fabulously interesting career. At 32 I had a very demanding role in emergency medicine.

Once I became a father and there were some extra stresses at work, it became too much and I decided to resign, despite loving the work. I was lucky because one of my old professors contacted me and I began teaching part-time. Training nurses is the best job in the world!

JOSIE: My first job was as a financial assistant. This was great experience and it helped me get a job as a corporate banker. I always met my targets, so I was quickly promoted and rewarded with large pay raises. I was quite wealthy by the time I was 35.

Then came the worldwide financial slump. My bank lost money and many highly paid executives lost their jobs, including me. I was now unemployed for the first time in my working life. I worked freelance, as a consultant, and then opened my own consultancy, which now employs 50 staff.

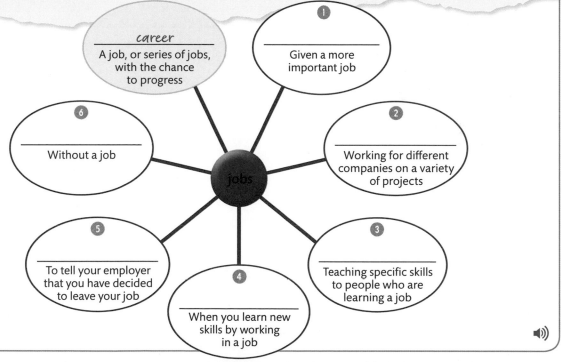

career
A job, or series of jobs, with the chance to progress

1. _____
Given a more important job

2. _____
Working for different companies on a variety of projects

3. _____
Teaching specific skills to people who are learning a job

4. _____
When you learn new skills by working in a job

5. _____
To tell your employer that you have decided to leave your job

6. _____
Without a job

jobs

---

07 ✓ CHECKLIST

⚙ "Job" and "work" ☐   **Aa** Jobs and professions ☐   🧩 Talking about your career ☐

08 Routine and free time

You can use adverbs of frequency to talk accurately about your daily routine and how often you do work and leisure activities.

⚙ **New language** Adverbs of frequency
Aa Vocabulary Leisure activities
✦ **New skill** Talking about routines

8.1 KEY LANGUAGE ADVERBS OF FREQUENCY

Adverbs of frequency sit between the subject of the sentence and the main verb.

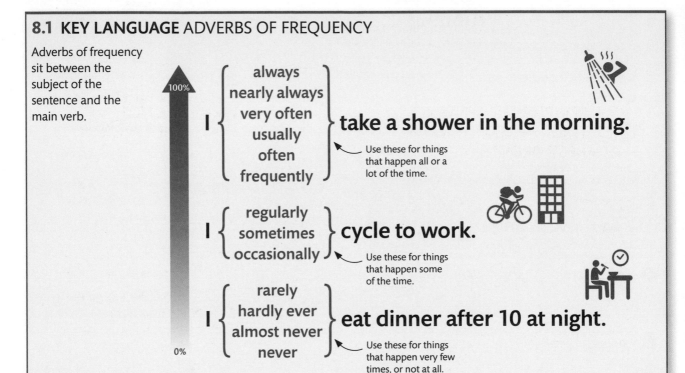

100%

I
- always
- nearly always
- very often
- usually
- often
- frequently

take a shower in the morning.

Use these for things that happen all or a lot of the time.

I
- regularly
- sometimes
- occasionally

cycle to work.

Use these for things that happen some of the time.

I
- rarely
- hardly ever
- almost never
- never

eat dinner after 10 at night.

Use these for things that happen very few times, or not at all.

0%

8.2 CROSS OUT THE INCORRECT WORDS TO MAKE PAIRS OF SENTENCES WITH SIMILAR MEANINGS

| We go to the theater a few times a year. | = | We **occasionally** / ~~often~~ go to the theater. |

① We spend every Christmas together. = We **usually** / **always** spend Christmas together.

② It rains here about three times a week. = It **frequently** / **hardly ever** rains here.

③ She goes swimming six days a week. = She **very often** / **sometimes** goes swimming.

④ They go to the gym twice a week. = They **regularly** / **nearly always** go to the gym.

⑤ I stay late at work about once a month. = I **often** / **rarely** stay late at work.

8.3 KEY LANGUAGE WORD ORDER

You can also describe frequency with more precise expressions.
Unlike adverbs of frequency, these must sit at the end of a phrase.

The verb usually goes after the adverb of frequency.

Precise expressions usually go at the end of a phrase.

I { often / regularly / hardly ever } go running.

I go running { five times a week. / every Tuesday. / once a year. }

8.4 REWRITE THE SENTENCES, PUTTING THE WORDS IN THE CORRECT ORDER

occasionally | a book. | reads | He

He occasionally reads a book.

1. once a week. | play | We | tennis

_____

2. home | rarely | They | get | early.

_____

3. breakfast | every morning. | She | eats

_____

4. hardly ever | I | TV. | watch

_____

5. cooks | nearly always | He | dinner.

_____

6. the dentist | twice a year. | We | see

_____

8.5 REWRITE THE NOTE, CORRECTING THE ERRORS

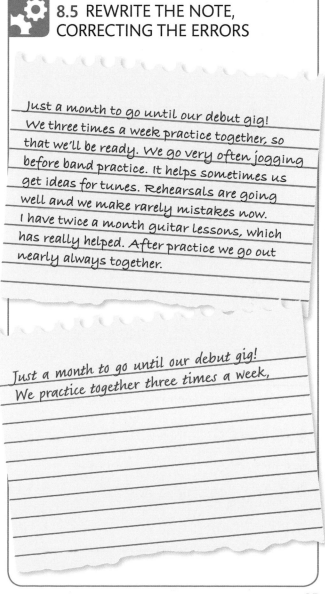

Just a month to go until our debut gig!
We three times a week practice together, so
that we'll be ready. We go very often jogging
before band practice. It helps sometimes us
get ideas for tunes. Rehearsals are going
well and we make rarely mistakes now.
I have twice a month guitar lessons, which
has really helped. After practice we go out
nearly always together.

Just a month to go until our debut gig!
We practice together three times a week,

8.6 KEY LANGUAGE WORD ORDER WITH "BE"

If the main verb in a sentence is "be," adverbs of frequency go after the verb, not before it.

Adverbs of frequency go before most verbs.

I often take the train.

The traffic is often very bad.

Adverbs of frequency go after the verb "be."

8.7 FURTHER EXAMPLES WORD ORDER WITH "BE"

The weather is usually nice here.

I'm always tired in the morning.

He's often late for meetings.

You're hardly ever sick.

8.8 MARK THE SENTENCES THAT ARE CORRECT

I carry nearly always a bag. ☐
I nearly always carry a bag. ☑

1. My house is sometimes too cold. ☐
   My house sometimes is too cold. ☐

2. She almost never walks to work. ☐
   She walks almost never to work. ☐

3. It very often is his fault. ☐
   It is very often his fault. ☐

4. They are rarely at home. ☐
   They rarely are at home. ☐

5. He has usually coffee with his lunch. ☐
   He usually has coffee with his lunch. ☐

6. My boss hardly ever is angry with me. ☐
   My boss is hardly ever angry with me. ☐

7. We often invite friends to our house. ☐
   We invite often friends to our house. ☐

8.9 SAY THE SENTENCES OUT LOUD, PUTTING THE ADVERB OF FREQUENCY IN THE CORRECT PLACE

I get up early. [rarely]

I rarely get up early.

1. She has lunch with her friends. [frequently]

2. He meets clients in London. [occasionally]

3. It's great to see you. [always]

4. You're late for work. [almost never]

5. I read on train trips. [usually]

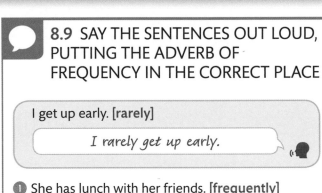

8.10 LISTEN TO THE AUDIO AND WRITE HOW OFTEN EACH ACTIVITY IS DONE

Lucy is an artist who has recently retired and moved to a small town. Her friend Michael is asking her about her new life.

often

1 _____

2 _____

3 _____

4 _____

5 _____

occasionally   frequently   always

often   hardly ever   rarely

8.11 READ THE ARTICLE AND ANSWER THE QUESTIONS

YOUR HEALTH

BEACH LIVING

Renshu talks about his new life in Barbados

When my wife Zoe and I lived in London, every day was stressful. We almost never went out, because we were too tired. One day I saw this hotel and diving center for sale in Barbados. We left our jobs, bought the business and moved to paradise! Now we work as diving instructors. After breakfast, I usually check the diving gear and load it onto the boat. Zoe occasionally does breakfast for our guests, but our staff usually do that. Zoe and I teach diving courses five days a week. We miss our families and friends, but we regularly call our parents, and visit friends in London twice a year. We love our new life!

Renshu and Zoe never went out in London.
True ☐   **False** ☐   **Not given** ☑

1 Zoe usually checks the diving gear.
True ☐   **False** ☐   **Not given** ☐

2 Renshu and Zoe's staff usually make breakfast.
True ☐   **False** ☐   **Not given** ☐

3 Renshu and Zoe rarely teach diving courses.
True ☐   **False** ☐   **Not given** ☐

4 Renshu and Zoe frequently call their parents.
True ☐   **False** ☐   **Not given** ☐

5 Renshu and Zoe's friends sometimes visit them.
True ☐   **False** ☐   **Not given** ☐

08 ✓ CHECKLIST

⚙ Adverbs of frequency ☐   **Aa** Leisure activities ☐   🧩 Talking about routines ☐

09 Everyday activities

English often uses phrasal verbs to talk about routine activities. Phrasal verbs are two-part verbs that are mostly used in informal, conversational English.

⚙ **New language** Phrasal verbs
Aa Vocabulary Work and leisure
🧩 **New skill** Talking about everyday activities

9.1 KEY LANGUAGE PHRASAL VERBS

Phrasal verbs consist of a verb followed by a particle. The particle often changes the usual meaning of the verb.

TIP
Most, but not all, particles in phrasal verbs are also prepositions.

PHRASAL VERB

I get up early every day.

verb — particle

🔊

9.2 HOW TO FORM PHRASAL VERBS

The particle always comes after the verb. The particle never changes, even if the verb changes.

The "he" form of the verb has an "s."

He gets up. ✓

This is wrong. The particle should never change.

He get ups. ✗

This is wrong. The particle should come after the verb.

He up gets. ✗

9.3 FURTHER EXAMPLES PHRASAL VERBS

 You work out at the gym.

 She chills out in the evening.

 My cat sometimes runs away.

 They meet up on weekends.

 She eats out every Friday.

 We check into the hotel.

 Do you always turn up late?

 She stays in when she's tired.

🔊

9.4 REWRITE THE SENTENCES, CORRECTING THE ERRORS

> He **work outs** at the gym.
> *He works out at the gym.*

1 I don't usually **out eat** in restaurants.

_____

2 She **chill outs** on weekends.

_____

3 I **up get** at six in the morning

_____

4 They **check** the hotel **into**.

_____

5 He **meet ups** with his friends after work.

🔊

Aa 9.5 READ THE ARTICLE AND MATCH THE PHRASAL VERBS TO THEIR DEFINITIONS

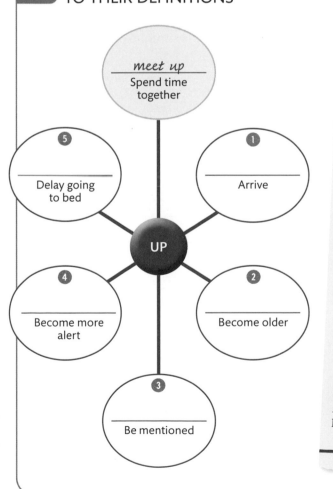

meet up
Spend time together

5
_____
Delay going to bed

1
_____
Arrive

UP

4
_____
Become more alert

2
_____
Become older

3
_____
Be mentioned

26 **BUSINESS TODAY**

BUSINESS LIFE

A day in the life of businesswoman Lou Milton

I own an international business consultancy. After a busy morning, my clients and I sometimes **meet up** for lunch. The clients really enjoy eating great food, so it's good business to go out for a meal and spend some time with them.

After lunch, we'll have group meetings. Once all the clients **turn up**, we have coffee, which always helps me **wake up**. All kinds of important issues can **come up** at these meetings, and I don't want to miss even a tiny detail. After work, I always hurry home to see my family.

Kids **grow up** so quickly, and it's important to spend time with them. I don't usually **stay up** too late. The next day could be a long one!

🔊

9.6 KEY LANGUAGE PHRASAL VERBS IN DIFFERENT TENSES

When phrasal verbs are used in different tenses,
the verb changes but the particle remains the same.

The particle
never changes.

PRESENT SIMPLE	I work **out** every week.
PAST SIMPLE	I worked **out** yesterday.
PRESENT CONTINUOUS	I am working **out** right now.
FUTURE WITH "WILL"	I will work **out** tomorrow.

◀))

9.7 REWRITE THE SENTENCES, CORRECTING THE ERRORS

I just **chill out** right now.
I'm just chilling out right now.

① Don't **running away** from me!

_____

② She **stays in** last night.

_____

③ We **are meeting up** last Thursday.

_____

④ She **ate out** next Saturday.

_____

⑤ He **turns up** late to work yesterday.

_____

◀))

9.8 LISTEN TO THE AUDIO AND ANSWER THE QUESTIONS

Teresa meets her friend Paul for coffee, and they talk about what they've been doing.

Paul arrived at work on time today.
True ☐   **False** ☐   **Not given** ☑

① Teresa never gets up early.
True ☐   **False** ☐   **Not given** ☐

② Teresa thinks it's important to relax.
True ☐   **False** ☐   **Not given** ☐

③ Teresa likes exercising.
True ☐   **False** ☐   **Not given** ☐

④ Paul will see his best friend on Saturday.
True ☐   **False** ☐   **Not given** ☐

⑤ Paul won't go to a restaurant this weekend.
True ☐   **False** ☐   **Not given** ☐

9.9 SAY THE SENTENCES OUT LOUD, USING THE GIVEN PHRASAL VERBS

I exercise three times a week. **[work out]**

I work out three times a week.

1 It's nice to have dinner in a restaurant. **[eat out]**

2 I often spend time with friends. **[meet up]**

3 He doesn't usually arrive late. **[turn up]**

4 Are you going to stay at home tonight? **[stay in]**

5 She likes to relax after work. **[chill out]**

Aa 9.10 LOOK AT THE PICTURES AND USE PHRASAL VERBS TO COMPLETE THE SENTENCES

They are _____*checking into*_____ the hotel.

1 I usually _____ on weekends.

2 We _____ last night.

3 She's _____ at the gym.

4 We're going to _____ tomorrow.

5 The bus has _____ .

Vocabulary

10.1 THE BODY

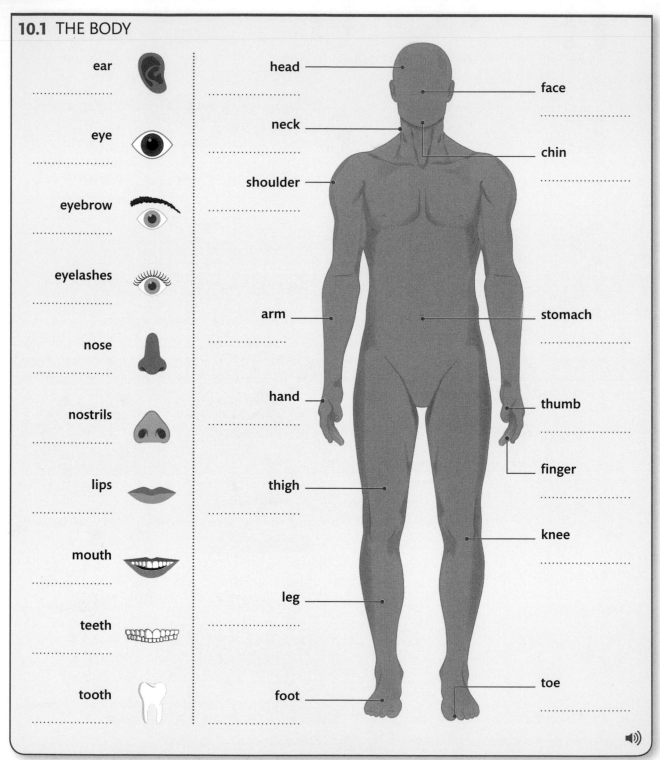

ear
....

eye
....

eyebrow
....

eyelashes
....

nose
....

nostrils
....

lips
....

mouth
....

teeth
....

tooth
....

head
....

face
....

neck
....

chin
....

shoulder
....

arm
....

stomach
....

hand
....

thumb
....

finger
....

thigh
....

knee
....

leg
....

foot
....

toe
....

10.2 HAIR

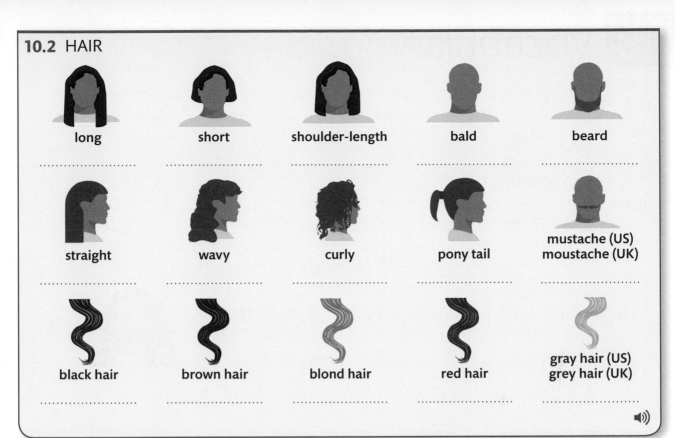

long

short

shoulder-length

bald

beard

straight

wavy

curly

pony tail

mustache (US)
moustache (UK)

black hair

brown hair

blond hair

red hair

gray hair (US)
grey hair (UK)

10.3 APPEARANCE

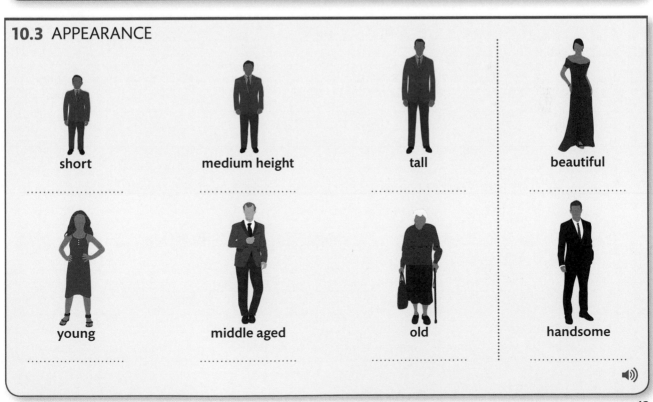

short

medium height

tall

beautiful

young

middle aged

old

handsome

11 Describing people

You often use more than one adjective in a row, for example when describing people. In English, adjectives must be written in a particular order, according to their meaning.

⚙ **New language** Adjective order
Aa Vocabulary Adjectives for describing people
🧩 **New skill** Describing people in detail

11.1 KEY LANGUAGE ADJECTIVE ORDER

The meaning of an adjective decides its order in a sentence. Opinions come first, followed by different types of facts.

Fact adjectives also have their own order, depending on their meaning.

TIP
Don't use more than two or three adjectives in a sentence.

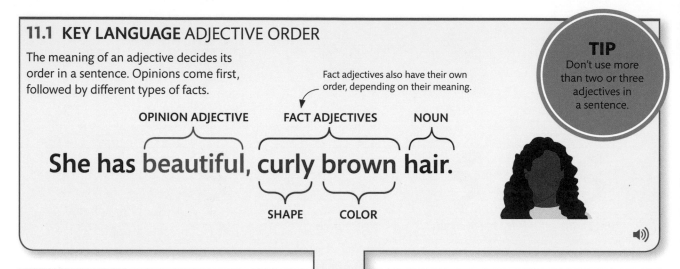

OPINION ADJECTIVE   FACT ADJECTIVES   NOUN

She has beautiful, curly brown hair.

SHAPE   COLOR

11.2 KEY LANGUAGE ADJECTIVE ORDER IN DETAIL

	OPINION	SIZE	SHAPE	AGE	COLOR	NOUN
She has	beautiful,		curly		brown	hair.
He is a		tall,	slim	old		man.

⚙ 11.3 WRITE THE WORDS FROM THE PANEL IN THE CORRECT GROUPS

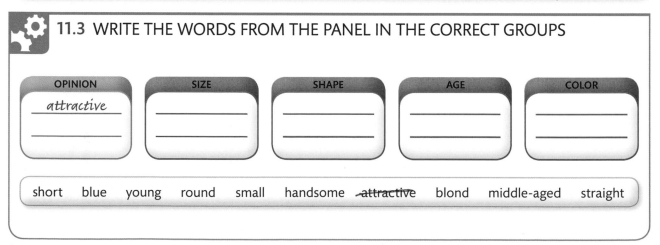

OPINION	SIZE	SHAPE	AGE	COLOR
attractive				

short   blue   young   round   small   handsome   ~~attractive~~   blond   middle-aged   straight

11.4 REWRITE THE SENTENCES, PUTTING THE WORDS IN THE CORRECT ORDER

She | has | hair. | blond | straight | short

She has short, straight, blond hair.

① She | has | brown | large | eyes. | round

_____

② He | has | blue | big | beautiful | eyes.

_____

③ He | is an | middle-aged | attractive | man.

_____

④ He | has a | red | beard. | curly | long

_____

⑤ He | is a | man. | young | thin | short

_____

⑥ She | has | red | hair. | attractive | wavy

_____

⑦ She | has | brown | eyes. | round | small

_____

🔊

11.5 LISTEN TO THE AUDIO AND MATCH THE NAMES TO THE PORTRAITS

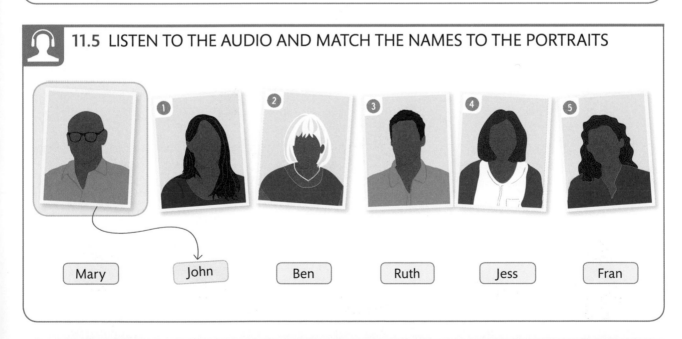

Mary   John   Ben   Ruth   Jess   Fran

11 ✓ CHECKLIST

⚙ Adjective order ☐   **Aa** Adjectives for describing people ☐   👥 Describing people in detail ☐

45

12.1 CLOTHES

t-shirt

shirt

collar

suit

pajamas

shorts

blouse

tie

dress

skirt

cardigan

pants (US)
trousers (UK)

jeans

sweater (US)
jumper (UK)

coat

jacket

raincoat

socks

boots

shoes

high-heels

sandals

sneakers (US)
trainers (UK)

12.2 ACCESSORIES AND STYLES

hat

purse (US)
handbag (UK)

scarf

gloves

laces

belt

buttons

zipper (US)
zip (UK)

smart

casual

12.3 CLOTHING MATERIALS

plain

polka dot (US)
spotted (UK)

striped

checked

woolen hat (US)
woollen hat (UK)

silk scarf

denim jacket

leather bag

cotton socks

suede boots

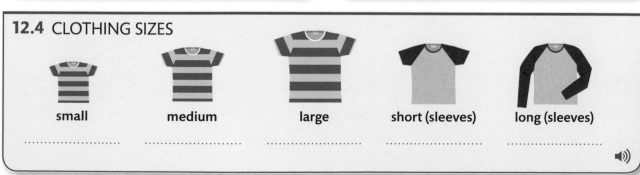

12.4 CLOTHING SIZES

small

medium

large

short (sleeves)

long (sleeves)

13 What I'm wearing

The present continuous is used to talk about ongoing actions that are happening now. It also describes the current state of things, such as what a person is wearing.

⚙ **New language** Present continuous
Aa Vocabulary Clothes and fashion
🧩 **New skill** Describing clothes

13.1 KEY LANGUAGE PRESENT CONTINUOUS

The present continuous is formed using the verb "to be" and the present participle.

She is wearing a red dress.

The present continuous uses the verb "be."

Add "-ing" to the main verb.

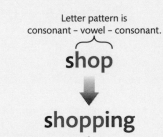

13.2 HOW IT IS FORMED PRESENT PARTICIPLES

The present participle is usually formed by adding "-ing" to the end of the verb. Some participles are formed slightly differently.

Main verb.

wear

⬇

wearing

Add "-ing" to form regular present participles.

Last letter is "e."

choose

⬇

choosing

Leave out "e" and add "-ing."

Last letters are "ie."

tie

⬇

tying

Change "ie" to "y."

Letter pattern is consonant – vowel – consonant.

shop

⬇

shopping

Double the last letter, unless it's "w" or "y."

⚙ 13.3 FILL IN THE GAPS BY PUTTING THE VERBS IN THE PRESENT CONTINUOUS

I _____ *am shopping* _____ **(shop)** for a new wool cardigan.

① They _____ **(buy)** pink cotton dresses.

② I _____ **(wear)** my new leather sandals.

③ He _____ **(try on)** different suits.

④ She _____ **(mend)** her yellow polka dot shirt.

13.4 READ THE BLOG AND ANSWER THE QUESTIONS

Jane's style

HOME | FASHION | BEAUTY | ABOUT | CONTACT

 POSTED TUESDAY, 11:24AM

CREATING YOUR SUMMER STYLE

Summer's coming, so it's time to think about shopping for the new season's gorgeous styles!

This summer's designs are inspired by the dresses of the 1920s and 1950s. There are so many beautiful clothes this season that it makes it difficult when deciding between a cotton or wool cardigan or a silk dress. I'm currently wearing a light-blue dress with a leather belt from a wonderful new collection by Belinda Flynn.

Other amazing items in this collection include cotton cardigans with zips instead of buttons, and shirts with wide collars. I tuck the flowing shirts into smart skirts for work. To make the outfit more casual, I like tying a silk scarf around my waist. If I'm going out in the evening, the only option is Flynn's knee-length silk dress. Wearing a pair of No. 43's fashionable white high heels completes the look.

ABOUT ME

I'm a fashion writer living and working in London. As well as writing about the latest trends, I also enjoy taking photographs of interesting clothes and shoes that I see when I'm walking around the city. Browsing in fabulous clothing stores, trying on clothes, and buying them is my passion. I call it research!

Jane finds it hard to decide what new clothes to buy.
True ☑ **False** ☐

❶ Jane is wearing a light-blue dress with a leather belt.
True ☐ **False** ☐

❷ Belinda Flynn's cotton cardigans have wide collars.
True ☐ **False** ☐

❸ Jane wears a casual skirt to work.
True ☐ **False** ☐

❹ No. 43 is a great shop for buying silk dresses.
True ☐ **False** ☐

❺ White high heels are fashionable this summer.
True ☐ **False** ☐

❻ Jane is a fashion writer living in New York.
True ☐ **False** ☐

❼ Jane likes taking photographs of shoes.
True ☐ **False** ☐

13.5 REWRITE THE SENTENCES, CORRECTING THE ERRORS

Sophie is wearring a blue cottonne dress.
Sophie is wearing a blue cotton dress.

❶ Alice is bying the shirt with pretty butons.

_____

❷ George has five pairs of jeens.

_____

❸ Shinko loves wearring high-heeled botts.

_____

❹ John prefers plane cloths.

_____

❺ Farah is shoping for a party dress.

_____

◀))

 13.6 DESCRIBE WHAT EACH PERSON IS WEARING USING THE WORDS IN THE PANEL, SPEAKING OUT LOUD

He's wearing
_____*checked*_____
pajamas.

❸ He's wearing
a jacket with
a _____ .

❶ He's wearing
boots with
_____ .

❹ She's wearing a
_____ dress with
black _____ .

❷ She's wearing a
_____ with
large _____ .

❺ She's wearing
_____
sandals.

checked   leather   smart   laces   cardigan   high heels   zip   buttons

◀))

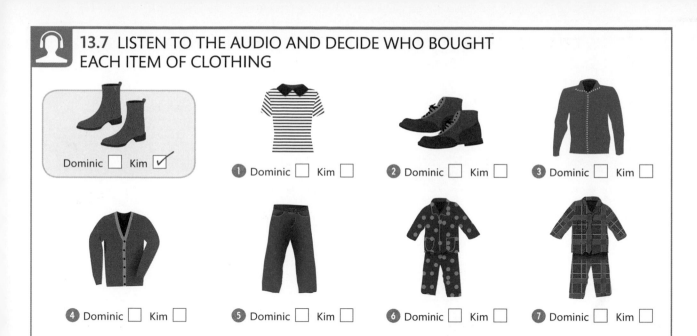

13.7 LISTEN TO THE AUDIO AND DECIDE WHO BOUGHT EACH ITEM OF CLOTHING

Dominic ☐ Kim ☑

1 Dominic ☐ Kim ☐

2 Dominic ☐ Kim ☐

3 Dominic ☐ Kim ☐

4 Dominic ☐ Kim ☐

5 Dominic ☐ Kim ☐

6 Dominic ☐ Kim ☐

7 Dominic ☐ Kim ☐

13 ✓ CHECKLIST

⚙ Present continuous ☐   **Aa** Clothes and fashion ☐   🧩 Describing clothes ☐

↻ REVIEW THE ENGLISH YOU HAVE LEARNED IN UNITS 07–13

NEW LANGUAGE	SAMPLE SENTENCE	☑	UNIT
"JOB" OR "WORK"	I enjoy my job. I work in an office.	☐	7.4
ADVERBS OF FREQUENCY	I always take a shower in the morning. I regularly cycle to work.	☐	8.1
DESCRIPTIONS OF FREQUENCY WORD ORDER	I go running five times a week.	☐	8.3
ADVERBS OF FREQUENCY WORD ORDER WITH "BE"	I often take the train. The traffic is often very bad.	☐	8.6
PHRASAL VERBS	I get up early every day.	☐	9.1
ADJECTIVE ORDER	She has beautiful, curly, brown hair.	☐	11.1
PRESENT CONTINUOUS	She is wearing a red dress.	☐	13.1

14.1 ROOMS AND FURNITURE

plants	yard (US) garden (UK)	lawn	lawn mower	door
bed	closet (US) wardrobe (UK)	chest of drawers	bedside table	mirror
computer	desk	table	chair	lamp
television	armchair	couch (US) sofa (UK)	cushion	rug
basin	bathtub (US) bath (UK)	shower	toilet	towel

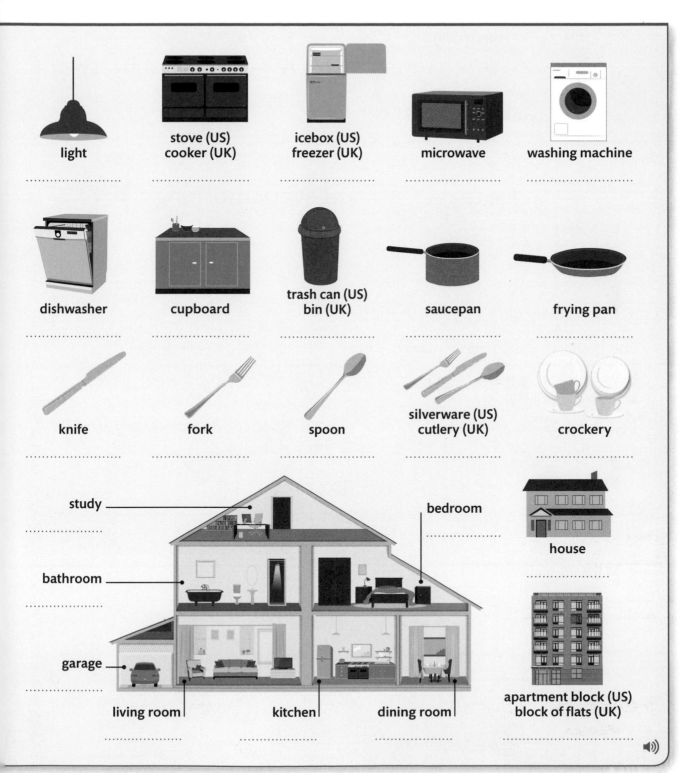

light

stove (US)
cooker (UK)

icebox (US)
freezer (UK)

microwave

washing machine

dishwasher

cupboard

trash can (US)
bin (UK)

saucepan

frying pan

knife

fork

spoon

silverware (US)
cutlery (UK)

crockery

study

bedroom

house

bathroom

garage

living room

kitchen

dining room

apartment block (US)
block of flats (UK)

15 Daily routines

Collocations are groups of words that are often used together in English. You can use them to make your spoken English sound more natural.

🔧 **New language** Collocations
Aa Vocabulary Routines and chores
🧩 **New skill** Talking about your day

15.1 KEY LANGUAGE COLLOCATIONS

Many household chores are described using collocations. Often the definite article ("the") is included.

COLLOCATION

He makes the bed every morning.

English speakers would usually say "make" rather than "do" or "tidy" in this sentence.

"The" sounds more natural than "his" in this sentence.

15.2 FURTHER EXAMPLES COLLOCATIONS

She mows the lawn every week.

I do the cooking every evening.

I walk the dog every day.

They do the laundry every Sunday.

 15.3 LISTEN TO THE AUDIO, THEN NUMBER THE PICTURES IN THE ORDER THEY ARE DESCRIBED

Tatiana is visiting her friend Laura and they are talking about household chores.

Ⓐ ☐

Ⓑ 1

Ⓒ ☐

Ⓓ ☐

Ⓔ ☐

15.4 KEY LANGUAGE COLLOCATIONS IN DIFFERENT TENSES

Collocations can be used in different tenses by changing the form of the verb.

PAST SIMPLE

He folded the towels this morning.

She did the dishes this afternoon.

PRESENT CONTINUOUS

He's watering the plants now.

They're clearing the table after lunch.

FUTURE WITH "WILL"

I'll sweep the floor this afternoon.

I'll load the dishwasher in a minute.

15.5 REWRITE THE NOTE, CORRECTING THE ERRORS

Hi Bill,
The landlord is visiting tomorrow so please could you broom the floor, water the dishes, wet the plants, set the dishwasher, and cut the lawn?
Thanks,
Mandy

Hi Bill,
The landlord is visiting tomorrow so please could you sweep the floor,

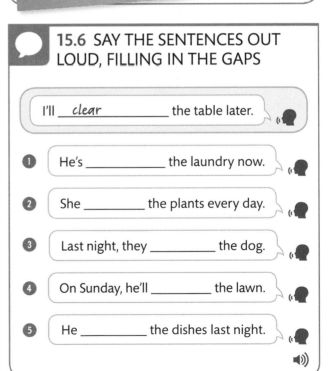

15.6 SAY THE SENTENCES OUT LOUD, FILLING IN THE GAPS

I'll __clear__ the table later.

① He's _____ the laundry now.

② She _____ the plants every day.

③ Last night, they _____ the dog.

④ On Sunday, he'll _____ the lawn.

⑤ He _____ the dishes last night.

15.7 KEY LANGUAGE PRESENT SIMPLE AND PRESENT CONTINUOUS

The present simple describes routine actions. The present
continuous describes actions that are occurring right now.

PRESENT SIMPLE (ROUTINE ACTION)   PRESENT CONTINUOUS (ACTION HAPPENING NOW)

I usually cook at home, but I'm eating out tonight.

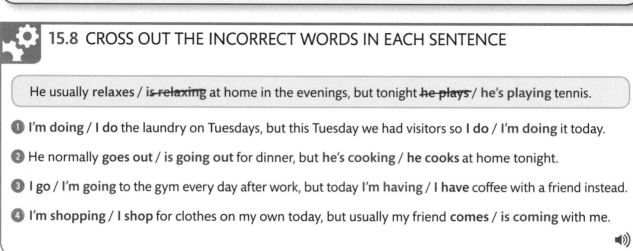

15.8 CROSS OUT THE INCORRECT WORDS IN EACH SENTENCE

He usually **relaxes** / ~~is relaxing~~ at home in the evenings, but tonight ~~he plays~~ / **he's playing** tennis.

1 **I'm doing** / **I do** the laundry on Tuesdays, but this Tuesday we had visitors so **I do** / **I'm doing** it today.

2 He normally **goes out** / **is going out** for dinner, but **he's cooking** / **he cooks** at home tonight.

3 **I go** / **I'm going** to the gym every day after work, but today **I'm having** / **I have** coffee with a friend instead.

4 **I'm shopping** / **I shop** for clothes on my own today, but usually my friend **comes** / **is coming** with me.

15.9 LISTEN TO THE AUDIO AND ANSWER THE QUESTIONS

Maya visits her sister, Gita, to go shopping,
but Gita is busy with chores.

Do Maya and Gita go shopping on Mondays?
Never ☐ **Usually** ☐ **Always** ☑

1 When does Gita usually do her laundry?
Weekends ☐ **Fridays** ☐ **Tuesdays** ☐

2 When is Gita cleaning the house?
Tuesday ☐ **Now** ☐ **Tomorrow** ☐

3 Is this Gita's normal routine?
Yes ☐ **No** ☐ **Sometimes** ☐

4 What do Gita and Maya usually do after shopping?
Go for a run ☐ **Have lunch** ☐ **Go home** ☐

5 Who usually sweeps her floor?
Raj ☐ **Maya** ☐ **Gita** ☐

15.10 READ THE ARTICLE AND ANSWER THE QUESTIONS

CELEBRITY INTERIORS

HOME | ABOUT | CONTACT

AT HOME WITH POP ICON SUSIE TAYLOR

So what's a normal day like for you, Susie?
Well, it starts early in the morning when I'm not on tour. I walk Missy, my dog. After that, I do normal things; I do the laundry and the cleaning.

Really?
Yes, and I use the time to sing scales and practice my songs. I usually write songs and practice for about six hours in my studio every day as well.

That's a lot of time to fit into your schedule.
It's all part of the job. I don't normally wear such elegant clothes at home, but today I dressed up for this interview and photo shoot.

**That is a lovely dress and you do have a beautiful home, Susie.
Doesn't anyone help you keep it looking so gorgeous?**
Sure. You can hear Kurt loading the dishwasher, and I have a gardener, Jack. He's outside mowing the lawn now. I don't do that as I don't like the noise.

Well, I'm glad to hear you have some help.

What does Susie do every morning?

Susie walks the dog every morning.

❸ What is Susie doing at the moment?

_____

❶ What does Susie also usually do when cleaning?

_____

❷ Does she usually wear elegant clothes at home?

_____

❹ Who normally helps Susie with the chores?

_____

❺ Why doesn't Susie like mowing the lawn?

_____

---

15 ✓ CHECKLIST

⚙ Collocations ☐   **Aa** Routines and chores ☐   🧩 Talking about your day ☐

16 Separable phrasal verbs

All phrasal verbs consist of a verb and a particle. Some must have the verb and particle together, but with others, the object can appear in between.

⚙ **New language** Separable phrasal verbs
Aa Vocabulary Around town
🧩 **New skill** Describing a town in detail

16.1 KEY LANGUAGE SEPARABLE PHRASAL VERBS

With separable phrasal verbs, the object of the sentence can go before or after the particle. The meaning is the same.

The object can go after the particle.

He is picking up litter.

The object can also go between the verb and the particle.

He is picking litter up.

16.2 FURTHER EXAMPLES SEPARABLE PHRASAL VERBS

He is cutting down trees.

He is cutting trees down.

She gave out the town maps.

She gave the town maps out.

16.3 REWRITE THE SENTENCES BY CHANGING THE POSITION OF THE PARTICLE

The theater is putting on a show.
The theater is putting a show on.

① We'll pick up the shopping.

_____

② Those people are giving leaflets out.

_____

③ Can you check out the menu?

_____

④ They're filling that hole in the road in.

_____

⑤ I'm taking back those library books.

_____

Aa 16.4 READ THE PASSAGE AND WRITE THE HIGHLIGHTED PHRASES NEXT TO THEIR DEFINITIONS

26   LOCAL NEWS

BRAND NEW SPORTS CENTER ARRIVING SOON!

The new sports center will open later this month. There will be many opportunities for people to take up exciting activities, show off their talents, and find out what suits them best.

The surrounding area has been cleaned up and the beautiful Brock park has just been reopened. Just one year since the previous owners sold off the derelict site to Haven Sports Centers, the town has a great new sports venue. Come along and try out the facilities.

Start doing	=	_take up_
❶ Improved	=	_____
❷ Test	=	_____
❸ Discover	=	_____
❹ Exhibit	=	_____
❺ Sold cheaply	=	_____

16.5 COMMON MISTAKES SEPARABLE PHRASAL VERBS WITH PRONOUNS

If the object of a sentence with a separable phrasal verb is a pronoun, it must go between the verb and the particle.

This is correct. The pronoun must go between the verb and the particle.

He is picking it up. ✔
He is picking up it. ✘

This is wrong. The pronoun cannot go after the particle.

⚙ 16.6 REWRITE THE SENTENCES USING THE OBJECT PRONOUN "IT"

She's looking up the location.
She's looking it up.

❶ They're closing down the factory.

❷ She's renting out her house.

❸ He's cleaning up the front of the shop.

❹ He's showing off his new car.

❺ They tore down the building.

16.7 VOCABULARY AROUND TOWN

government building ....

law court ....

shopping mall (US)
shopping centre (UK) ....

skyscraper ....

art gallery ....

16.9 LISTEN TO THE AUDIO AND NUMBER THE PICTURES IN THE ORDER THEY ARE DESCRIBED

A ☐

B 1  INFORMATION

C ☐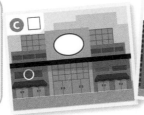

D ☐

E ☐

16.10 READ THE EMAIL AND ANSWER THE QUESTIONS

✉ ∨ ✕

To: Jane Warren

Subject: Welcome!

Hi Jane,
Welcome to Boston! I can't wait to show my city off to you! Because you love art, I want to take you to the art gallery in the city center. The law court is a beautiful building, so you should also see that. We should take a tour of the historic quarter as well. I'll find the details out for this tour soon. There are more tourist attractions to visit, but I'll let you know about them later. Looking forward to seeing you, Anne

↰ ↰↰   📎 🗑

Jane doesn't like art at all.
True ☐ **False** ☐ **Not given** ✓

❶ The art gallery is a beautiful building.
True ☐ **False** ☐ **Not given** ☐

❷ Anne wants to do the historic quarter tour.
True ☐ **False** ☐ **Not given** ☐

❸ Jane will have to research the tour details.
True ☐ **False** ☐ **Not given** ☐

❹ Anne wants Jane to go to a palace.
True ☐ **False** ☐ **Not given** ☐

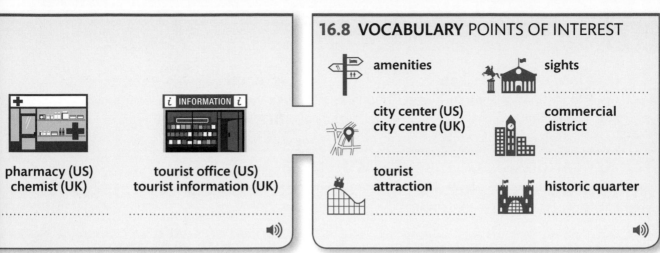

16.8 VOCABULARY POINTS OF INTEREST

amenities

sights

city center (US)
city centre (UK)

commercial
district

tourist
attraction

historic quarter

pharmacy (US)
chemist (UK)

tourist office (US)
tourist information (UK)

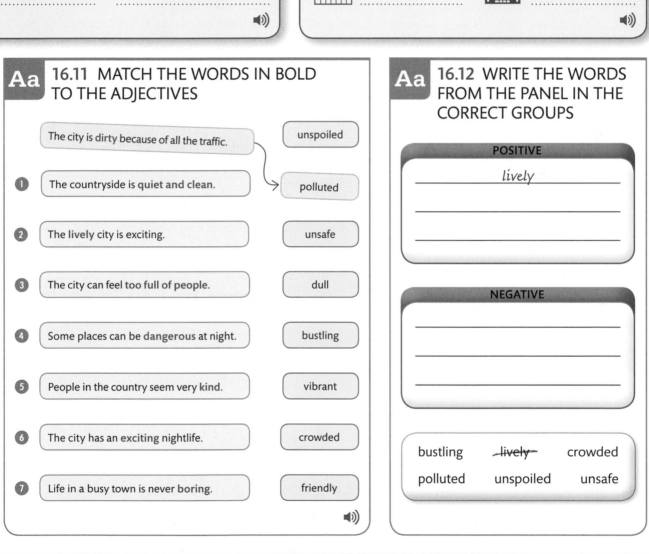

Aa 16.11 MATCH THE WORDS IN BOLD TO THE ADJECTIVES

The city is **dirty** because of all the traffic. — unspoiled

1. The countryside is **quiet and clean**. → polluted

2. The **lively** city is exciting. — unsafe

3. The city can feel too **full of people**. — dull

4. Some places can be **dangerous** at night. — bustling

5. People in the country seem very **kind**. — vibrant

6. The city has an **exciting nightlife**. — crowded

7. Life in a **busy** town is never boring. — friendly

Aa 16.12 WRITE THE WORDS FROM THE PANEL IN THE CORRECT GROUPS

POSITIVE

lively

NEGATIVE

bustling   ~~lively~~   crowded
polluted   unspoiled   unsafe

16 ✓ CHECKLIST

⚙ Separable phrasal verbs ☐   Aa Around town ☐   🧩 Describing a town in detail ☐

61

17 Comparing places

You can use modifiers before comparatives and superlatives to compare places, such as geographical features, in more detail.

⚙ **New language** Modifiers
Aa Vocabulary Geographical terms
🏃 **New skill** Describing and comparing places

17.1 KEY LANGUAGE COMPARATIVES WITH MODIFIERS

Use modifiers before comparatives to be more precise about the comparison you are making.

> **TIP**
> You can't modify comparatives with "very."

modifier

comparative

The tree is { **a lot** / **much** } **taller than the building.**

These modifiers mean there is a big difference between the things you are comparing.

These modifiers mean there is only a small difference between the things you are comparing.

The tree is { **a bit** / **slightly** } **taller than the building.**

🔊

17.2 KEY LANGUAGE LONG COMPARATIVES WITH MODIFIERS

The palace is much more beautiful than the factory.

The modifier goes before "more."

Form long comparatives by putting "more" before the adjective.

🔊

⚙ 17.3 LOOK AT THE PICTURES AND CROSS OUT THE INCORRECT WORDS IN EACH SENTENCE

 The tree is ~~a bit~~ / much taller than the house.

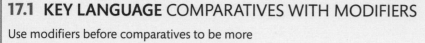

❶  The mountain is **much** / **a bit** taller than the hill.

❷ The church is **a lot** / **slightly** taller than the café.

❸ The window is **slightly** / **much** wider than the door.

❹ The lighthouse is **a bit** / **a lot** taller than the statue.

❺  The castle is **much** / **slightly** bigger than the hotel.

🔊

17.4 KEY LANGUAGE SUPERLATIVES WITH MODIFIERS

You can use "easily" or "by far" to make superlative adjectives stronger,
or "one of" to show that the superlative belongs to a group of things.

The clock tower is $\left\{ \begin{array}{l} \text{easily} \\ \text{by far} \end{array} \right\}$ **the tallest** building in the town.

These modifiers make the superlative stronger.
You cannot use them with comparatives.

The clock tower is **one of the tallest** buildings in the town.

"One of" makes the
superlative part of a group.

If you use "one of" with superlatives,
the noun must be in plural form.

17.5 KEY LANGUAGE LONG SUPERLATIVES WITH MODIFIERS

This is **by far the most expensive** shop in the street.

The modifier
goes before "the."

Form long superlatives by putting
"the most" before the adjective.

17.6 SAY THE SENTENCES OUT LOUD, CORRECTING THE ERRORS

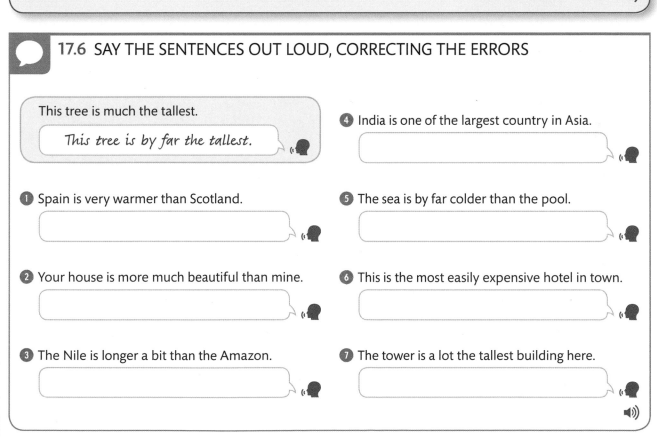

This tree is much the tallest.

This tree is by far the tallest.

1 Spain is very warmer than Scotland.

2 Your house is more much beautiful than mine.

3 The Nile is longer a bit than the Amazon.

4 India is one of the largest country in Asia.

5 The sea is by far colder than the pool.

6 This is the most easily expensive hotel in town.

7 The tower is a lot the tallest building here.

17.7 VOCABULARY GEOGRAPHICAL TERMS

volcano	mountain range	glacier	valley
....	....	....	....

 ## 17.8 LISTEN TO THE AUDIO AND ANSWER THE QUESTIONS

 Umar and Sharon are taking a quiz about places around the world.

Umar thinks the Himalayas are...

the tallest mountain range ✓

the highest mountain ☐

much longer than the Andes ☐

1 Sharon thinks the Andes are...

a bit longer than the Himalayas ☐

much longer than the Himalayas ☐

slightly longer than the Himalayas ☐

2 What does Umar say about the Niagara Falls?

It's one of the tallest waterfalls ☐

It's the longest river ☐

It's by far the tallest waterfall ☐

3 What does Umar say is off the coast of Japan?

The highest mountain ☐

The Khone Falls ☐

The biggest volcano ☐

4 What does Umar think is found in Antarctica?

The largest glacier ☐

The coldest glacier ☐

The widest glacier ☐

5 Umar says the Pacific Ocean is...

a bit bigger than the Atlantic Ocean ☐

easily the biggest ocean ☐

much bigger than the Atlantic Ocean ☐

6 Umar says Canada's coastline is...

longer than Australia's coastline ☐

by far the longest coastline ☐

shorter than Australia's coastline ☐

7 Sharon says Canada is...

the world's biggest country ☐

a lot bigger than Australia ☐

a bit bigger than Australia ☐

rainforest

waterfall

cliff

ocean

....

17.9 READ THE ARTICLE AND ANSWER THE QUESTIONS

Antarctica is easily the coldest continent on Earth.
True ✓ **False** ☐

1 Death Valley is the driest place in the world.
True ☐ **False** ☐

2 The Atacama Desert is a lot drier than Death Valley.
True ☐ **False** ☐

3 Helsinki has much more daylight time than Reykjavik.
True ☐ **False** ☐

4 The Congo rainforest is the largest one on Earth.
True ☐ **False** ☐

5 The Amazon is slightly bigger than the Congo.
True ☐ **False** ☐

6 The wettest place on Earth is in India.
True ☐ **False** ☐

 Did you know?

🌍 **Antarctica** is by far the coldest and windiest continent on Earth. It's covered by permanently frozen ground.

🌍 **Death Valley** in California is the hottest place in the world, with temperatures of around 130°F. It's also one of the driest places in the world.

🌍 **The Atacama Desert**, in Chile, is much drier than Death Valley. Some parts of the desert have had no rain for more than 400 years.

🌍 **Reykjavik**, in Iceland, has only 4.07 hours of daylight in December. Helsinki has slightly more daylight time than Reykjavik; around 5.5 hours.

🌍 The two largest rainforests on Earth are the **Amazon** and **the Congo**, but the Amazon is much bigger than the Congo.

🌍 The wettest place on Earth is **Mawsynram**, in India, where the average rainfall is 11,871 mm per year.

---

17 ✓ **CHECKLIST**

⚙ Modifiers ☐   **Aa** Geographical terms ☐   🧩 Describing and comparing places ☐

18 Likes and dislikes

In English, many adjectives are formed by adding "-ing" or "-ed" to verbs. These adjectives often have different meanings and can be used to describe likes and dislikes.

⚙ **New language** Adjectives with "-ing" and "-ed"
Aa Vocabulary Feelings and emotions
🧩 **New skill** Talking about likes and dislikes

18.1 KEY LANGUAGE ADJECTIVES WITH "-ING" AND "-ED"

Adjectives that end in "-ing" describe the effect something has.
Adjectives ending in "-ed" describe how something is affected.

The spider causes fright.

The spider is frightening.
The man is frightened.

The man experiences fright.

🔊

18.2 FURTHER EXAMPLES ADJECTIVES WITH "-ING" AND "-ED"

The fireworks are amazing.
She is amazed.

The wasp is annoying.
He is annoyed.

The roller coaster was thrilling.
They were thrilled.

The vacation is relaxing.
He is relaxed.

🔊

⚙ 18.3 CROSS OUT THE INCORRECT WORD IN EACH SENTENCE

I am ~~exciting~~ / excited about the football game.

 ❶ This movie is really **bored** / **boring**.

❷ That meal was **disgusting** / **disgusted**.

 ❸ Your lecture was really **interested** / **interesting**.

 ❹ I'm really **thrilled** / **thrilling** about our trip!

❺ The movie was very **exciting** / **excited**.

 ❻ I always feel **relaxing** / **relaxed** after a bath.

❼ I'm really **shocked** / **shocking** by the news.

🔊

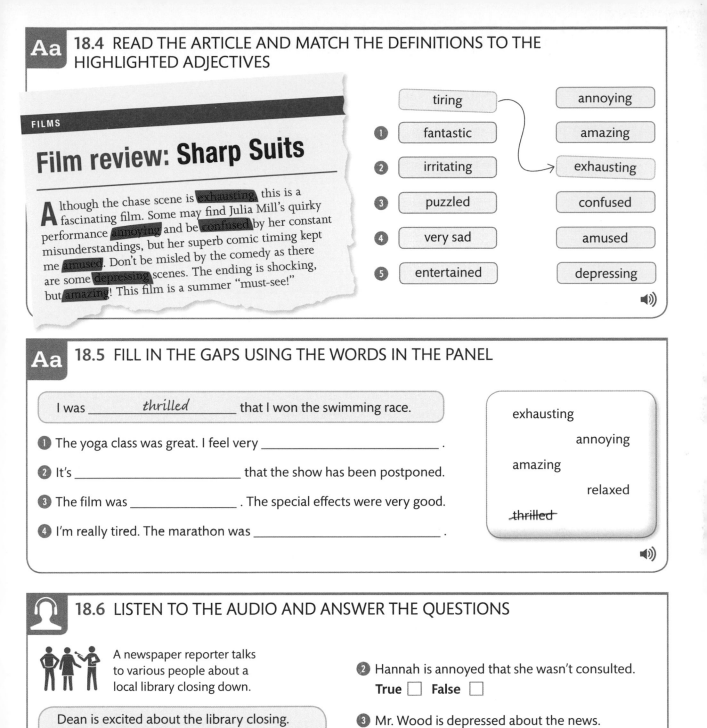

Aa 18.4 READ THE ARTICLE AND MATCH THE DEFINITIONS TO THE HIGHLIGHTED ADJECTIVES

FILMS

Film review: Sharp Suits

Although the chase scene is **exhausting**, this is a fascinating film. Some may find Julia Mill's quirky performance **annoying** and be **confused** by her constant misunderstandings, but her superb comic timing kept me **amused**. Don't be misled by the comedy as there are some **depressing** scenes. The ending is shocking, but **amazing**! This film is a summer "must-see!"

tiring	annoying
➊ fantastic	amazing
➋ irritating	exhausting
➌ puzzled	confused
➍ very sad	amused
➎ entertained	depressing

Aa 18.5 FILL IN THE GAPS USING THE WORDS IN THE PANEL

I was _____*thrilled*_____ that I won the swimming race.

➊ The yoga class was great. I feel very _____ .

➋ It's _____ that the show has been postponed.

➌ The film was _____ . The special effects were very good.

➍ I'm really tired. The marathon was _____ .

> exhausting
> annoying
> amazing
> relaxed
> ~~thrilled~~

18.6 LISTEN TO THE AUDIO AND ANSWER THE QUESTIONS

A newspaper reporter talks to various people about a local library closing down.

Dean is excited about the library closing.
True ☑ **False** ☐

➊ Aki understands why the decision was made.
True ☐ **False** ☐

➋ Hannah is annoyed that she wasn't consulted.
True ☐ **False** ☐

➌ Mr. Wood is depressed about the news.
True ☐ **False** ☐

➍ Mrs. Tana thinks the committee's plan is funny.
True ☐ **False** ☐

18.7 KEY LANGUAGE MODIFYING WORDS

"Quite," "really," and "absolutely" can be used to modify how much you like or don't like something. These modifying words must go before the verb.

In UK English "quite" doesn't have as strong an emphasis as "really." In US English the emphasis is stronger.

I quite enjoy cycling.
You can use "quite" before "enjoy" and "like."

"Really" is used when you mean "a lot more."

I really like cycling.
You can use "really" before "like," "love," "enjoy," "don't like," and "hate."

"Absolutely" is used in extreme forms.

I absolutely love cycling.
You can use "absolutely" before "love" and "hate."

18.8 FURTHER EXAMPLES MODIFYING WORDS

 He quite likes **playing tennis.**

 I really don't like **cooking.**

 He really loves **eating cake.**

 She really hates **waking up early.**

 She really enjoys **playing guitar.**

 They absolutely hate **singing.**

18.9 ⚠ COMMON MISTAKES

Some combinations of modifying words and verbs are wrong.

I quite love cycling. ✗
Don't use "quite" before "love," "don't like," or "hate."

I absolutely enjoy cycling. ✗
Don't use "absolutely" before "like," "enjoy," or "don't like."

⚙ 18.10 CROSS OUT THE INCORRECT WORD IN EACH SENTENCE

I ~~quite~~ / really love going to the movie theater.

1 I absolutely / quite hate traveling to the city.

2 I really / absolutely enjoy reading books.

3 I absolutely / quite like swimming.

4 I quite / really hate driving to work.

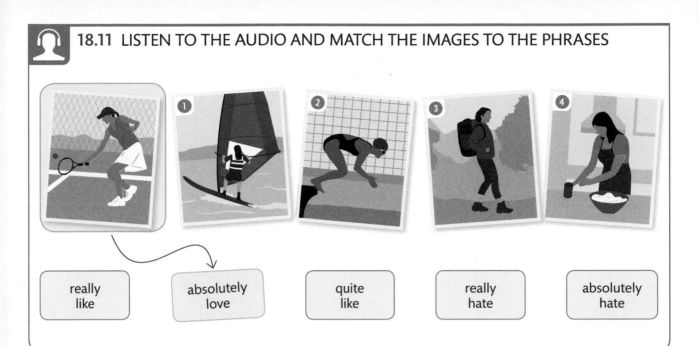

18.11 LISTEN TO THE AUDIO AND MATCH THE IMAGES TO THE PHRASES

really like

absolutely love

quite like

really hate

absolutely hate

18 ✓ CHECKLIST

⚙ Adjectives with "-ing" and "-ed" ☐   **Aa** Feelings and emotions ☐   🧩 Talking about likes and dislikes ☐

↻ REVIEW THE ENGLISH YOU HAVE LEARNED IN UNITS 15–18

NEW LANGUAGE	SAMPLE SENTENCE	☑	UNIT
COLLOCATIONS	**He** makes the bed **every morning**.	☐	15.1
PRESENT SIMPLE AND PRESENT CONTINUOUS	I **usually** cook **at home, but** I'm eating out **tonight**.	☐	15.7
SEPARABLE PHRASAL VERBS	**He** is picking up **litter.** **He** is picking **litter** up	☐	16.1
COMPARATIVES WITH MODIFIERS	**The tree is** a lot taller **than the building.** **The tree is** slightly taller **than the building.**	☐	17.1
SUPERLATIVES WITH MODIFIERS	**The clock tower is** easily the tallest **building in the town.**	☐	17.4
ADJECTIVES WITH "-ING" AND "-ED"	**The spider is frighten**ing. **The man is frighten**ed.	☐	18.1
MODIFYING WORDS	I quite enjoy **cycling.** I really like **cycling.**	☐	18.7

19.1 HENRY'S FAMILY

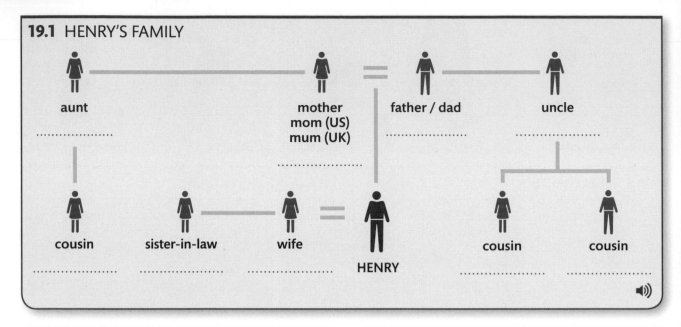

aunt

mother
mom (US)
mum (UK)

father / dad

uncle

cousin

sister-in-law

wife

HENRY

cousin

cousin

19.2 SARAH'S FAMILY

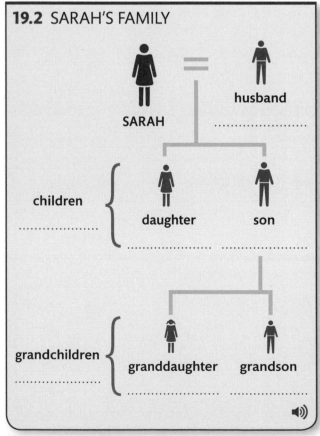

husband

SARAH

children

daughter

son

grandchildren

granddaughter

grandson

19.3 MIA'S FAMILY

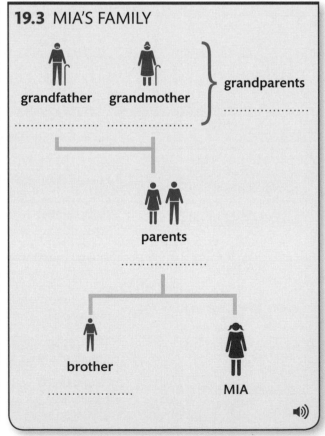

grandfather

grandmother

grandparents

parents

brother

MIA

19.4 GROWING UP

baby   toddler   girl   boy   teenagers   adults

....

19.5 TIM'S FAMILY

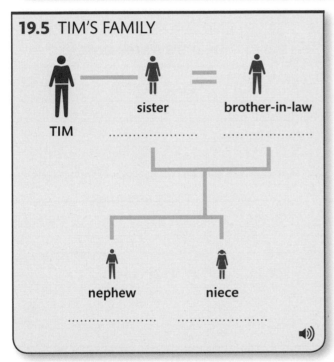

TIM   sister   brother-in-law

....

nephew   niece

....

19.6 VIC'S FAMILY

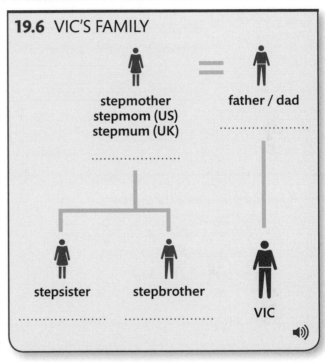

stepmother
stepmom (US)
stepmum (UK)   father / dad

....

....

stepsister   stepbrother   VIC

....

19.7 RELATIONSHIPS

male   female   boyfriend and girlfriend   partner   husband and wife

....

20 Early years

In English, the word "did" can be used for emphasis to assure someone that a past action really happened. It's useful for describing past events and memories.

⚙ **New language** "Did" for emphasis
Aa Vocabulary Baby equipment and parenting
🧩 **New skill** Describing your childhood

20.1 KEY LANGUAGE PAST SIMPLE WITH EMPHASIS

To emphasize a verb in the past simple, replace it with "did" plus the base form of the verb.

Past simple.

You called your dad about babysitting Kim tonight, didn't you?

The word "did" gives emphasis.

"Did" is followed by the base form of the main verb.

No, but I did call Aunt Sue. She'll be here soon.

◀))

20.2 FURTHER EXAMPLES PAST SIMPLE WITH EMPHASIS

I thought you asked Maya to put away these toys.

I did ask her. I think she forgot.

Are you sure you bought the birthday cake?

Yes, I did buy it. It's on the top shelf.

◀))

20.3 REWRITE THE SENTENCES USING THE PAST SIMPLE WITH EMPHASIS

She worked hard at her homework.
She did work hard at her homework.

❶ I behaved well as a child.

_____

❷ He took his lunchbox to school.

_____

❸ I enjoyed the children's performance.

_____

❹ He gave his teacher a birthday card.

_____

❺ She played quietly at Anita's house.

_____

◀))

20.4 KEY LANGUAGE SPOKEN EMPHASIS

The important words in a sentence may be said more loudly or in a different pitch to make them more emphatic.

Are you <u>sure</u> you called her?

Yes, I <u>did</u> call her.

20.5 UNDERLINE THE WORD IN EACH SENTENCE THAT SHOULD BE STRESSED, THEN SAY THE SENTENCES OUT LOUD

Jane really <u>did</u> love that story about the bear.

1 I did tell the babysitter to arrive early.

2 It's true! She did say "papa" today!

3 We did invite her to the birthday party.

4 I really did enjoy the cake Lucy baked.

5 Molly did ask if she could play with your toys.

20.6 MARK THE SENTENCES THAT ARE CORRECT

I did tell her mother. ☑
I did told her mother. ☐

1 She did played nicely with her toys. ☐
She did play nicely with her toys. ☐

2 We did ask them to be quiet. ☐
We did asked them to be quiet. ☐

3 I did love that trip to the beach. ☐
I did loved that trip to the beach. ☐

4 He did left the room in a messy. ☐
He did leave the room in a mess. ☐

5 Tommy did enjoy the magic show. ☐
Tommy did enjoyed the magic show. ☐

6 Raj really did loved playing that game. ☐
Raj really did love playing that game. ☐

7 We did give Lucy's doll back to her. ☐
We did gave Lucy's doll back to her. ☐

20.7 VOCABULARY EARLY YEARS

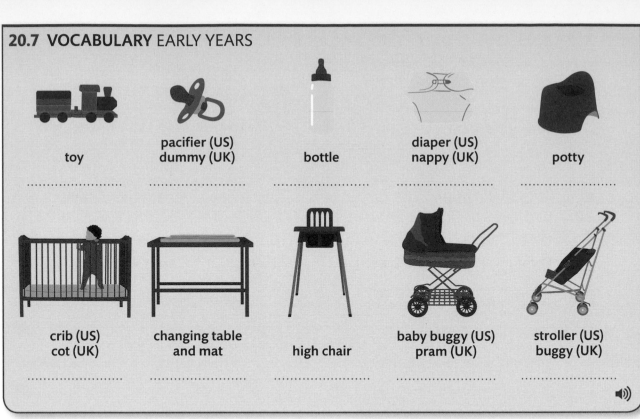

toy

pacifier (US)
dummy (UK)

bottle

diaper (US)
nappy (UK)

potty

crib (US)
cot (UK)

changing table
and mat

high chair

baby buggy (US)
pram (UK)

stroller (US)
buggy (UK)

20.8 READ THE EMAIL AND ANSWER THE QUESTIONS

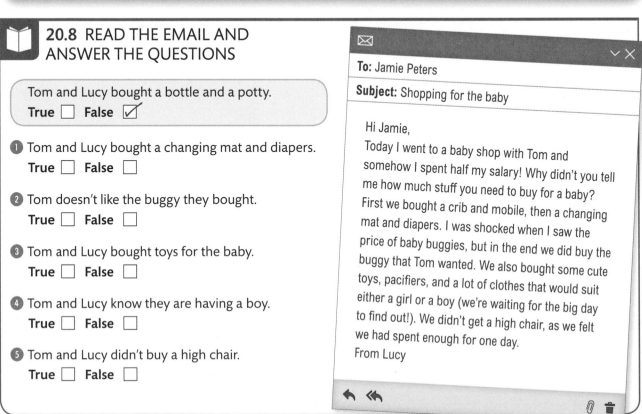

Tom and Lucy bought a bottle and a potty.
True ☐ False ☑

① Tom and Lucy bought a changing mat and diapers.
True ☐ False ☐

② Tom doesn't like the buggy they bought.
True ☐ False ☐

③ Tom and Lucy bought toys for the baby.
True ☐ False ☐

④ Tom and Lucy know they are having a boy.
True ☐ False ☐

⑤ Tom and Lucy didn't buy a high chair.
True ☐ False ☐

To: Jamie Peters

Subject: Shopping for the baby

Hi Jamie,
Today I went to a baby shop with Tom and somehow I spent half my salary! Why didn't you tell me how much stuff you need to buy for a baby? First we bought a crib and mobile, then a changing mat and diapers. I was shocked when I saw the price of baby buggies, but in the end we did buy the buggy that Tom wanted. We also bought some cute toys, pacifiers, and a lot of clothes that would suit either a girl or a boy (we're waiting for the big day to find out!). We didn't get a high chair, as we felt we had spent enough for one day.
From Lucy

20.9 VOCABULARY PAST SIMPLE IRREGULAR VERBS

Most English verbs take "-ed" in the past simple, but some irregular verbs have very different past forms.

feed
She **fed** the baby.

sink
The toy ship **sank** in the bathtub.

bite
She **bit** the apple.

draw
He **drew** a nice picture today.

hide
They **hid** behind the tree.

lead
Her older brother **led** the way.

20.10 FILL IN THE GAPS BY PUTTING THE IRREGULAR VERBS IN THE PAST SIMPLE

She ___*drew*___ (draw) a picture of a cat.

1 He _____ (feed) her in the high chair.

2 Archie _____ (hide) from his sister.

3 Francis _____ (bite) into the pie.

4 Carly _____ (lead) her brother to the park.

5 Soolin's toy _____ (sink) in the pond.

20.11 LISTEN TO THE AUDIO AND ANSWER THE QUESTIONS

Jo is telling Georgia about her first day at school.

How did Jo feel before her first day at school?
Bored ☐ **Excited** ☑ **Scared** ☐

1 What did Jo do when her dad left?
Ran after him ☐ **Nothing** ☐ **Cried** ☐

2 What did Jo get stuck in?
A bucket ☐ **A fence** ☐ **A ladder** ☐

3 Who found Jo stuck outside the school?
Her dad ☐ **The teacher** ☐ **Joan** ☐

4 Who got her out?
Joan ☐ **Her mom** ☐ **The fire department** ☐

---

20 ✓ CHECKLIST

⚙ "Did" for emphasis ☐   **Aa** Baby equipment and parenting ☐   🧩 Describing your childhood ☐

21 Vocabulary

21.1 EDUCATION

English

art

history

geography

science

biology

physics

chemistry

math (US)
maths (UK)

medicine

economics

law

business studies

engineering

architecture

psychology

philosophy

school

college (US)
university (UK)

library

classroom

laboratory

class

exam

sit an exam

essay

 desk

 pen

 pencil

 pencil sharpener

 homework

 exercise book

 text book

 eraser (US) rubber (UK)

 ruler

 thesis

 review (US) revise (UK)

 resit

 lecture

 study a subject

 test

 grade

 pass

 fail

 diploma (US) qualification (UK)

 degree

 teacher

 lecturer

 student

 graduate

22 Changing meaning

Prefixes are small groups of letters that can be added to the beginnings of words to change their meaning. Suffixes are similar, but are added to the ends of words.

✿ **New language** Prefixes and suffixes
Aa Vocabulary Studying
🧩 **New skill** Changing the meaning of words

22.1 KEY LANGUAGE PREFIXES AND SUFFIXES

Each prefix or suffix has its own meaning, which modifies whatever word it is added to.

 Jane is unlikely to study history because she prefers science.

un- = not

 Tom was rewriting his essay because his teacher gave him a low grade.

re- = again

 The principal was so pleased that the play was successful.

-ful = full of

 I don't like the food in the cafeteria. It is tasteless.

-less = without

🔊

22.2 FURTHER EXAMPLES PREFIXES AND SUFFIXES

 Please clean up your desk. It's very **un**tidy.

 I didn't work very hard this year. I'll have to **re**take my exams.

 Now that I've passed my exams, I am hope**ful** for the future.

 What a boring lecture. Being there was point**less**.

🔊

78

22.3 FILL IN THE GAPS BY ADDING PREFIXES OR SUFFIXES TO THE HIGHLIGHTED WORDS

My teacher asked me to _____rewrite_____ (write) my essay.

1 I'm _____ (hope) that I will do well in my English exam.

2 You are _____ (likely) to pass the exam if you don't work harder.

3 The old science laboratories have been _____ (built).

4 I think that worrying about exams is _____ (healthy).

5 I think this plan can be _____ (organized) so it works better.

6 Thanks for all your help. You've been absolutely _____ (wonder).

7 I had a very _____ (rest) night, as I was worrying about my geography test.

22.4 LISTEN TO THE AUDIO AND ANSWER THE QUESTIONS

Wei Pan talks about her experience teaching students from two different schools.

The first school's students respected teachers.
True ☑ **False** ☐ **Not given** ☐

1 Some of the first school's classes were small.
True ☐ **False** ☐ **Not given** ☐

2 The large classes meant teachers had to shout.
True ☐ **False** ☐ **Not given** ☐

3 Being creative helps teachers succeed.
True ☐ **False** ☐ **Not given** ☐

4 Students went home earlier at the second school.
True ☐ **False** ☐ **Not given** ☐

5 Some of Wei's current students don't concentrate.
True ☐ **False** ☐ **Not given** ☐

6 Students from both schools have good handwriting.
True ☐ **False** ☐ **Not given** ☐

7 Wei doesn't think her current students will pass.
True ☐ **False** ☐ **Not given** ☐

22 ✓ CHECKLIST

⚙ Prefixes and suffixes ☐   **Aa** Studying ☐   🧩 Changing the meaning of words ☐

23.1 TRANSPORTATION

car

taxi

bus

coach

plane

train

tram

bicycle

motorcycle (US)
motorbike (UK)

helicopter

23.2 TRAVEL

on time

pack your bags

luggage

vacation (US)
holiday UK

train ride

set off on a journey

fly in a plane

go cycling / ride a bike

drive a car

get on a bus

get off a bus

arrive at the airport

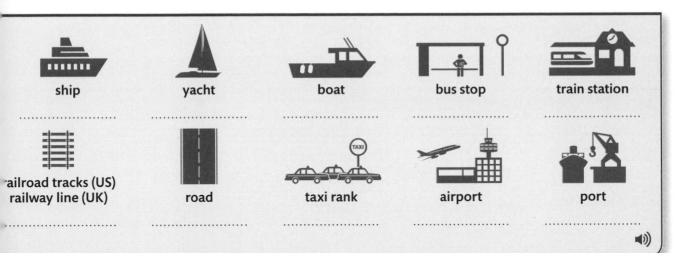

ship

yacht

boat

bus stop

train station

railroad tracks (US)
railway line (UK)

road

taxi rank

airport

port

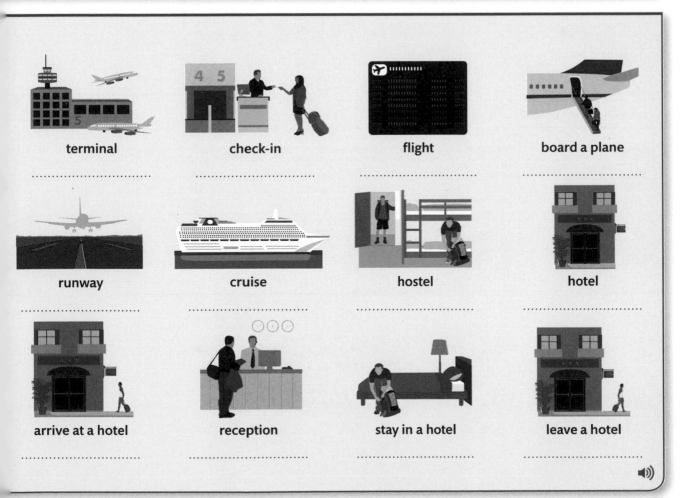

terminal

check-in

flight

board a plane

runway

cruise

hostel

hotel

arrive at a hotel

reception

stay in a hotel

leave a hotel

24 Places I have been

In English, the present perfect tense is used to talk about recent or repeated past events. The past simple is used to say exactly when those events happened.

⚙ **New language** Present perfect tense
Aa Vocabulary Travel experiences
🧩 **New skill** Talking about the recent past

24.1 KEY LANGUAGE PRESENT PERFECT

The present perfect can be used to talk about the past in three different ways.

SUBJECT + HAVE/HAS + PAST PARTICIPLE

To give new information or "news."

Hi! I have arrived in London! My plane landed five minutes ago.

To talk about a repeated action that continues to happen.

I have visited California every summer since I was 18.

To talk about an event that started in the past and is still happening now.

Olivia has gone on a trip to Egypt.

🔊

24.2 FILL IN THE GAPS BY PUTTING THE VERBS IN THE PRESENT PERFECT

We ___*have left*___ (leave) and are on our way to the airport.

① They _____ (set off) on the Pilgrims' Way walk to Santiago de Compostela.

② He _____ (not finish) cycling through Europe.

③ They _____ (go) on a cruise to the Caribbean.

④ She _____ (visit) her family in Cuba every year since 2004.

🔊

24.3 KEY LANGUAGE PRESENT PERFECT AND PAST SIMPLE

The present perfect is used for talking about a recent event or ongoing action.

SUBJECT + "HAVE / HAS" + PAST PARTICIPLE

Olivia **has gone** to Egypt on vacation.

The past simple gives specific details about when a completed event happened.

SUBJECT + PAST SIMPLE   **TIME MARKER**

Olivia **went** to Egypt last week.

24.4 MARK THE SENTENCES THAT ARE CORRECT

I has cycled in Holland several times. ☐
I have cycled in Holland several times. ☑

1. Annie went to Kenya last winter. ☐
   Annie has gone to Kenya last winter. ☐

2. Uma has visited Cuba every year since 2011. ☐
   Uma have visit Cuba every year since 2011. ☐

3. I've flown to Spain for a vacation last month. ☐
   I flew to Spain for a vacation last month. ☐

4. Liam has gone on a bus tour of Ireland. ☐
   Liam have gone on a bus tour of Ireland. ☐

5. Nada studied Tai Chi in China last year. ☐
   Nada have studied Tai Chi in China last year. ☐

6. Andrew gone to Australia. ☐
   Andrew has gone to Australia. ☐

7. They have reached the North Pole! ☐
   They has reached the North Pole! ☐

24.5 LISTEN TO THE AUDIO AND ANSWER THE QUESTIONS

Jodie and Trina are talking about Trina's travel adventures and what she has learned along the way.

Where has Trina been?
Trina has been out of the country.

1. Was this Trina's first road trip?

_____

2. What did she learn to do in the Sierra Nevada?

_____

3. Does she own hang gliding equipment?

_____

4. What other skill has Trina learned?

_____

5. How did she get to Egypt?

_____

24.6 READ THE ARTICLE AND ANSWER THE QUESTIONS IN FULL SENTENCES

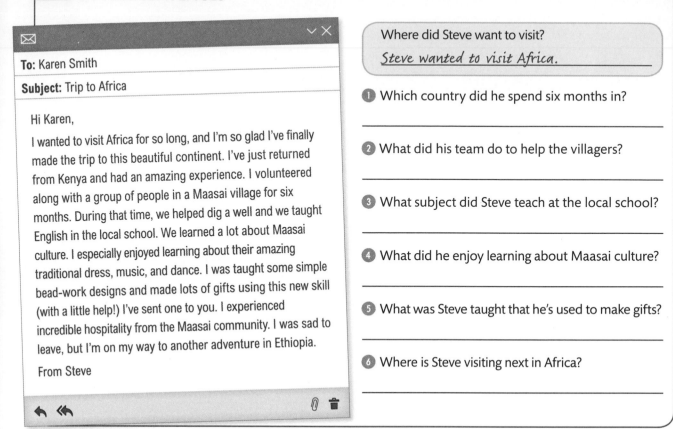

To: Karen Smith

Subject: Trip to Africa

Hi Karen,

I wanted to visit Africa for so long, and I'm so glad I've finally made the trip to this beautiful continent. I've just returned from Kenya and had an amazing experience. I volunteered along with a group of people in a Maasai village for six months. During that time, we helped dig a well and we taught English in the local school. We learned a lot about Maasai culture. I especially enjoyed learning about their amazing traditional dress, music, and dance. I was taught some simple bead-work designs and made lots of gifts using this new skill (with a little help!) I've sent one to you. I experienced incredible hospitality from the Maasai community. I was sad to leave, but I'm on my way to another adventure in Ethiopia.

From Steve

Where did Steve want to visit?

Steve wanted to visit Africa.

❶ Which country did he spend six months in?

_____

❷ What did his team do to help the villagers?

_____

❸ What subject did Steve teach at the local school?

_____

❹ What did he enjoy learning about Maasai culture?

_____

❺ What was Steve taught that he's used to make gifts?

_____

❻ Where is Steve visiting next in Africa?

_____

24.7 SAY THE SENTENCES OUT LOUD, FILLING IN THE GAPS

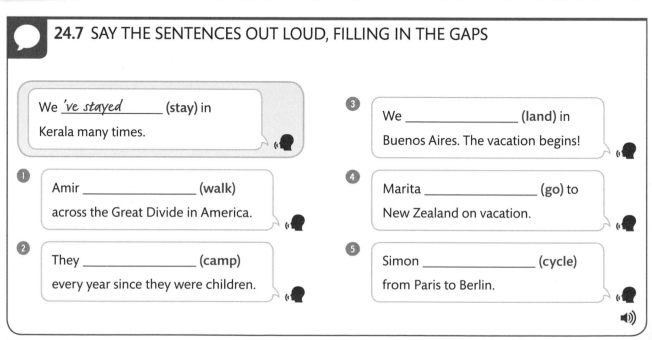

We _'ve stayed_ (stay) in Kerala many times.

❶ Amir _____ (walk) across the Great Divide in America.

❷ They _____ (camp) every year since they were children.

❸ We _____ (land) in Buenos Aires. The vacation begins!

❹ Marita _____ (go) to New Zealand on vacation.

❺ Simon _____ (cycle) from Paris to Berlin.

24.8 KEY LANGUAGE PRESENT PERFECT AND PAST SIMPLE IN US ENGLISH

US English often uses the past simple when
UK English would use the present perfect.

No dessert for me! I ate too much. (US)
No dessert for me! I've eaten too much. (UK)

I can't find my passport. Did you see it? (US)
I can't find my passport. Have you seen it? (UK)

24.9 CROSS OUT THE INCORRECT WORD IN EACH SENTENCE

> Did you **see** / ~~seen~~ the Statue of Liberty?

1. **I** / **I've** ate so much pizza when I was in Italy.

2. **They've** / **They** received our postcard yesterday.

3. Didn't you **arrive** / **arrived** here on Friday?

4. **Did** / **Have** you go to Finland this year?

5. **She** / **She's** found her passport on Tuesday.

6. Did he **write** / **wrote** this travel guide book?

7. **We've** / **We** taught English in Peru last summer.

8. Did they **cycled** / **cycle** all the way to Spain?

9. **Have** / **Did** you hike to the top of that mountain?

24.10 REWRITE THE SENTENCES IN THE PAST SIMPLE

> I've told you about my vacation.
> _I told you about my vacation._

1. Have you visited Peru?

   _____

2. Have you finished your packing yet?

   _____

3. We've had a wonderful time at the beach.

   _____

4. I love Spain. Have you gone there before?

   _____

5. Are you hungry again? Haven't you just eaten?

   _____

6. I've just seen an amazing opera in Rome.

   _____

---

24 ✓ CHECKLIST

⚙ Present perfect ☐   **Aa** Travel experiences ☐   🧩 Talking about the recent past ☐

25 Things I have done

You can use the present perfect to talk about personal achievements. Modifying adverbs can help you to be precise about when the achievements happened.

⚙ **New language** Modifying adverbs
Aa Vocabulary Adventure sports
🧩 **New skill** Talking about your achievements

25.1 KEY LANGUAGE PRESENT PERFECT WITH MODIFYING ADVERBS

Modifying adverbs give more information about when or if an action happened.

The adverb "already" means that something has happened or been completed, possibly earlier than expected.

"Already" is usually placed before the main verb.

I've already packed my bags, so I can relax now.

"Just" is placed before the main verb.

**I've just called a cab.
It should be here soon.**

The adverb "just" means "a short time ago."

The adverb "yet" is used to talk about something that is expected to happen. It is used only in questions and negative sentences.

"Yet" is usually placed at the end of the sentence.

**The cab hasn't arrived yet.
I hope I won't be late.**

"Still" is usually placed after the subject.

**The cab still hasn't arrived.
Where can it be?**

The adverb "still" means an action or situation is ongoing.

🔊))

25.2 REWRITE THE SENTENCES, PUTTING THE MODIFYING ADVERB IN THE CORRECT PLACE

> I've run a marathon. **(just)**
> _I've just run a marathon._

1 She hasn't been hiking. **(yet)**

_____

2 I've learned three languages. **(already)**

_____

3 They've finished canoeing down the river. **(just)**

_____

4 He's swum in a coral reef. **(already)**

_____

5 Our flight to Madrid is delayed. **(still)**

_____

25.3 READ THE POSTCARD AND ANSWER THE QUESTIONS

Hi Dad,

My trip to Australia continues to be incredible! I'm in Sydney and I've already climbed the Harbour Bridge. Another highlight was Bondi Beach, where I learned to surf! I still haven't gone on a boat trip around Darling Harbour. I've just returned from a hiking tour of the Blue Mountains. It was amazing! When I was in Queensland, we swam in the Great Barrier Reef, but I haven't seen any dolphins yet. I still haven't seen a kangaroo, but I hope I will on the long drive to Melbourne.

Love, Anita

> What has Anita climbed in Sydney?
> **A mountain** ☐ **A reef** ☐ **Harbour bridge** ☑

1 What did Anita learn to do at Bondi Beach?
Sunbathe ☐ **Surf** ☐ **Dive** ☐

2 What does Anita hope to do in Darling Harbour?
Take a boat trip ☐ **Swim** ☐ **Sunbathe** ☐

3 What activity did Anita do in the Blue Mountains?
Hiking ☐ **Climbing** ☐ **Surfing** ☐

4 Which animal hasn't Anita seen in the ocean yet?
Koala ☐ **Dolphin** ☐ **Whale** ☐

5 What animal does Anita hope to see?
Whale ☐ **Koala** ☐ **Kangaroo** ☐

25.4 VOCABULARY ADVENTURE SPORTS

scuba diving

hang gliding

sky diving

snorkeling

go on safari

windsurfing

25.5 READ THE ARTICLE AND ANSWER THE QUESTIONS IN FULL SENTENCES

HOLIDAY TIPS

Five Things to Do This Summer

By Ian Freshman

1 Snorkeling in the Red Sea
I've loved snorkeling since I was a kid. It's still my favorite hobby and the Red Sea is amazing. It's also fantastic for scuba-diving.

2 Windsurfing in Venezuela
If, like me, you love windsurfing, you should go to Margarita Island, off the coast of Venezuela. With perfect winds, it's a windsurfer's paradise.

3 Hang gliding in Interlaken
Viewing the awe-inspiring scenery from above is the nearest I've been to "hang gliding heaven!" I've just returned from Interlaken and I've already booked my next trip.

4 Safari in South Africa
I haven't been on nearly enough safaris yet. Driving around in a big open vehicle, hoping to see a "big cat," is an exciting experience.

5 Skydiving in Hawaii
I went last year and discovered the ultimate thrill for adrenalin lovers. While you're "diving," keep your eyes open because the view's stunning!

What is Ian's favorite thing to do?
Ian's favorite thing to do is snorkeling.

❶ Where does Ian enjoy snorkeling?

_____

❷ Where is Margarita Island?

_____

❸ What activity has Ian just done in Interlaken?

_____

❹ Does Tim want to hang glide again in Interlaken?

_____

❺ What does Ian hope to see when in South Africa?

_____

❻ What did Ian do last year?

_____

❼ What should you do while skydiving?

_____

88

25.6 LISTEN TO THE AUDIO AND ANSWER THE QUESTIONS

Maria and Kevin are talking about the things they've done since they got married, three years ago.

They have done many things together.
True ☑ False ☐

1 Maria and Kevin haven't visited every country.
True ☐ False ☐

2 They have been hang gliding in Switzerland.
True ☐ False ☐

3 Maria and Kevin have been skydiving in Australia.
True ☐ False ☐

4 Maria hasn't tried windsurfing yet.
True ☐ False ☐

5 Maria learned French a long time ago.
True ☐ False ☐

6 Kevin hasn't done much surfing this year.
True ☐ False ☐

25 ✓ CHECKLIST

⚙ Modifying adverbs ☐   **Aa** Adventure sports ☐   🧩 Talking about your achievements ☐

↻ REVIEW THE ENGLISH YOU HAVE LEARNED IN UNITS 20–25

NEW LANGUAGE	SAMPLE SENTENCE	☑	UNIT
PAST SIMPLE WITH EMPHASIS	I thought you asked Maya to tidy her room. I did ask her. I think she forgot.	☐	20.2
PAST SIMPLE IRREGULAR VERBS	They hid behind the tree.	☐	20.9
PREFIXES AND SUFFIXES	Jane is unlikely to study history. Mr. Ri was pleased the play was successful.	☐	22.1
PRESENT PERFECT: TO GIVE NEW INFORMATION	I have arrived in London! My plane landed five minutes ago.	☐	24.1
PRESENT PERFECT: TO TALK ABOUT A REPEATED ACTION	I have visited California every summer since I was 18.	☐	24.1
PRESENT PERFECT: TO TALK ABOUT AN EVENT THAT IS STILL HAPPENING NOW	Olivia has gone on a trip to Egypt.	☐	24.3
PRESENT PERFECT AND PAST SIMPLE	Olivia has gone to Egypt on vacation. Olivia went to Egypt in September.	☐	24.3
PRESENT PERFECT WITH MODIFYING ADVERBS	I've already packed my bag, so I can relax now. The cab still hasn't arrived. Where can it be?	☐	25.1

26 Activities in progress

Use the present perfect continuous to talk about ongoing activities in the past. Use "for" and "since" to talk about the length or starting point of an activity.

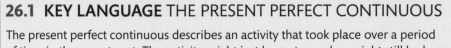 **New language** Present perfect continuous
Aa Vocabulary Home improvements
New skill Talking about activities in the past

26.1 KEY LANGUAGE THE PRESENT PERFECT CONTINUOUS

The present perfect continuous describes an activity that took place over a period of time in the recent past. The activity might just have stopped or might still be happening.

PRESENT PERFECT CONTINUOUS

The past activity often affects the present moment.

I have been painting the house all day. I'm exhausted!

26.2 FURTHER EXAMPLES THE PRESENT PERFECT CONTINUOUS

"I have" can be shortened to "I've."

I've been cooking this evening. Now I have to do the dishes.

"He has" can be shortened to "He's."

He's been waiting for the bus for an hour. He is going to be late for work.

26.3 HOW TO FORM THE PRESENT PERFECT CONTINUOUS

SUBJECT	"HAS/HAVE"	"BEEN"	VERB + "-ING"	OBJECT
I	have	been	painting	the house.

Use "have" or "has," depending on the subject.

"Been" stays the same for all subjects.

Add "ing" to the main verb.

26.4 FILL IN THE GAPS BY PUTTING THE VERBS IN THE PRESENT PERFECT CONTINUOUS

I _have been cooking_ (cook) dinner all afternoon. I'm having a dinner party tonight.

1 They _____ (play) tennis this morning. Now they're very tired.

2 Tom _____ (fish) today. He's caught lots of fish.

3 We _____ (watch) TV all evening. Now it's time to go to bed.

4 Irina _____ (read) a book in the park. She says it's really good.

5 You _____ (clean) the apartment all day. It's time for a break.

6 I _____ (listen) to music on the way to work. It helps me relax.

🔊

Aa   26.5 READ THE ARTICLE AND MATCH THE PICTURES TO THE PHRASES

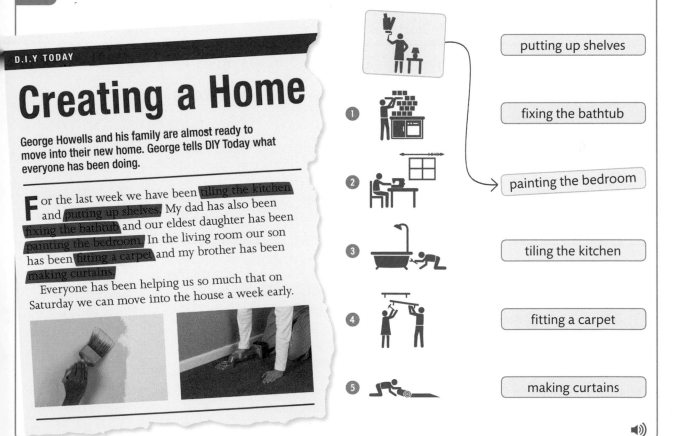

D.I.Y TODAY

Creating a Home

George Howells and his family are almost ready to move into their new home. George tells DIY Today what everyone has been doing.

For the last week we have been tiling the kitchen and putting up shelves. My dad has also been fixing the bathtub and our eldest daughter has been painting the bedroom. In the living room our son has been fitting a carpet and my brother has been making curtains.

Everyone has been helping us so much that on Saturday we can move into the house a week early.

putting up shelves

fixing the bathtub

painting the bedroom

tiling the kitchen

fitting a carpet

making curtains

🔊

91

26.6 KEY LANGUAGE "FOR" AND "SINCE"

English uses "for" with the present perfect continuous to show the length of time that an action has taken. "Since" is used to show the starting point of the action.

"FOR" + QUANTITY OF TIME

I have been painting **the house** for **three hours.**

This means the speaker started painting three hours ago.

"SINCE" + TIME OR DATE

I have been painting **the house** since **3 o'clock.**

This means the speaker started painting at 3pm.

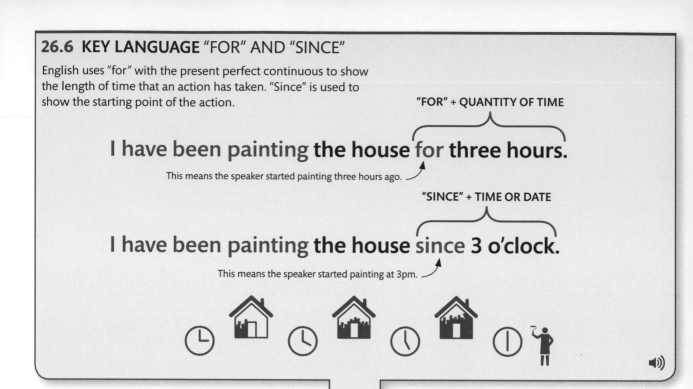

26.7 FURTHER EXAMPLES "FOR" AND "SINCE"

He's been tiling **the kitchen** for **a week.**
He's been tiling **the kitchen** since **last Wednesday.**

26.8 USE THE CHART TO CREATE 16 CORRECT SENTENCES AND SAY THEM OUT LOUD

I've been tiling the bathroom for three weeks.

| I've / She's | been | tiling the bathroom / painting the walls | for / since | three weeks. / noon. / two days. / April. |

26.9 FILL IN THE GAPS WITH "FOR" OR "SINCE"

 He's been cleaning ____*for*____ five hours. His parents are visiting the apartment tonight.

1 It's been raining _____ Saturday morning. I hope the weather gets better soon!

2 You've been gardening _____ 9 o'clock. You should take a break.

3 I've been swimming _____ 20 minutes. I'm quite tired, but I'll keep going.

4 She's been baking _____ 11 o'clock this morning. We'll have lots of cookies to eat later.

5 He's been tiling the wall _____ three hours. I think it will be finished today.

26.10 LISTEN TO THE AUDIO AND WRITE HOW LONG THE ACTIVITY IN EACH PICTURE HAS BEEN GOING ON FOR

for three weeks

1 _____

2 _____

3 _____

4 _____

5 _____

---

26 ✓ CHECKLIST

⚙ Present perfect continuous ☐   **Aa** Home improvements ☐   🧩 Talking about activities in the past ☐

93

27 My talents and skills

When you see evidence that something has happened, you can use the present perfect continuous to ask questions about it.

⚙ **New language** Present perfect continuous question
Aa Vocabulary Hobbies and interests
🧩 **New skill** Asking about past events

27.1 KEY LANGUAGE PRESENT PERFECT CONTINUOUS QUESTIONS

English uses present perfect continuous questions to ask about ongoing actions in the recent past, especially when there is evidence that an action has taken place.

The subject goes between "have" and "been."

Have you been baking a cake?
It smells delicious!

27.2 FURTHER EXAMPLES PRESENT PERFECT CONTINUOUS QUESTIONS

Have you been gardening? Your flowers look nice.

Have you been learning the guitar?

James looks good. Has he been working out?

27.3 HOW TO FORM PRESENT PERFECT CONTINUOUS QUESTIONS

In present perfect continuous questions, the subject comes between "has" or "have" and "been."

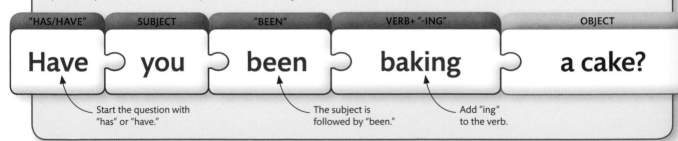

"HAS/HAVE"	SUBJECT	"BEEN"	VERB+ "-ING"	OBJECT
Have	**you**	**been**	**baking**	**a cake?**

Start the question with "has" or "have."

The subject is followed by "been."

Add "ing" to the verb.

27.4 REWRITE THE STATEMENTS AS QUESTIONS

He's been playing the drums.
Has he been playing the drums?

1 She's been training for a race.

_____

2 He's been learning the violin.

_____

3 They've been playing music together.

_____

4 She's been taking photos of the city.

_____

5 You've been painting her portrait.

_____

27.5 LISTEN TO THE AUDIO AND ANSWER THE QUESTIONS

Cath is going to Vikram's house for dinner. The two friends haven't seen each other for a long time.

Vikram has been cooking for Cath.
True ☑ **False** ☐

1 Cath has been making a curry.
True ☐ **False** ☐

2 Cath has been working for a magazine.
True ☐ **False** ☐

3 Cath has been painting her apartment.
True ☐ **False** ☐

4 Vikram hasn't been designing menus.
True ☐ **False** ☐

5 Vikram will open a new restaurant.
True ☐ **False** ☐

27.6 MATCH THE STATEMENTS TO THE QUESTIONS

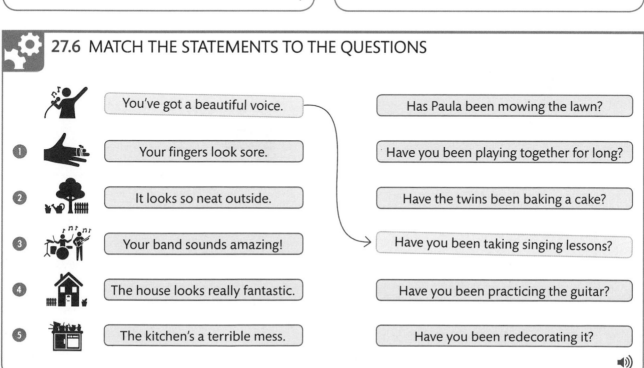

You've got a beautiful voice. — Has Paula been mowing the lawn?

1 Your fingers look sore. — Have you been playing together for long?

2 It looks so neat outside. — Have the twins been baking a cake?

3 Your band sounds amazing! → Have you been taking singing lessons?

4 The house looks really fantastic. — Have you been practicing the guitar?

5 The kitchen's a terrible mess. — Have you been redecorating it?

27.7 KEY LANGUAGE "HOW LONG?"

You can add "how long" to the beginning of present perfect continuous questions to ask about the duration of actions in the past. Answers to these questions use the present perfect continuous with "for" or "since."

"How long" is added to the beginning of the question.

How long have you been playing the guitar?

I've been playing the guitar { **for five months.**
since January.

🔊

27.8 FURTHER EXAMPLES "HOW LONG?"

How long has he been learning the piano?

He's been learning the piano since last May.

How long has she been singing in the choir?

She's been singing in the choir for nine months.

🔊

27.9 REWRITE THE SENTENCES, PUTTING THE WORDS IN THE CORRECT ORDER

the | playing | been | How | have | long | you | trumpet?
How long have you been playing the trumpet?

① long | Melissa | How | writing | has | novel? | been | her
_____

② house? | the | painting | have | long | been | they | How
_____

③ Savannah | has | practicing | long | recorder? | How | the | been
_____

④ learning | been | long | drive? | How | to | Alejandro | has
_____

🔊

96

27.10 READ THE ARTICLE AND ANSWER THE QUESTIONS

When did The Tangs start working on their album?
Two years ago ✓ **Last year** ☐ **Six months ago** ☐

❶ Where did The Tangs start playing music together?
At college ☐ **At work** ☐ **At school** ☐

❷ What instrument did Dan learn to play?
Piano ☐ **Guitar** ☐ **Drums** ☐

❸ How long has Jules been playing the saxophone?
Five years ☐ **Seven years** ☐ **He can't play** ☐

❹ How long have The Tangs been writing songs?
Three years ☐ **Always** ☐ **A few years** ☐

❺ Has Jess been taking singing lessons?
Yes ☐ **No** ☐ **She doesn't say** ☐

MAD FOR MUSIC

5 mins with The Tangs

M4M: Your new album, Funk Family, is out next week. How long have you been working on it?
Jules: For two years. We wanted to get it just right!

M4M: And how long have you been playing music together?
Jess: Since we were at school. Jules couldn't even play the saxophone at first, and Dan took drumming lessons.
Jules: Now I've been playing the sax for seven years.
Dan: At first we played all sorts of music, but for the last three years, we've been writing our own songs.

M4M: And you sound great! Jess, you've got a beautiful voice. Have you been taking lessons?
Jess: Not to start with, but I have recently.

27.11 SAY THE PRESENT PERFECT CONTINUOUS QUESTIONS OUT LOUD, FILLING IN THE GAPS

How long ___*has*___ Jason ___*been learning*___ (learn) the guitar?

❶ How long _____ you _____ (play) the piano?

❷ How long _____ they _____ (perform) in public?

❸ How long _____ Ben _____ (take) singing lessons?

❹ How long _____ she _____ (learn) English?

27 ✓ CHECKLIST

⚙ Present perfect continuous questions ☐   **Aa** Hobbies and interests ☐   🧩 Asking about past events ☐

28 Activities and their results

English uses the present perfect continuous to talk about recent activities that are probably still ongoing. Use the present perfect simple to talk about finished activities.

⚙ **New language** Forms of the present perfect
Aa Vocabulary State and action verbs
🧩 **New skill** Talking about results of activities

28.1 KEY LANGUAGE PRESENT PERFECT CONTINUOUS AND PRESENT PERFECT SIMPLE

Use the present perfect continuous to emphasize the continuous nature of an activity in the past. It is possible that the activity is still going on.

PRESENT PERFECT CONTINUOUS

I've been fixing my car. I'm covered in oil.

Use the present perfect simple to emphasize the completion of an activity in the past. It is likely that the activity is finished.

PRESENT PERFECT SIMPLE

I've fixed my car. Now I can drive to work again.

🔊

28.2 FURTHER EXAMPLES PRESENT PERFECT CONTINUOUS AND PRESENT PERFECT SIMPLE

I've been cooking **dinner. It will be ready soon.**

I've cooked **dinner. It's ready now.**

Vicky has been running **today. Now she's really tired!**

Vicky has just run **a race. Now she's receiving a medal.**

I've been eating **too much cake. I must eat less!**

I've eaten **all the cake. The plate is empty.**

🔊

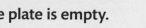

28.3 MARK THE SENTENCES THAT ARE CORRECT

I've been playing rugby all afternoon. I'm exhausted and covered in mud. ☑
I've played rugby all afternoon. I'm exhausted and covered in mud. ☐

1. He's washed the car for half an hour. There's water all over our driveway. ☐
   He's been washing the car for half an hour. There's water all over our driveway. ☐

2. Her room looks so neat and tidy. She's put all her clothes away now. ☐
   Her room looks so neat and tidy. She's been putting all her clothes away now. ☐

3. How long have you walked in the rain? You're both soaking wet. ☐
   How long have you been walking in the rain? You're both soaking wet. ☐

4. You've been sunbathing for far too long. Please go and sit in the shade now. ☐
   You've sunbathed for far too long. Please go and sit in the shade now. ☐

5. Riley has just broken a glass. There are pieces on the floor, so be careful. ☐
   Riley has just been breaking a glass. There are pieces on the floor, so be careful. ☐

6. Has Oliver eaten chocolate all morning? He won't want any lunch. ☐
   Has Oliver been eating chocolate all morning? He won't want any lunch. ☐

7. I've just finished a really good book. You can borrow it now if you like. ☐
   I've just been finishing a really good book. You can borrow it now if you like. ☐

28.4 LISTEN TO THE AUDIO AND MARK WHETHER THE ACTIVITY IN EACH PICTURE IS IN PROGRESS OR FINISHED

In progress ☑
Finished ☐

1. In progress ☐
   Finished ☐

2. In progress ☐
   Finished ☐

3. In progress ☐
   Finished ☐

4. In progress ☐
   Finished ☐

28.5 ⚠ COMMON MISTAKES STATE VERBS AND ACTION VERBS

State verbs describe feelings or a state of mind.
Action verbs describe an action. You cannot
normally use state verbs in the continuous form.

I've always loved classical music. ✓

"Love" is a state verb, so it is correct
to use it in the present perfect simple.

I've always been loving classical music. ✗

It is incorrect to use "love" in
the present perfect continuous.

28.6 READ THE ARTICLE AND WRITE ANSWERS TO THE QUESTIONS AS FULL SENTENCES

PROPERTY NEWS

A perfect home?

Buying an apartment is harder than you think,
says property expert Stella Parnell

've always loved
property. It's
fascinating to see how
people have decorated
their homes. It's always
been easy for me to have
an opinion about
properties when I've
been viewing them with
friends, because I can
easily imagine how
places might look.

Of course, it's also
important to realize
how much apartment
maintenance costs. In
my current apartment,
I've been repairing
hundreds of little faults
for years. My friend
Sadiq has almost
completely rebuilt his
apartment in the same
amount of time! This
week I have been
calculating roughly how
much time and money
I've spent on repairs
over the years. It's
expensive, but now I
understand how
important it is to look
after your property. This
month I've been
painting my living room
and tiling the kitchen.
The apartment will look
great when it's all done!

What has Stella Parnell always loved?

She has always loved property.

❶ What does she say is fascinating to see?

_____

❷ What can she easily imagine?

_____

❸ What has she been doing in her apartment?

_____

❹ What has Sadiq done with his apartment?

_____

❺ What has Stella been doing this week?

_____

❻ What does she understand now?

_____

❼ What has she been doing this month?

_____

28.7 DESCRIBE THE PICTURES OUT LOUD USING THE PRESENT PERFECT CONTINUOUS OR PRESENT PERFECT SIMPLE

He _has been repairing_ his bike and he's covered in oil.

1. I _____ all the cake. There are only crumbs left.

2. Luca _____ just _____ a big fish.

3. We _____ in the rain. We're all soaking wet!

4. She _____ for an hour. The food smells delicious!

28.8 REWRITE THE LETTER, CORRECTING THE ERRORS

Hi Jacob,
I hear you've been passing your driving test and that Uncle George has been buying you a car. Congratulations! I suppose you've driven around ever since. I'm so jealous. I've always been wanting to learn to drive. You should visit me soon! I've worked too hard recently and I've been realizing that I need a break.
Love Alice

Hi Jacob,
I hear you've passed your driving test

28 ✓ CHECKLIST

🗗 Forms of the present perfect ☐   **Aa** State and action verbs ☐   👥 Talking about results of activities ☐

29 Everyday problems

Prefixes that mean "not" are called negative prefixes. Many words that have negative prefixes are useful for talking about everyday workplace and urban problems.

⚙ **New language** Negative prefixes
Aa Vocabulary Urban problems
New skill Talking about everyday problems

29.1 KEY LANGUAGE NEGATIVE PREFIXES

Negative prefixes change a word's meaning to its opposite.

Maria is very organized. Her desk is always tidy.

Kevin is very disorganized. His desk is always untidy.

The opposite of "organized."   The opposite of "tidy."

29.2 FURTHER EXAMPLES NEGATIVE PREFIXES

The traffic is so bad it's impossible to get to work on time.

I think you've misunderstood what I was trying to say.

It's irresponsible to drive faster than the speed limit.

It's illegal to park in the middle of the road.

Aa 29.3 FILL IN THE GAPS USING THE WORDS IN THE PANEL

They were so ___unlucky___ to miss the train this morning.

❶ It's _____ to solve a problem when you don't have all the facts.

❷ Her room is so _____ that you can't even see the floor.

❸ He's very _____ , so I always have to check to confirm our meetings.

❹ It's _____ to download that movie without paying for it.

> untidy
> illegal
> ~~unlucky~~
> impossible
> disorganized

Aa 29.4 READ THE ARTICLE AND FIND 11 MORE WORDS THAT BEGIN WITH NEGATIVE PREFIXES

1 im-
- immature

2 dis-

3 un-

4 ir-

Your problems solved!

Our experts are here to help solve all your problems

Bad Workplace Habits

Q I share my office with 20 young co-workers. Most are great, but some are really immature and it's almost impossible to work with them. They play unacceptable and irresponsible tricks on colleagues. For example, if I leave my desk tidy, I sometimes return to find it in total disorder. And they also swap computers around during lunch, leaving people unable to do their work. Actually, it's unusual to come back to the desk and find everything as we left it. These people think it's funny, but I disagree. I think it's disrespectful. I understand the irresistible if slightly irrational wish to break rules, but I'm getting very impatient with their behavior. Should I report them to our manager?

Jenny (via email)

29.5 SAY THE OPPOSITE OF THE STATEMENTS OUT LOUD, USING NEGATIVE PREFIXES

They were able to meet their deadline.

They were unable to meet their deadline.

1 You have made a very mature decision.

2 Speeding on the freeway is responsible.

3 Playing tricks on your colleagues is acceptable.

4 I completely agree with you.

5 Your remarks were very respectful.

103

29.6 VOCABULARY URBAN PROBLEMS

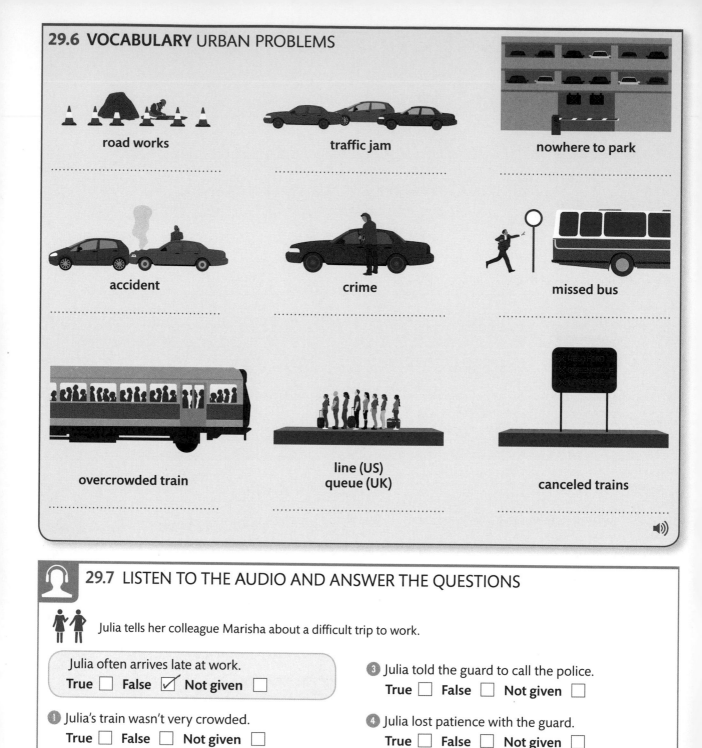

road works

traffic jam

nowhere to park

accident

crime

missed bus

overcrowded train

line (US)
queue (UK)

canceled trains

29.7 LISTEN TO THE AUDIO AND ANSWER THE QUESTIONS

Julia tells her colleague Marisha about a difficult trip to work.

Julia often arrives late at work.
True ☐ **False** ☐ **Not given** ☑

1 Julia's train wasn't very crowded.
True ☐ **False** ☐ **Not given** ☐

2 Julia thought the students were childish.
True ☐ **False** ☐ **Not given** ☐

3 Julia told the guard to call the police.
True ☐ **False** ☐ **Not given** ☐

4 Julia lost patience with the guard.
True ☐ **False** ☐ **Not given** ☐

5 The next train was on time.
True ☐ **False** ☐ **Not given** ☐

Aa 29.8 FILL IN THE GAPS USING THE WORDS IN THE PANEL

I'm stuck in a _____ *traffic jam* _____ on the highway.

Panel words:
- accident
- delayed
- road works
- unusual
- ~~traffic jam~~
- impatient
- impossible
- Unfortunately
- overcrowded

1 _____ there's been an _____ 2 miles south of us.

2 It's _____ to move, and we could be _____ for another 2 hours.

3 The highway was already jammed because of the _____ .

4 The traffic is so bad that the highway is like an _____ parking lot.

5 People are getting very _____ , which I suppose isn't _____ .

🔊

---

29 ✓ CHECKLIST

⚙ Negative prefixes ☐　　**Aa** Urban problems ☐　　🧩 Talking about everyday problems ☐

🔄 REVIEW THE ENGLISH YOU HAVE LEARNED IN UNITS 26–29

NEW LANGUAGE	SAMPLE SENTENCE	☑	UNIT
PRESENT PERFECT CONTINUOUS	I have been painting **the house all day.**	☐	26.1
"FOR" AND "SINCE"	I've been painting the house for three hours. I've been painting the house since three o'clock.	☐	26.6
PRESENT PERFECT CONTINUOUS QUESTIONS	Have you been baking a cake? How long have you been playing the guitar?	☐	27.1, 27.7
PRESENT PERFECT CONTINUOUS FOR ONGOING ACTIVITIES	I've been fixing my car. I'm covered in oil.	☐	28.1
PRESENT PERFECT SIMPLE FOR FINISHED ACTIVITIES	I've fixed my car. Now I can drive to work again.	☐	28.1
STATE VERBS	I've always loved classical music.	☐	28.5
NEGATIVE PREFIXES	Kevin is very disorganized. His desk is always untidy.	☐	29.1

30 General and specific things

Articles sit before the noun in English, and give more information about which item is being described. Use "the" to talk about specific items.

⚙ **New language** Definite and zero articles
Aa Vocabulary Possessions
🧩 **New skill** Talking about the things you own

30.1 KEY LANGUAGE DEFINITE AND ZERO ARTICLES

English uses no article (zero article) to talk about things in general. Use "the" (definite article) to talk about specific things.

GENERAL

Sam is always buying clothes.

SPECIFIC

The clothes he bought yesterday were expensive.

30.2 FURTHER EXAMPLES DEFINITE AND ZERO ARTICLES

I like reading books.
The last book I read was very good.

You take great photos.
The photo in your living room is beautiful.

I usually save money, but I'm going
to spend the money I got for my birthday.

Jenny has lots of shoes.
The shoes she's wearing today are green.

30.3 REWRITE THE SENTENCES, CORRECTING THE ERRORS

I love eating the vegetables.
I love eating vegetables.

① Waiter is just getting us a menu.

② I enjoy shopping for the shoes.

③ Jo's back at school now vacation is over.

④ Has he paid you money that he owes you?

⑤ I like watching the exciting movies.

30.4 READ THE ARTICLE AND WRITE ANSWERS TO THE QUESTIONS AS FULL SENTENCES

COLLEGE LIFE

STARTING COLLEGE

Ex-student Emilia offers some advice to new students

You'll have to cook your own meals now.

When you see the student room you're going to live in, it looks great. It feels like freedom. But remember: you have to do your own cleaning now. Your parents won't be cooking meals for you either, so write down the recipes of dishes that you love. Money can be another problem. Speak to the student adviser at your local bank, who can help you budget properly and manage your money.

The social life in college is very exciting, with so many parties and people to meet. Enjoy everything, but remember that you have to study, too. Although exams don't seem important to you now, the final exams come around faster than you think. They could affect your future career, so play hard if you must, but remember to work too!

What will look great to new students?
Their new rooms will look great.

① What must new students do now?

② What won't students' parents do for them?

③ What should students write down?

④ What can be another problem for students?

⑤ Who can help students budget?

⑥ What is very exciting at college?

⑦ Why are the final exams so important?

30.5 KEY LANGUAGE "HAVE" AND "HAVE GOT"

You can use "have" or "have got" to talk about the things you own. "Have" is appropriate in all situations, but "have got" is only used in spoken UK English.

I have a new phone.
"Have" becomes "has" in the third person singular.

I've got a new phone.
"Got" doesn't change when the subject changes.

I don't have a dishwasher.
Always use "have" in the negative.

I haven't got a dishwasher.
"Have not" can be shortened to "haven't."

Do you have your keys?
The subject sits between "do" and "have" in questions.

Have you got your keys?
The subject sits between "have" and "got" in questions.

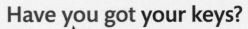

 30.6 USE THE CHART TO CREATE 6 CORRECT QUESTIONS AND SAY THEM OUT LOUD

Do you have your laptop?

| Do you / Have you | have / got | your | laptop? / wallet? / passport? |

 30.7 LISTEN TO THE AUDIO, THEN NUMBER THE PICTURES IN THE ORDER THEY ARE DESCRIBED

 A ☐

 B ①

 C ☐

 D ☐

 E ☐

 F ☐

30.8 LISTEN TO THE AUDIO FROM 30.7 AGAIN AND MARK THE THINGS THAT YOU HEAR

A ✓ B ☐ C ☐ D ☐ E ☐

F ☐ G ☐ H ☐ I ☐ J ☐

30.9 READ THE ARTICLE AND ANSWER THE QUESTIONS

Digital natives have few digital devices.
True ☐ **False** ☐ **Not given** ✓

① Some digital natives are tired of texting.
True ☐ **False** ☐ **Not given** ☐

② All older people have digital devices.
True ☐ **False** ☐ **Not given** ☐

③ Older people don't like using social media.
True ☐ **False** ☐ **Not given** ☐

④ Older people use apps to contact their friends.
True ☐ **False** ☐ **Not given** ☐

⑤ Some people don't have the latest devices.
True ☐ **False** ☐ **Not given** ☐

⑥ All smartphone users have a camera.
True ☐ **False** ☐ **Not given** ☐

---

94 **BUSINESS TODAY**

LIVING IN A DIGITAL WORLD

How to cope with today's digital lifestyle

These days, digital natives (people who have been brought up using digital technology) have many digital devices that they use every day. But the digital native who would rather talk than text is becoming more common.

Some elderly people still don't have any digital devices. But increasingly, older users are embracing the latest forms of communication, because they love keeping in contact with their family via social media apps.

Not everyone has the most up-to-date version of devices, but smartphones are very popular, and are replacing more traditional gadgets. Many people no longer have a camera, for example, because they can take photos with a smartphone.

---

30 ✔ **CHECKLIST**

⚙ Definite and zero articles ☐   **Aa** Possessions ☐   🧩 Talking about the things you own ☐

31 Vocabulary

31.1 FOOD AND DRINK

 fish

 meat

 seafood

 fruit

 vegetables

 herbs

 pork

 chicken

 lamb

 beef

 onion

garlic

 potatoes

 avocado

 mushrooms

 pepper

 zucchini (US) courgette (UK)

 lettuce

 tomato

 pineapple

 melon

 mango

 orange

lemon

 banana

 strawberry

 raspberries

 apple

 peach

 fruit salad

110

flour	dough	bread	pasta	noodles	rice

milk	cream	cheese	butter	yogurt	eggs

sandwich	soup	salad	burger	fries (US) chips (UK)	spaghetti

sugar	cookie	chocolate	cake	ice cream	cereal

coffee	tea	hot chocolate	juice	water	lemonade

32 Myself, yourself

English uses reflexive pronouns when the subject of the verb is the same as the object. They show that the action affects the person who is carrying it out.

🔧 **New language** Reflexive pronouns
Aa Vocabulary Measurements and flavors
🧩 **New skill** Talking about food and recipes

32.1 KEY LANGUAGE REFLEXIVE PRONOUNS

Reflexive pronouns in English include the word "self" (or "selves" in the plural).

He cut himself while chopping vegetables.

The subject pronoun refers to the person doing the action.

Use a reflexive pronoun when the same person is affected by the action.

🔊))

32.2 FURTHER EXAMPLES REFLEXIVE PRONOUNS

 She's teaching herself to cook.

He introduced himself to the other party guests.

 That pan is very hot. Don't burn yourself.

 Did they enjoy themselves at the party?

🔊))

32.3 KEY LANGUAGE REFLEXIVE PRONOUNS

SUBJECT PRONOUNS

me	you	he	she	it	we	they
⬇	⬇	⬇	⬇	⬇	⬇	⬇
myself	yourself 👤 yourselves 👥	himself	herself	itself	ourselves	themselves

REFLEXIVE PRONOUNS

🔊))

32.4 FILL IN THE GAPS USING THE WORDS IN THE PANEL

I think Elizabeth's enjoying ___*herself*___ .

1 I hope the children exhaust _____ and sleep tonight.

2 Look at baby Callum trying to feed _____ . Isn't he smart?

3 I can't find my keys. I hope we haven't locked _____ out.

4 Oh dear. I cut _____ while I was peeling potatoes.

5 You should take a break. You'll wear _____ out.

6 The dishwasher will turn _____ off when it's finished.

ourselves

~~herself~~   yourself

themselves

itself   himself

myself

 32.5 LISTEN TO THE AUDIO AND WRITE THE REFLEXIVE PRONOUN YOU HEAR UNDER EACH IMAGE

himself

 32.6 CROSS OUT THE INCORRECT WORDS IN EACH SENTENCE

I've burned ~~me~~ / **myself** on a hot pan.

1 The baby can pull **her** / **herself** up.

2 I'm teaching **them** / **themselves** to swim.

3 You really enjoyed **you** / **yourself** tonight.

4 Have you introduced **you** / **yourselves** to him?

5 Ouch! That wasp stung **me** / **myself**.

6 The cake's all gone. I've eaten **it** / **itself**.

7 The car's dirty. Please wash **it** / **itself**.

8 Don't tease the cat. You'll scare **her** / **herself**.

9 The oven will turn **it** / **itself** off now.

32.7 VOCABULARY MEASUREMENTS

The most common measurements of weight and volume are written and abbreviated as follows.

IMPERIAL MEASUREMENTS	
pound	**lb**
ounce	**oz**
fluid ounce	**fl. oz**
gallon	**gal**
quart	**qt**
pint	**pt**
cup	**c**
tablespoon	**tbsp**
teaspoon	**tsp**

METRIC MEASUREMENTS	
liter	**l**
milliliter	**ml**
gram	**g**
kilogram	**kg**

32.8 READ THE LIST OF INGREDIENTS OUT LOUD

Two pounds of dark chocolate

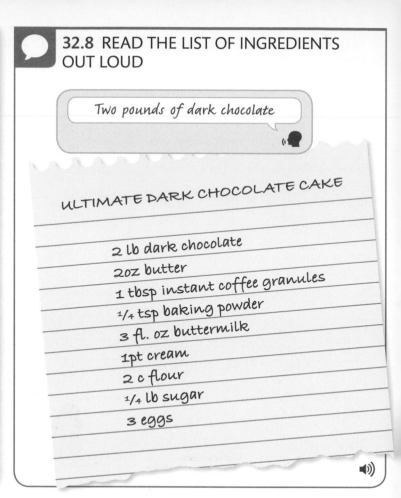

ULTIMATE DARK CHOCOLATE CAKE

2 lb dark chocolate

2oz butter

1 tbsp instant coffee granules

1/4 tsp baking powder

3 fl. oz buttermilk

1pt cream

2 c flour

1/4 lb sugar

3 eggs

32.9 VOCABULARY ADJECTIVES TO DESCRIBE FOOD AND DRINK

sweet chocolate

savory pasta

tasty cake

chilled water

salty pretzels

bitter lemons

mixed salad

spicy curry

fresh fruit

strong coffee

Aa 32.10 CROSS OUT THE INCORRECT WORDS IN EACH SENTENCE

I enjoy eating ~~sweet~~ / savory / ~~spicy~~ food, like meat, cheese, and vegetables.

1 I'm so tired this morning. I need a **tasty** / **mixed** / **strong** cup of coffee to wake me up.

2 I'd like some **chilled** / **salty** / **bitter** fruit juice, please. It's a hot day, and I need a refreshing drink.

3 That curry was too **mixed** / **chilled** / **spicy**. I'll follow a different recipe next time I make it.

4 Remember to buy lots of **fresh** / **strong** / **bitter** fruit. We're making a fruit salad tonight.

5 The chocolate mousse was too **salty** / **sweet** / **tasty** for me, but I think the guests will love it.

32.11 READ THE TEXT MESSAGES AND ANSWER THE QUESTIONS

Gemma had fun at the party.
True ✓ **False** ☐

1 Gemma thought the drinks were colorless.
True ☐ **False** ☐

2 Hannah asked Gemma if she liked the food.
True ☐ **False** ☐

3 Gemma said the curry didn't taste good.
True ☐ **False** ☐

4 The salad had lots of different ingredients.
True ☐ **False** ☐

5 Hannah was very pleased with the chocolate cake.
True ☐ **False** ☐

6 Gemma likes eating sugary food.
True ☐ **False** ☐

Gemma

Great party last night, Hannah! I really enjoyed myself. The drinks were delicious, and so colorful!

Thanks, Gemma. What did you think of the food?

Delicious! The curry was so tasty, and I loved your mixed salad.

Did you try the chocolate cake? I thought it was a bit too sweet.

I thought it was great! I love eating sweet things. Thank you for a wonderful party.

You're welcome. I'm glad you had a good time.

---

32 ✓ CHECKLIST

⚙ Reflexive pronouns ☐   **Aa** Measurements and flavors ☐   🧩 Talking about food and recipes ☐

115

33 What things are for

English uses gerunds and infinitives to talk about why people use things. This is useful for describing the purpose of everyday objects and household gadgets.

⚙ **New language** Gerunds and infinitives
Aa Vocabulary Household gadgets
🧩 **New skill** Talking about why you use things

33.1 KEY LANGUAGE GERUNDS AND INFINITIVES

When you talk about why you generally use things, you can use "for" with a gerund, or the infinitive ("to" plus verb). The meaning is the same.

"For" with a gerund

I **use** my blender { **for making** / **to make** } soup.

The present simple expresses a routine action.

Infinitive

33.2 FURTHER EXAMPLES GERUNDS AND INFINITIVES

 She uses her laptop { **for writing** / **to write** } emails.

 He uses this cloth { **for washing** / **to wash** } the dishes.

33.3 FILL IN THE GAPS USING THE WORDS IN THE PANEL

I use this knife to ___*chop*___ vegetables.

❶ They use the microwave for _____ food.

❷ We use our juicer to _____ fruit juice.

❸ She uses her phone for _____ her friends.

❹ They use this corkscrew to _____ bottles of wine.

❺ He uses his laptop for _____ movies.

texting	~~chop~~
open	watching
heating	make

33.4 KEY LANGUAGE INFINITIVES FOR SPECIFIC ACTIONS

When you talk about why someone does a specific action rather than what you do with something in general, you must use the infinitive. It is incorrect to use "for" and a gerund in this case.

Sentence refers to a specific action, not a routine action.

Sentence refers to one particular email, not emails in general.

I turned on my laptop to write an email. ✓

I turned on my laptop for writing an email. ✗

33.5 MATCH THE BEGINNINGS OF THE SENTENCES TO THE CORRECT ENDINGS

I went to the washing machine

1 I turned on the heating

2 You use a refrigerator

3 He uses this remote control

4 We turned on our sound system

5 I sometimes use my smartphone

to keep food fresh.

for taking photos.

to warm up the house.

to do the laundry.

for turning on the TV.

to listen to music.

33.6 LISTEN TO THE AUDIO AND ANSWER THE QUESTIONS

On a radio show, three inventors present their new gadgets.

Bilal's gadget is for household cleaning.
True ☑ **False** ☐

1 Bilal's gadget can find dirt on the floor.
True ☐ **False** ☐

2 Harry's gadget is for opening bottles.
True ☐ **False** ☐

3 You press a button to use Harry's gadget.
True ☐ **False** ☐

4 You use Lauren's gadget when you are at home.
True ☐ **False** ☐

5 Lauren's gadget can keep your house secure.
True ☐ **False** ☐

33.7 KEY LANGUAGE PHRASAL VERBS

Things you do with gadgets are often explained in English using separable phrasal verbs.

The particle can come straight after the verb.

  It's too hot in here. Let's { turn **on** the fan. / turn the fan **on**. }

The particle can come after the object.

 Can you { turn the radio **up**? / turn **up** the radio? } I can't hear it.

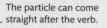

33.8 FILL IN THE GAPS USING THE WORDS IN THE PANEL

I always __turn__ the light __off__ when I leave a room.

1. He sometimes _____ the TV _____ too loud.

2. My laptop has a low battery. I need to _____ it _____ .

3. You shouldn't _____ emails _____ . It wastes paper.

4. Remember to _____ the computer _____ after work.

down	plug
out	turns
in	~~turn~~
shut	up
print	~~off~~

33.9 USE THE WORDS IN THE PANEL TO DESCRIBE THE GADGETS, SPEAKING OUT LOUD

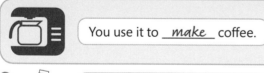 You use it to __make__ coffee.

3 It's for _____ to music.

1 It's for _____ your phone.

4 It's for _____ cans.

2 You use it to _____ your hair.

5 You use it to _____ photos.

| listening | take | ~~make~~ | opening | dry | charging |

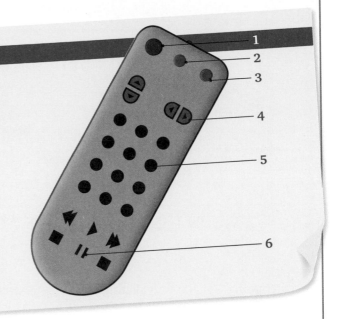

YOUR GUIDE TO YOUR NEW ALL-IN-ONE REMOTE

This versatile remote is for controlling all the audio-visual equipment in your home.

1 The red button is for turning the TV on and off.

2 Use the blue button to control the DVD player.

3 The yellow button is for turning the sound system on and off.

4 Use these buttons to change TV channels, or skip tracks when you listen to music.

5 The round black buttons are for selecting a particular TV channel.

6 Use this button to pause DVDs, music, or live TV.

What gadget can't you control using the all-in-one remote?

The television ☐

The refrigerator ☑

The sound system ☐

❶ What can you do if you press the red button on the remote control?

Turn on the TV ☐

Turn the TV up ☐

Pause the TV ☐

❷ Which button are you most likely to use for watching movies?

The red button ☐

The blue button ☐

The yellow button ☐

❸ Why would you press the yellow button on the remote control?

To watch a documentary ☐

To listen to music ☐

To change TV channels ☐

❹ What gadget can't you control using the buttons labeled 4?

The DVD player ☐

The sound system ☐

The TV ☐

❺ Which gadget are the round black buttons for?

The sound system ☐

The DVD player ☐

The TV ☐

---

33 ✓ CHECKLIST

⚙ Gerunds and infinitives ☐   **Aa** Household gadgets ☐   🧩 Talking about why you use things ☐

34 Vocabulary

34.1 SPORTS

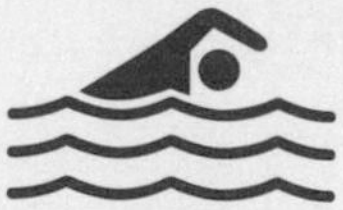
swimming

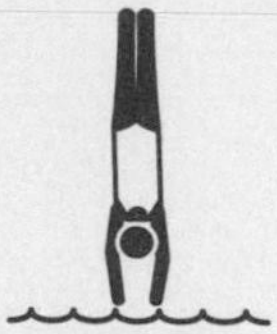
diving

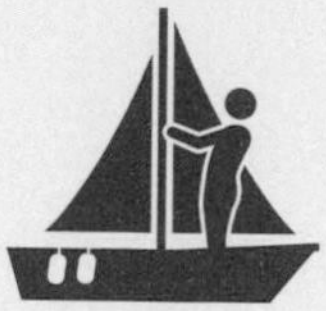
sailing

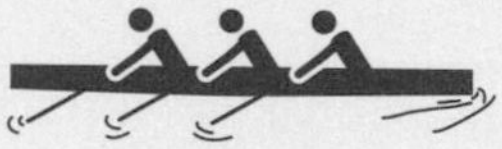
rowing

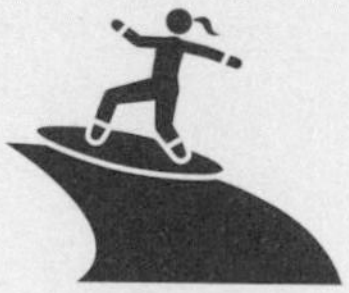
surfing

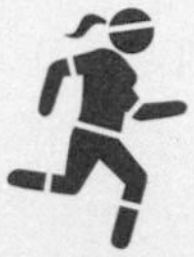
running

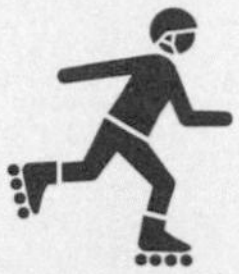
skating

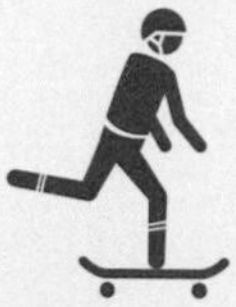
skateboarding

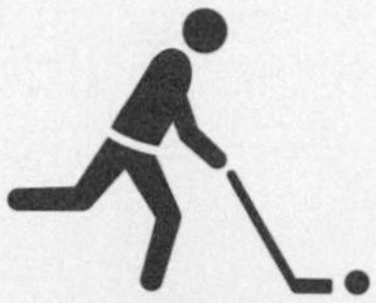
hockey

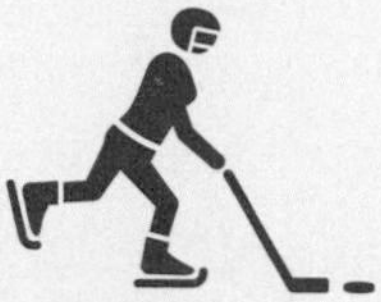
ice hockey

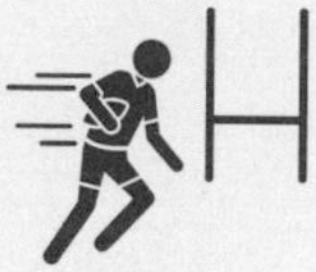
rugby

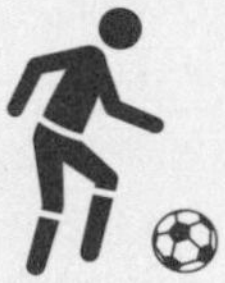
soccer (US)
football (UK)

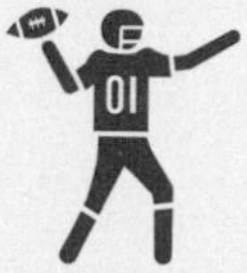
football (US)
American football (UK)

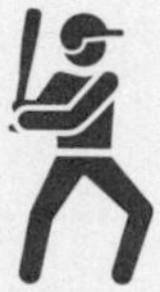
baseball

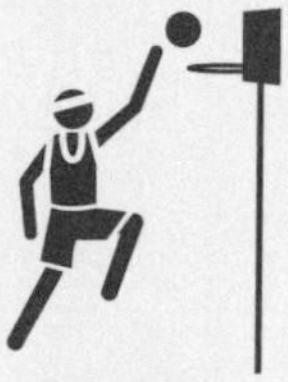
basketball

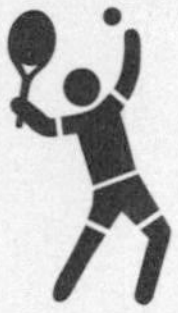
tennis

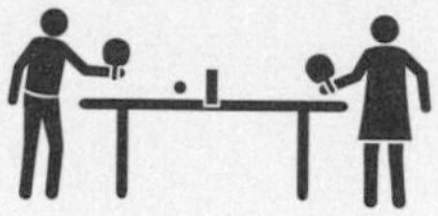
table tennis

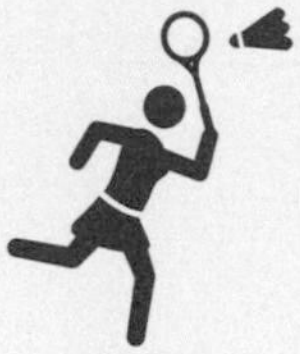
badminton

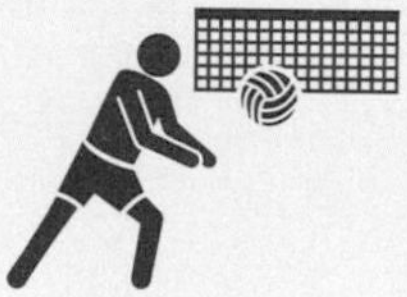
volleyball

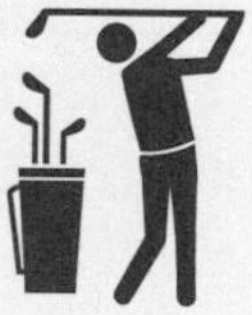
golf

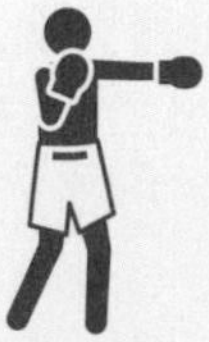
boxing

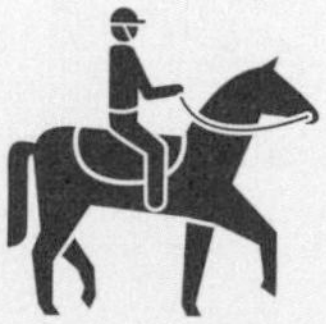
horse riding

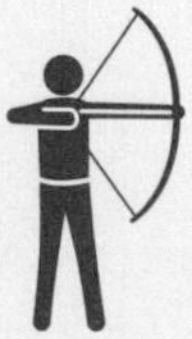
archery

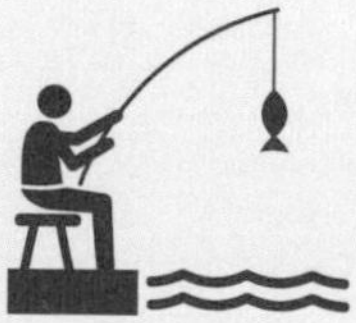
fishing

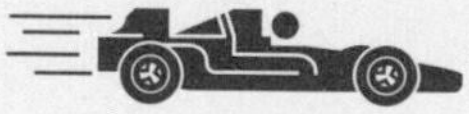
motor racing

snowboarding

skiing

cycling

running
a marathon

throwing
the javelin

throwing
the discus

judo

gymnastics

high jump

long jump

34.2 EQUIPMENT

baseball bat

golf club

tennis racket

ball

skateboard

surfboard

skis

snowboard

net

34.3 VENUES

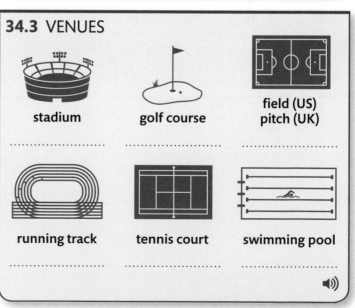

stadium

golf course

field (US)
pitch (UK)

running track

tennis court

swimming pool

35 Opinions and plans

When you give opinions on activities such as sports, you often use verbs with gerunds. When you talk about plans to do an activity, you use verbs with infinitives.

⚙ **New language** Simple verb patterns
Aa Vocabulary Sports and leisure
🧩 **New skill** Talking about opinions and plans

35.1 KEY LANGUAGE VERBS WITH GERUNDS

English uses gerunds after certain verbs that say how a person feels about an activity.

I enjoy swimming.

The verb describes feelings about an activity. ⤴

⤴ The word for the activity is in gerund form.

🔊

35.2 FURTHER EXAMPLES VERBS WITH GERUNDS

He doesn't feel like playing tennis tonight.

We can't stand jogging. We're so unfit!

Do you miss skiing now that summer's here?

I'm looking forward to running the marathon.

🔊

35.3 FILL IN THE GAPS BY PUTTING THE VERBS IN GERUND FORM

I've missed _____ *playing* _____ (**play**) soccer since I broke my leg.

1 I don't feel like _____ (**run**) in the park with you now. I'm too tired.

2 I can't stand _____ (**work out**) in the gym. It's so boring.

3 He likes _____ (**watch**) basketball, and he plays it on weekends, too.

4 She absolutely loves _____ (**dive**), and she's very good at it.

🔊

35.4 READ THE ARTICLE AND ANSWER THE QUESTIONS

OLYMPIC FOCUS

Keep on running

Isabella Woods, 21, is a talented marathon runner who hopes to win Olympic gold. Here she tells us about her training and her ambitions.

" I love running marathons. I always look forward to challenging myself so that I run faster each time I train. I never put off training, because it helps me to get ready for competitions. Even when the weather is really bad, I still feel like getting my running shoes on and getting out on the road. I couldn't cope with doing a desk job. It'd be torture! When I'm on vacation, I'm usually miserable because I miss training. I can't stand sitting around doing nothing. For me, it's a waste of time. I've got more important things to do."

What does Isabella hope to do?
Run a marathon ☐
Win an Olympic gold medal ☑

1 What does Isabella say is a challenge for her?
Going faster every time she runs ☐
Getting ready for competitions ☐

2 How does Isabella get ready for competitions?
She buys new running shoes ☐
She always makes time for training ☐

3 Isabella wants to go running...
only if the weather is good ☐
whatever the weather is like ☐

4 Where would Isabella hate to work?
In an office ☐
Outside ☐

5 Why doesn't Isabella enjoy vacations?
She wants to relax more ☐
She wants to train ☐

Aa 35.5 MATCH THE DEFINITIONS TO THE WORDS

Want to do something ——————— Look forward to

1 Successfully manage something ——— Put off

2 Do something later than planned ——→ Feel like

3 Be happy that something is going to happen — Miss

4 Feel sad because something isn't happening — Can't stand

5 Strongly dislike or hate ——————— Cope with

🔊

123

35.6 KEY LANGUAGE VERBS WITH INFINITIVES

English uses the infinitive with "to" after certain verbs
that describe someone's plans or wishes to do an activity.

They arranged to play tennis this weekend.

Main verb describes a plan
or wish to do an activity.

Infinitive with "to"
describes the activity.

35.7 FURTHER EXAMPLES VERBS WITH INFINITIVES

The infinitive doesn't change no matter what tense the main verb is in.

I'm waiting to play badminton, but my friend's running late.

Will you promise to teach me to swim?

We wanted to play baseball yesterday, but it was raining.

35.8 CROSS OUT THE INCORRECT WORDS IN EACH SENTENCE

I've arranged ~~going~~ / **to go** swimming today.

❶ You enjoy **dancing** / **to dance**, don't you?

❷ Do you want **seeing** / **to see** the match tonight?

❸ He can't stand **watching** / **to watch** soccer.

❹ You promised **playing** / **to play** golf with me.

❺ I don't mind **training** / **to train** with you.

35.9 USE THE CHART TO CREATE 12 CORRECT SENTENCES AND SAY THEM OUT LOUD

*I enjoy
playing tennis.*

I

enjoy arranged miss decided

to play playing

tennis. basketball. squash.

35.10 LISTEN TO THE AUDIO AND ANSWER THE QUESTIONS

   Cyclist Kofi Osei talks about last year's Olympics.

Kofi said he would coach the team.
True ☑ **False** ☐

❸ Kofi's training wasn't very successful.
True ☐ **False** ☐

❶ The directors chose Kofi for the squad.
True ☐ **False** ☐

❹ Kofi wants to win the Tour de France next year.
True ☐ **False** ☐

❷ Kofi thought he would easily win a medal.
True ☐ **False** ☐

❺ Kofi wants a long break from competitions now.
True ☐ **False** ☐

🔊

---

35 ✔ CHECKLIST

⚙ Simple verb patterns ☐   **Aa** Sports and leisure ☐   🧩 Talking about opinions and plans ☐

♻ REVIEW THE ENGLISH YOU HAVE LEARNED IN UNITS 30–35

NEW LANGUAGE	SAMPLE SENTENCE	☑	UNIT
DEFINITE AND ZERO ARTICLES	Sam is always buying clothes. The clothes he bought yesterday are expensive.	☐	30.1
"HAVE" AND "HAVE GOT"	I have a new phone. I have got a new phone.	☐	30.5
REFLEXIVE PRONOUNS	He cut himself while chopping vegetables.	☐	32.1
"FOR" WITH A GERUND	I use my blender for making soup.	☐	33.1
INFINITIVES FOR PURPOSE	I use my blender to make soup.	☐	33.1
PHRASAL VERBS FOR USING GADGETS	It's too hot in here. Let's turn the fan on.	☐	33.7
VERBS WITH GERUNDS FOR OPINIONS	I enjoy swimming.	☐	35.1
VERBS WITH INFINITIVES FOR PLANS	They arranged to play tennis this weekend.	☐	35.6

36 Future arrangements

In English, the present continuous can be used when talking about future arrangements that have already been planned for a specific time.

⚙ **New language** Present continuous for plans
Aa **Vocabulary** Collocations with "take"
🧩 **New skill** Talking about future arrangements

36.1 KEY LANGUAGE PRESENT CONTINUOUS FOR FUTURE PLANS

You can use present continuous verbs paired with future time clauses to talk about future events that are already planned.

PRESENT CONTINUOUS   FUTURE TIME CLAUSE

Jane is having lunch with friends next Tuesday.

🔊

36.2 FURTHER EXAMPLES PRESENT CONTINUOUS FOR FUTURE PLANS

 She is going **to the ballet** tonight.

 I'm seeing **the dentist** tomorrow.

 She's having **coffee with Paul** later.

 We're playing **tennis** this evening.

🔊

⚙ 36.3 FILL IN THE GAPS BY PUTTING THE VERBS IN THE PRESENT CONTINUOUS

Alannah ___*is playing*___ (play) tennis with Carrie on Saturday at 2pm.

① Thomas _____ (catch) the train at 6pm, so he can get to the restaurant by 7pm.

② Nahid and Eric _____ (go) to Sally's birthday party next Friday.

③ We _____ (meet) Nicole and Yuri at the beach this Saturday.

④ Sonia _____ (work out) at the gym tomorrow because she's training for a marathon.

⑤ Lottie _____ (sing) in a concert this weekend at the city's concert hall.

🔊

36.4 REWRITE THE SENTENCES CORRECTING THE ERRORS

> Hugo and Laura are see a play at the Palace Theater on Saturday night.
> _Hugo and Laura are seeing a play at the Palace Theater on Saturday night._

1 Susan playing chess with Kai on Tuesday at 8pm to prepare for the championships.

_____

2 Vicky visits her grandmother in Finland next week. She's really looking forward to the trip.

_____

3 Michelle are going to Roy's surprise birthday party on Friday night. It should be a fun night!

_____

4 Andrew have lunch with Rosi and Maggie on Thursday at 1:30pm at their local café.

_____

36.5 LISTEN TO THE AUDIO AND ANSWER THE QUESTIONS

Maria is on the phone to Catherine, arranging a time to meet up for a coffee or lunch.

What is Maria doing on Monday before work?
- **Going swimming** ☑
- **Playing tennis** ☐
- **Going to the beach** ☐

1 When is Maria having lunch with Adrian?
- **Monday at 1pm** ☐
- **Tuesday at noon** ☐
- **Thursday at 1pm** ☐

2 Who is coming for lunch on Thursday?
- **Jude** ☐
- **Adrian** ☐
- **Omar's brother** ☐

3 What evening is Omar returning home?
- **Monday** ☐
- **Thursday** ☐
- **Saturday** ☐

4 Who is visiting Maria's family for the weekend?
- **Catherine** ☐
- **Jude** ☐
- **Omar's brother** ☐

5 Where are Maria and Catherine going to meet?
- **Ricky's Café** ☐
- **Skating rink** ☐
- **Catherine's house** ☐

36.6 KEY LANGUAGE COLLOCATIONS WITH "TAKE"

The verb "take" often appears in English collocations.

She's taking a trip to the beach next weekend.

He takes care of his dog by feeding him healthy snacks.

She took a look at the paintings at her local art gallery.

After his performance, he took a bow as the audience clapped.

They got on the train and took their seats.

He's taking time off work this month to go on holiday.

I took time out from my busy day to eat lunch with a friend.

I took a picture of the sunrise from my bedroom window.

Aa 36.7 MATCH THE DEFINITIONS TO THE COLLOCATIONS

Sit down	Take a look
① Look at something	Take care of
② Look after	Take a seat
③ Go somewhere for pleasure	Take a bow
④ Photograph something	Take a trip
⑤ Acknowledge applause	Take time out
⑥ Stop working for a short time	Take a picture

36.8 LISTEN TO THE AUDIO, THEN NUMBER THE PICTURES IN THE ORDER THEY ARE DESCRIBED

A ☐   B 1   C ☐   D ☐   E ☐

36.9 SAY THE SENTENCES OUT LOUD, FILLING IN THE GAPS

Adam is going to ___*take a picture*___ of the beach at sunset.

taking time out

~~take a picture~~

1 Violet is _____ Stella's dog this weekend.

2 The children are _____ to the ice rink tomorrow.

taking time off

3 I'm _____ from work this afternoon because I don't feel well.

take a look

4 Connor is planning to _____ at the competition entries today.

taking a trip

5 I'm _____ from my schedule to meet friends this weekend.

taking care of

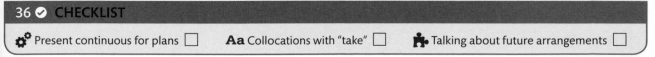

36 ✓ CHECKLIST

⚙ Present continuous for plans ☐   Aa Collocations with "take" ☐   Talking about future arrangements ☐

37 Planning the future

You can use "going to" when talking about something you've decided to do in the future, such as getting fit. This is useful for discussing intentions and predictions.

🕸 **New language** "Going to"
Aa Vocabulary Healthy living
🧩 **New skill** Talking about plans to keep fit

37.1 KEY LANGUAGE DECISION BEFORE SPEAKING

Use "going to" when you have already decided to do something before speaking.

Angus has decided he is going to swim every week to get fit.

Put "to be" + "going to" before the main verb.

Base form of the verb.

37.2 FILL IN THE GAPS USING THE FUTURE WITH "GOING TO"

Harry *'s going to play* _____ **(play)** more football with his friends this year.

1 Jingjing _____ **(walk)** to work every day, unless it's raining or snowing.

2 Tilly _____ **(join)** the new pilates class starting at the gym near her house.

3 Sam _____ **(learn)** judo this year with his friends Shankar and Belinda.

4 Kadija _____ **(start)** jogging to work and back home from next week.

37.3 READ THE LIST AND ANSWER THE QUESTIONS

New year's resolutions

Lose weight
Join a yoga class
Get up earlier
Cycle to work
Exercise on weekends

Joe's going to do yoga. **True** ☑ **False** ☐

1 Joe's going to join a gym. **True** ☐ **False** ☐

2 Joe's going to use his bike for transportation. **True** ☐ **False** ☐

3 Joe's going to gain weight. **True** ☐ **False** ☐

4 Joe's going to be more active on the weekend. **True** ☐ **False** ☐

37.4 KEY LANGUAGE PREDICTION BASED ON EVIDENCE

You can also use "going to" when making a prediction about the future based on something you know is true when you are speaking.

This is the future outcome.

You know this is true.

PREDICTION

EVIDENCE

Angie is going to lose weight because she's stopped eating unhealthy food.

37.5 MATCH THE BEGINNINGS OF THE SENTENCES TO THE CORRECT ENDINGS

Peter's going to feel more relaxed

as she's in the lead by a long way.

1 Carly's going to get better at tennis

because he's started weight lifting.

2 Collette's going to win the race

because she's starting lessons next week.

3 Abdel's going to be healthier

as he's now doing yoga every day.

4 Rob's going to be stronger

because he's on a low-sugar diet.

37.6 LISTEN TO THE AUDIO AND PUT THE PICTURES IN THE ORDER THEY ARE DESCRIBED

Paul and Anya are discussing Anya's plans to lose weight and get fit.

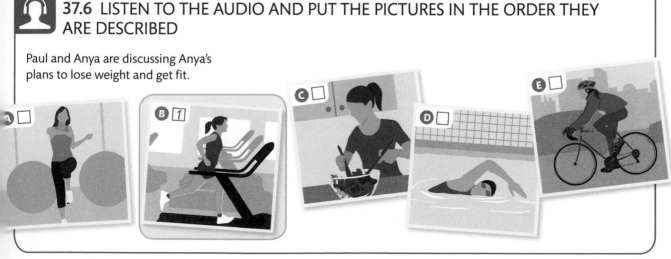

A ☐   B ☐ 1   C ☐   D ☐   E ☐

37.7 KEY LANGUAGE ADVERB MODIFIERS WITH "GOING TO"

English uses modifiers to show how definite the future action will be.

Ewan's probably going to get fit this summer.
└ Something is likely.

Linda's definitely going to try harder at karate.
└ There is no doubt about something happening.

Maya's certainly going to eat healthier food.
└ A more emphatic form of "definitely."

37.8 KEY LANGUAGE VERB MODIFIERS WITH "GOING TO"

You can also change the verb to make the prediction more or less certain.

George doubts he's ever going to give up eating burgers.

Raj hasn't decided, but he thinks he's going to join a gym.

Anya hopes she's going to get on the basketball team.

Cristina knows she's going to do well in the marathon.

37.9 CROSS OUT THE INCORRECT WORDS IN EACH SENTENCE

Annabelle ~~probably~~ / **knows** she's going to start swimming lessons next week.

1. Gary's **certainly** / **doubts he's** going to run the next marathon to raise money for charity.

2. Helena's **definitely** / **hopes she's** going to improve her fitness level by going to the gym.

3. Ahmed **certainly** / **thinks he's** going to try kick boxing after his judo classes have finished.

4. James **doubts he's** / **definitely** going to stop eating fatty food, but he'll try to eat more fruit.

132

37.10 REWRITE THE SENTENCES, CORRECTING THE ERRORS

The other team is really good! I doubt we going to win.
The other team is really good! I doubt we're going to win.

1 I think I'm go to go jogging, but I might read a book instead.

_____

2 They're probably going to finishing the marathon, but it's a long way to run.

_____

3 She's not going to plays tennis now, is she? It's raining!

_____

4 You're going to definitely look great after working out so much.

_____

5 It's too late to going out. I think I'm going to go to bed.

_____

🔊

37.11 USE THE CHART TO CREATE EIGHT CORRECT SENTENCES AND SAY THEM OUT LOUD

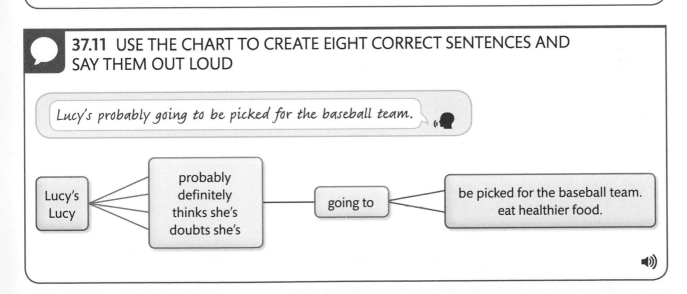

Lucy's probably going to be picked for the baseball team.

| Lucy's / Lucy | probably / definitely / thinks she's / doubts she's | going to | be picked for the baseball team. / eat healthier food. |

🔊

38.1 WEATHER AND CLIMATE

temperature

mild

warm

hot

boiling

cool

chilly

cold

freezing

snow drift

raindrop

drizzle

light shower

downpour

hail

blustery

gale

hurricane /
typhoon / cyclone

tornado

blizzard

lightning

thunder

sandstorm

hailstorm

snowstorm

gray sky (US)
grey sky (UK)

blue sky

clear sky

smog

overcast

rainbow

puddle

snowflake

hailstone

flood

drought

heatwave

wet

dry

humidity

38.2 WEATHER ADJECTIVES

sun ➡ sunny

cloud ➡ cloudy

fog ➡ foggy

rain ➡ rainy

snow ➡ snowy

ice ➡ icy

frost ➡ frosty

wind ➡ windy

storm ➡ stormy

thunder ➡ thundery

39 Predictions and promises

You can talk about future events in English using the verb "will." This construction has several meanings, which are all different from the future using "going to."

⚙ **New language** Future tense with "will"
Aa Vocabulary Weather
🧩 **New skill** Making predictions and promises

39.1 KEY LANGUAGE THE FUTURE USING "WILL"

English uses "will" when talking about the future in four main ways:

TIP
Remember to use the future with "going to" for predictions based on current evidence, and for decisions made before the time of speaking.

To make a prediction about what you think will happen.

Wait a few minutes. I think it will stop raining soon.

This prediction is not based on evidence.

To offer to do something for someone.

You look frozen. I'll make you some hot soup.

To make a promise.

We'll be there by eight. Don't worry!

This decision was not planned in advance.

To describe a decision you've just made.

I know! I'll buy Aaron a surfboard for his birthday.

◀))

39.2 FILL IN THE GAPS WITH EITHER "WILL" OR "TO BE" WITH "GOING TO"

Zoe _'s going to_____ meet Hannah and Ketil in the park this afternoon by the fountain.

1 Have a rest, and I _____ cook a warm stew for us to eat tonight.

2 I _____ take the dog for a walk after it stops raining, I promise!

3 Amelia and Jill _____ buy dresses tomorow to wear to Tom's birthday party.

4 You _____ be cold playing football today. It was snowing this morning!

◀))

39.3 MARK WHETHER EACH SENTENCE IS A PREDICTION, OFFER, PROMISE, OR DECISION

Don't worry, I'll make sure I get there in time for the start of your show.
Prediction ☐ **Offer** ☐ **Promise** ☑ **Decision** ☐

1. What a great idea! It's such a hot day. I'll have some ice cream, too.
Prediction ☐ **Offer** ☐ **Promise** ☐ **Decision** ☐

2. Make sure you take a coat, warm hat, and a scarf. It'll be cold tonight.
Prediction ☐ **Offer** ☐ **Promise** ☐ **Decision** ☐

3. It's started raining! I'll make sure I finish painting the fence when the weather is better.
Prediction ☐ **Offer** ☐ **Promise** ☐ **Decision** ☐

4. I'll look after your dog for you while you're on vacation. I'd be pleased to do it.
Prediction ☐ **Offer** ☐ **Promise** ☐ **Decision** ☐

39.4 LISTEN TO THE AUDIO AND WRITE ANSWERS TO THE QUESTIONS IN FULL SENTENCES

Carla is talking to her sister Stacey on the phone about her plans for the evening.

What does Stacey think will happen with the traffic?
Stacey thinks the traffic will get very heavy.

1. What will Carla make to eat tonight?

_____

2. What will Carla do after Kevin's guitar lesson?

_____

3. Did Stacey accept Carla's offer to eat with Stacey and Kevin this evening?

_____

4. When will Carla pick up Stacey?

_____

39.5 KEY LANGUAGE ADVERBS WITH "WILL"

Add an adverb after "will" to show how likely
you think the future action is to occur.

He'll probably go **skiing when it snows.**

They'll definitely go **hiking if it's sunny.**

It'll certainly be **easier to run in this cool weather.**

39.6 KEY LANGUAGE VERBS THAT MODIFY THE FUTURE WITH "WILL"

Like the future with "going to," the future with "will" is often used
to say what someone thinks or knows about the future.

Shows the "will" phrase is unlikely.

Hamid doubts **the storm will be dangerous.**

Claire thinks **it'll snow later on.**

Sita hopes **the rain will soon stop.**

Jo knows **it'll be difficult to surf because of the wind.**

Shows the "will" phrase is certain.

39.7 CROSS OUT THE INCORRECT WORDS IN EACH SENTENCE

I **know** / ~~definitely~~ we'll go to the festival tomorrow, whether it's sunny or not.

1 I'll **doubt** / **definitely** be at the airport by 7pm so I have enough time to catch the plane.

2 You'll **certainly** / **hope** look handsome in your new suit. It's a really nice color and cut.

3 I **know** / **doubt** you'll win the race because you've not been training very hard.

4 I **hope** / **definitely** I'll pass my geography exam tomorrow. I'm very nervous about it.

39.8 READ THE ARTICLE AND ANSWER THE QUESTIONS

GREENWAY SPORTS FACILITIES
A Strategy for the Future

Following last year's extreme weather, we will need to make Greenway more accessible whatever the weather conditions are outside.

SHORT TERM
Adding to the existing outdoor tennis facilities, the new indoor tennis court will be finished this spring. This will offer a great alternative to the outdoor courts for rainy days.

LONG TERM
We need stands next to our outdoor sport fields suitable for all weather. Also, plans for a heated swimming pool are under way. We will introduce a reduced entry fee in the colder, darker months, as promised at the last meeting.

The weather was not unusual last year.
True ☐ **False** ☑

❶ The facilities will be made suitable for all weather.
True ☐ **False** ☐

❷ An outdoor tennis court is being built.
True ☐ **False** ☐

❸ The indoor tennis court will be good for rainy days.
True ☐ **False** ☐

❹ A heated swimming pool is part of the long-term plans.
True ☐ **False** ☐

❺ Pool entry will cost more in winter.
True ☐ **False** ☐

39.9 LISTEN TO THE AUDIO AND MATCH THE MODIFYING ADVERBS TO THE ACTIVITIES YOU HEAR

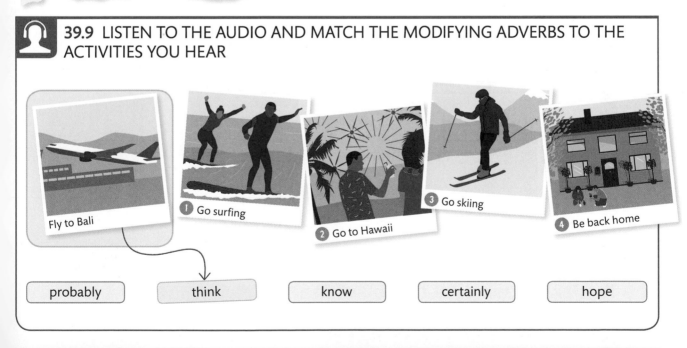

Fly to Bali

❶ Go surfing

❷ Go to Hawaii

❸ Go skiing

❹ Be back home

| probably | think | know | certainly | hope |

---

39 ✓ CHECKLIST

⚙ Future tense with "will" ☐   **Aa** Weather ☐   🧩 Making predictions and promises ☐

40 Possibility

The modal verb "might" is used to talk about things that are possible but not certain. It is often used when talking about the weather.

🔧 **New language** "Might" to show possibility
Aa Vocabulary Weather and landscape
🧩 **New skill** Discussing possibilities

40.1 KEY LANGUAGE "MIGHT" FOR POSSIBILITY

You can add "might" to different phrases to refer to past, present, or future possibilities.

___PAST POSSIBILITY___

MIGHT + HAS / HAVE + PAST PARTICIPLE

I can't find the compass. I might have dropped it earlier.

___PRESENT POSSIBILITY___

MIGHT + BE

I don't remember this path. We might be lost.

___FUTURE POSSIBILITY___

MIGHT + BASE VERB

It's very cold outside. It might snow later on.

40.2 FURTHER EXAMPLES "MIGHT" FOR POSSIBILITY

We might have taken a wrong turn at the river.

It might be windy at the top of the mountain.

Joe might not come walking with us next weekend.

"Not" always comes after "might" to form the negative.

> **TIP**
> Questions with "might" are only used in very formal English.

40.3 FILL IN THE GAPS USING THE PHRASES IN THE PANEL

Paris looks romantic. I _____*might take*_____ John there next weekend.

1 I can't find my purse. I _____ it on the metro.

2 Don't disturb him. He _____ .

3 I _____ out later if it stops raining.

4 I don't know where we are. We _____ the wrong turn.

5 I _____ , but I think the answer is A.

6 When we're in Venice, I _____ him to marry me.

7 Show everyone her photograph. Someone _____ her.

8 Cameron _____ stuck in traffic. He should be here by now.

might have left
~~might take~~
might have taken
might be
might ask
might be wrong
might go
might have seen
might be sleeping

◀))

40.4 REWRITE THE HIGHLIGHTED PHRASES, CORRECTING THE ERRORS

SPORTS WEEKLY

Mountain biker

Paul and Martin's mountain bike adventures

For last week's challenge, we thought it might been fun to try out the new mountain bike trail on Bluff Point. So we went last weekend and it didn't disappoint! I thought it might been too easy for experienced bikers like us but I think I might have get that wrong! The trail up through the forest was really tough and I thought we might fell into the valley. I know Jeff thought we might had lost our way at one point, but the track soon became clear. When we finally reached Bluff Point, it was

amazing. The downhill trail was scary and a bit crowded at times. There might have be as many as 30 bikers on the track that afternoon, but we had a great time. The jumps were awesome, and we think we might be go back next weekend. We also might taken some photos for the next week's column. Watch this space!

_____*might have been*_____

1 _____

2 _____

3 _____

4 _____

5 _____

6 _____

7 _____

40.5 KEY LANGUAGE CONTRACTIONS OF "MIGHT"

In spoken English, "have" is often contracted in phrases with "might."

He might have **got lost.**   **He** might not have **found the path.**

↓   ↓

He might've **got lost.**   **He** might not've **found the path.**

40.6 FILL IN THE GAPS BY CONTRACTING "HAVE"

Alan ___*might not've*___ (might not have) read the map correctly.

1. Georgia _____ (might have) walked around the lake.

2. They _____ (might not have) reached the valley yet.

3. We _____ (might have) left the supplies at the tent.

4. Horace _____ (might not have) climbed the mountain.

40.7 SAY THE SENTENCES OUT LOUD, CONTRACTING "HAVE"

I might not have seen Iris at the lake.

> *I might not've seen Iris at the lake.*

1. Dad might have bought me a new compass.

2. They might not have crossed the river yet.

3. Jonah might have pitched the tent by now.

4. I can't find my map. I might not have packed it.

5. Don might have hiked over the mountain already.

40.8 LISTEN TO THE AUDIO AND ANSWER THE QUESTIONS

Phoebe and Javid have become lost while hiking. They are deciding which way to go next.

Phoebe thinks they might be lost.
True ☑ False ☐

1 Javid thinks they might be in Reef Canyon.
True ☐ False ☐

2 They can see the forest marked on the map.
True ☐ False ☐

3 They might have seen Blue Mountain yesterday.
True ☐ False ☐

4 Phoebe thinks the forest might be dangerous.
True ☐ False ☐

40 ✓ CHECKLIST

⚙ "Might" to show possibility ☐   **Aa** Weather and landscape ☐   🧩 Discussing possibilities ☐

♻ REVIEW THE ENGLISH YOU HAVE LEARNED IN UNITS 36–40

NEW LANGUAGE	SAMPLE SENTENCE	☑	UNIT
PRESENT CONTINUOUS FOR FUTURE PLANS	Jane is having lunch with friends next Tuesday.	☐	36.1
COLLOCATIONS WITH "TAKE"	She's taking a trip to the beach this morning.	☐	36.6
USING "GOING TO" WHEN YOU HAVE MADE A DECISION BEFORE SPEAKING	I am going to play tennis every week.	☐	37.1
USING "GOING TO" TO MAKE A PREDICTION BASED ON EVIDENCE	Angie is going to lose weight because she's stopped eating unhealthy food.	☐	37.4
USING "WILL" TO MAKE A PREDICTION AND TO OFFER TO DO SOMETHING	Don't go out in the rain. You'll get soaked! You look frozen. I'll make you some hot soup.	☐	39.1
USING "WILL" WHEN PROMISING AND DECIDING AT THE TIME OF SPEAKING	We'll be there by seven. Don't worry! I know! I'll buy a surfboard for his birthday.	☐	39.1
"MIGHT" TO SHOW PAST POSSIBILITY	I can't find the compass. I might have dropped it earlier.	☐	40.1
"MIGHT" TO SHOW PRESENT POSSIBILITY	I don't remember this path. We might be lost.	☐	40.1
"MIGHT" TO SHOW FUTURE POSSIBILITY	It's very cold outside. It might snow later on.	☐	40.1

41 Vocabulary

41.1 SICKNESS AND HEALTH

unwell

sick

flu

fever (US) / high temperature (UK)

thermometer

cough

a cold

sneeze

runny nose

sore throat

ache

headache

backache

stomach ache

to vomit

pain

swollen

sore

appendicitis

tonsillitis

accident

broken bone

sprain

bandage

stitches

 symptoms

 medicine / medication

 pills / tablets

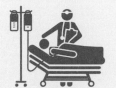 painkillers

 x-ray

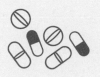 appointment

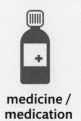 blood test

 test results

 treatment

 operation

 allergy

 hay fever

 rash

 itchy

 infection

 exercise

 lose weight

 gain weight

 drink water

 food poisoning

 lie down

 rest

 heal

 recovery

 feel better

42 Obligations

In English, you can use "have to" or "must" when talking about obligations or things that are necessary. You may hear it in important instructions such as medical advice.

- ⚙ **New language** "Must" and "have to"
- **Aa Vocabulary** Health and sickness
- 🧩 **New skill** Expressing obligation

42.1 KEY LANGUAGE OBLIGATIONS

"Must" and "have to" both express a strong need or obligation to do something.

 You $\left\{ \begin{array}{c} \text{must} \\ \text{have to} \end{array} \right\}$ rest, or your leg won't heal.

"Must not" is a strong negative obligation. It means something is not allowed.

 You **must not** get your bandage wet, or your leg might not heal properly.

"Don't have to" means something is not necessary, or there is no obligation.

 You **don't have to** come again. Your leg is better.

42.2 FURTHER EXAMPLES OBLIGATIONS

He **must** take two pills each morning and evening for the next two weeks.

She **mustn't** go back to work until her back is better.

Do I **have to** go back to the doctor again? I'm feeling so much better now.

42.3 HOW TO FORM OBLIGATIONS

"Must" does not change with the subject, but "have to" becomes "has to" in the third person singular. Both forms are followed by the base form of the main verb.

SUBJECT	"MUST / HAVE TO"	MAIN VERB	OBJECT
She	must / has to / must not / doesn't have to	take	this medicine

42.4 MATCH THE PHRASES THAT MEAN THE SAME THING

It's essential she exercises every day.

Everyone must wear a helmet.

① Eating too much sugar isn't allowed.

She has to exercise every day.

② Wearing a helmet is essential.

You mustn't eat too much sugar.

③ Running isn't allowed until your leg is better.

I don't have to take vitamins.

④ Taking vitamins isn't essential.

He has to lose weight.

⑤ It's essential that he loses weight.

You must not run while your leg is healing.

◀))

42.5 READ NADIA'S NOTE AND WRITE ANSWERS TO THE QUESTIONS AS FULL SENTENCES

Instructions from my doctor:

- I have to rest after my operation.
- I don't have to see the surgeon again. Instead, I can see Dr. Turner.
- I have to take my medication twice a day.
- I must eat before taking the pills.
- I mustn't go back to work for 14 days.
- I don't have to do any special exercises. A gentle daily walk is fine.
- I have to call Dr. Turner immediately if I feel sick again.
- Question for Dr. Turner: Do I have to go to the hospital to get my stitches out?

What does Nadia have to do after her operation?
She must rest after the operation.

❶ Does she have to see the surgeon again?

_____

❷ What must she do before taking her medication?

_____

❸ Can she go back to work immediately?

_____

❹ Does she have to do any special exercises?

_____

❺ What does she have to do if she feels sick again?

_____

42 ✔ CHECKLIST

⚙ "Must" and "have to" ☐   Aa Health and sickness ☐   🧩 Expressing obligation ☐

43 Making deductions

In English, you can add an extra verb (called a "modal verb") to show if a statement is likely or unlikely. You may hear modal verbs when people talk about sickness.

⚙ **New language** "Might" and "could"
Aa Vocabulary Health and sickness
🧩 **New skill** Talking about possibility

43.1 KEY LANGUAGE "MIGHT" AND "COULD"

The modal verbs "might" and "could" are useful for saying that you're not sure about something.

Use "might" and "could" when something is not certain.

John has a sore ankle. It { might / could } be broken.

The modal verb doesn't change with the subject.

The modal verb is usually followed by the base form of the main verb.

Use "might not" to describe a negative that is not certain.

It's not very swollen, so it might not be serious.

"Not" sits after the modal verb.

Use "could not" and "couldn't" to say that something was not possible in the past.

His ankle was so sore yesterday that he { could not / couldn't } walk.

Use "cannot" and "can't" when you're certain something is impossible.

It { cannot / can't } be broken because John walked to the doctor.

43.2 FURTHER EXAMPLES "MIGHT" AND "COULD"

Fay's got a sore throat and isn't feeling well. She might have a cold.

I was so sick last week that I couldn't get out of bed.

My eyes are itchy and I have a runny nose. It could be hay fever.

I can't have the flu because I don't have a high temperature.

43.3 FILL IN THE GAPS USING THE WORDS IN THE PANEL

I _____*might*_____ be able to change your doctor's appointment time for you.

1 Carla felt so sick last weekend that she _____ go back to work until Wednesday.

2 Bastian _____ be able to come over as he's allergic to most pets, and I have three dogs.

3 Your wrist _____ be broken as you're able to lean on it without much pain.

4 I recommend you go to the hospital. Your stomach pain _____ be appendicitis.

couldn't	~~might~~	can't	could	might not

🔊

43.4 LISTEN TO THE AUDIO AND ANSWER THE QUESTIONS

Jess and Boris are wondering why their manager, Selina, is not at work today.

Selina is at a marketing conference.
True ☐ **False** ☐ **Not given** ☑

1 Selina gets the bus to work.
True ☐ **False** ☐ **Not given** ☐

2 Selina can't be sick today.
True ☐ **False** ☐ **Not given** ☐

3 Selina might have caught the flu from James.
True ☐ **False** ☐ **Not given** ☐

4 Boris doesn't need Selina's help with the report.
True ☐ **False** ☐ **Not given** ☐

5 Jess says Boris might be able to contact Selina.
True ☐ **False** ☐ **Not given** ☐

43.5 RESPOND TO THE AUDIO, SPEAKING OUT LOUD

Doctor, my son's wrist is sore.

It _____*could*_____ be sprained.

1 Yes, I did walk here. But I think it's broken.

It _____ be broken.

2 My boss had a bad cough yesterday.

He _____ go to work today.

3 I've got a sore throat and a headache.

You _____ have a cold.

4 I heard you weren't very well yesterday.

I _____ get out of bed!

🔊

149

43.6 MATCH THE BEGINNINGS OF THE SENTENCES TO THE CORRECT ENDINGS

It can't be morning already;

so it might be lost.

1 I can't find my doctor's letter,

because it's red and swollen.

2 My hay fever could be getting worse

and might need an operation on her knee.

3 Marco's arm could be infected

I've hardly had any sleep.

4 I think my dad has a cold

because my eyes are itchy and sore.

5 Jackie had a skiing accident

you might need to go to the doctor.

6 If you don't feel any better soon,

because he can't stop sneezing.

7 That can't be Ailsa skating over there

so we might be late for the appointment.

8 We're stuck in traffic

because her ankle's broken.

43.7 CROSS OUT THE INCORRECT WORD IN EACH SENTENCE

 The doctor said I **might** / ~~can't~~ need an operation if my knee doesn't improve.

 1 Majeed **could** / **can't** be feeling very sick. He's playing soccer tonight.

 2 I'm starting to get a lot of headaches. My sister said I **might** / **cannot** need glasses.

 3 My shoulders ache. It **might not** / **could** be because I work all day at a desk.

 4 Your stomach ache **could** / **might not** be serious. It might just be something you ate.

 5 The reason you've got a pain in your foot **could** / **cannot** be because your shoes are too small.

43.8 READ THE EMAIL AND ANSWER THE QUESTIONS

✉

To: Julieta Fernández

Subject: re: Recovery

Hi Julieta,

It's great to hear from you. I haven't been very well recently. Last week, I was so sick that I couldn't go to work at all. At first I had a sore throat and a high temperature. I thought it could be tonsillitis. Then I got a terrible headache, and I couldn't stop vomiting. Ruby was sure I had food poisoning, but I thought it might not be that because I'd been feeling too sick to eat very much. I was afraid that it could be something really serious.

After a few days I felt a bit better, but I was still worried, so I made an appointment to see my doctor. I told her about my symptoms and she managed to reassure me. Now I know that it can't be tonsillitis because my tonsils aren't swollen, and it can't be food poisoning because I'm not vomiting any more. The doctor told me to get plenty of rest, drink lots of water, and take painkillers if I needed to. I still have a cough and a mild headache, but I'm feeling much better than I was this time last week. Want to meet for coffee once I've made a full recovery?

Hope to see you soon,

Xavier

↩ ↩↩

🔗 🗑

What couldn't Xavier do last week?

Get out of bed ☐

Leave the house ☐

Go to work ☑

1 What illness did Xavier think he could have?

Tonsillitis ☐

Food poisoning ☐

A headache ☐

2 What wasn't one of Xavier's symptoms?

A high temperature ☐

Backache ☐

A sore throat ☐

3 Xavier probably didn't have food poisoning...

because he wasn't vomiting ☐

because he hadn't eaten much ☐

because he was seriously sick ☐

4 Why can't Xavier have tonsillitis?

He has had it before ☐

He doesn't have a sore throat ☐

His tonsils aren't swollen ☐

5 The doctor didn't advise Xavier to...

go back to work ☐

take painkillers ☐

drink lots of water ☐

43 ✓ CHECKLIST

⚙ "Might" and "could" ☐   **Aa** Health and sickness ☐   🧩 Talking about possibility ☐

44 Polite requests

Use "can," "could," and "may" to ask permission to do something, or to ask someone to do something for you. Some constructions are more formal than others.

🔧 **New language** "Can," "could," and "may"
Aa Vocabulary Good manners
🧩 **New skill** Asking permission

44.1 KEY LANGUAGE "CAN," "COULD," AND "MAY"

Use "Can I" plus the verb to make a request. "Can" is mostly used in informal situations.

Ben, can I have some popcorn?

Informal answers use "can" as well.

Yes, you can.

"Could" replaces "can" for more formal situations, such as in business or to talk to strangers.

Excuse me, could I sit here, please?

Include "please" in polite requests.

Make negative answers more polite by adding "I'm sorry" or "I'm afraid."

I'm sorry, but that seat is taken.

"May" can also be used in formal situations.

May I take your coat?

Yes, thank you.

44.2 FURTHER EXAMPLES "CAN," "COULD," AND "MAY"

Can I borrow your pen?

Sure! Here you go.

Excuse me, could I have a glass of water?

Of course.

Good evening. May I reserve a table for 7pm?

I'm afraid we're completely full this evening.

TIP
"Could" and "may" are rarely used in short answers to polite questions.

44.3 MARK THE BEST REPLY TO EACH REQUEST

All of these replies are correct, but some are more appropriate for formal or informal situations.

Can I borrow your car, Harry?

No you can't, Joe. I need it today. ✓

No, you may not. ☐

1 Excuse me, do you know where the station is?

I'm afraid I don't know. ☐

No, I don't. ☐

2 Can we go soon? The show starts at 8pm.

Yes, when I've finished my coffee. ☐

I'm afraid that won't be possible. ☐

3 May I suggest we meet in the restaurant at 7pm?

Yes, see you later! ☐

Yes, that sounds perfect Ms. Eliker. ☐

4 Could we postpone our meeting until tomorrow?

I'm sorry, but I have meetings all day. ☐

No, we can't. ☐

44.4 RESPOND OUT LOUD TO THE AUDIO USING THE WORDS IN THE PANEL

Can I have some cake, Auntie Mel?

Yes, you ___can___ .

1 Could I please order a dozen red roses?

_____ , but I've sold out.

2 Could I please have the last sandwich?

_____ . Enjoy it.

3 Can I borrow your laptop?

No, you _____ . I need it.

4 Excuse me, may I sit next to you?

Yes, you _____ .

5 Could I speak to Rangit Singh, please?

_____ he's busy.

6 May I offer you a cup of coffee, Mrs. Soto?

Yes, _____ .

~~can~~	I'm afraid	may	can't
I'm sorry	please	Of course	

45 More phrasal verbs

Some phrasal verbs contain three words rather than two. Like two-word phrasal verbs, they are often used in informal spoken English.

⚙ **New language** Three-word phrasal verbs
Aa Vocabulary Personal relationships
🧩 **New skill** Understanding informal English

45.1 KEY LANGUAGE THREE-WORD PHRASAL VERBS

Three-word phrasal verbs consist of a verb, a particle, and a preposition. The particle and preposition often change the usual meaning of the verb.

VERB + PARTICLE + PREPOSITION

He **looks up to** his brother.

The verb changes with the subject.

The particle and preposition never change form.

🔊

Aa 45.2 MATCH THE SENTENCES WITH SIMILAR MEANINGS

He argued with his friend. ————→ He fell out with his friend.

We've run out of milk.

1. I have a bad relationship with my sister.

2. There's no milk left.

3. I won't tolerate his loud music.

4. Are you excited about the concert?

5. He thinks he's more important than everyone.

6. You thought of a great plan.

I don't get along with my sister.

Are you looking forward to the concert?

You came up with a great plan.

I won't put up with his loud music.

He looks down on everyone.

🔊

🎧 45.3 LISTEN TO THE AUDIO AND ANSWER THE QUESTIONS

 Amir tells Ruth about a difficult situation at work.

Amir's boss respects his staff.
True ☐ **False** ☑

1. Amir thinks it's hard to respect his boss.
True ☐ **False** ☐

2. Amir hasn't tried to like his boss.
True ☐ **False** ☐

3. Amir knows he can't argue with his boss.
True ☐ **False** ☐

4. Amir isn't losing patience with his boss.
True ☐ **False** ☐

5. Ruth thinks Amir's boss is treating him badly.
True ☐ **False** ☐

45.4 INTONATION THREE-WORD PHRASAL VERBS

When you say three-word phrasal verbs out loud, put the stress on the middle word.

look up to   **get along with**   **look forward to**

🔊

45.5 SAY THE SENTENCES OUT LOUD, FILLING IN THE GAPS USING THE WORDS IN THE PANEL

I'm making a cake, but I've _____ *run out of* _____ eggs. 🗣

1. Turn the radio down. I can't _____ that noise. 🗣

2. Our department works well because we _____ each other. 🗣

3. Dad _____ a great idea for Madison's birthday. 🗣

4. Don't _____ your staff. They're just as important as you! 🗣

look down on

came up with

put up with

get along with

~~run out of~~

🔊

45.6 REWRITE THESE SENTENCES USING THREE-WORD PHRASAL VERBS

Juan really admires his teacher.
Juan really looks up to his teacher.

1. Alexa is excited about her vacation.
_____

2. Trevor has a good relationship with Pam.
_____

3. Michelle always thinks of good ideas.
_____

4. Gavin thinks he's more important than us.
_____

5. I can't stand his behavior any longer!
_____

🔊

46 Asking for agreement

Use question tags in spoken English to encourage another person to agree with you, or to check that information is correct.

🔧 **New language** Question tags
Aa Vocabulary Travel and leisure plans
🧩 **New skill** Checking information

46.1 KEY LANGUAGE QUESTION TAGS

When you use question tags, a negative question tag follows a positive statement, and a positive question tag follows a negative statement. The verb that is used in the question tag depends on the verb that is used in the statement.

A present simple statement is followed by a question tag with the present simple form of "do."

PRESENT SIMPLE   QUESTION TAG

Mel plays the violin, doesn't she?

A past simple statement is followed by a question tag with the past simple form of "do."

PAST SIMPLE   QUESTION TAG

John studied art, didn't he?

A statement with an auxiliary verb is followed by a question tag with the same auxiliary verb.

AUXILIARY VERB   MAIN VERB   QUESTION TAG

You haven't seen my keys, have you?

Auxiliary verb.

Main verb describes the action.

Question tag uses the same auxiliary verb.

A statement with the verb "be" is followed by a question tag that also uses "be."

VERB "BE"   QUESTION TAG

He is annoyed, isn't he?

🔊

46.2 REWRITE THE SENTENCES, CORRECTING THE ERRORS

> Andy plays the piano, isn't he?
> _Andy plays the piano, doesn't he?_

1 We haven't met, are we?

_____

2 You walked the dog, don't you?

_____

3 She cycles to work, hasn't she?

_____

4 This book is amazing, doesn't it?

_____

🔊

46.3 ADD QUESTION TAGS TO THE SENTENCES

> It's not very warm today, ____is it____ ?

1 Ben has gone to China, _____ ?

2 That was a good concert, _____ ?

3 You're not upset, _____ ?

4 She doesn't like cheese, _____ ?

5 You went to work today, _____ ?

6 They haven't eaten yet, _____ ?

7 Luis speaks English, _____ ?

8 Zoe is working late, _____ ?

🔊

46.4 CHANGE THE QUESTIONS INTO SENTENCES WITH QUESTION TAGS, THEN SAY THEM OUT LOUD

> Have you seen my pen?
> _You haven't seen my pen, have you?_

1 Did Renata work in sales?

2 Were you listening to me?

3 Does he know the answer?

4 Is the phone ringing?

5 Was Will at the party?

6 Was that a good book?

7 Has Liam done the dishes?

🔊

157

46.5 KEY LANGUAGE QUESTION TAGS WITH MODAL VERBS

Statements with modal verbs such as "could," "would," and "should" are followed by question tags that use the same modal verb.

MODAL VERB

QUESTION TAG

Tim should be here by now, shouldn't he?

Use the same modal verb in the statement and the question tag.

46.6 FURTHER EXAMPLES QUESTION TAGS WITH MODAL VERBS

I heard the house is haunted. We shouldn't be here, should we?

You could teach me to drive, couldn't you?

She would love this restaurant, wouldn't she?

46.7 ADD QUESTION TAGS TO THE SENTENCES

They couldn't come earlier, _could they_ ?

1 You wouldn't go alone, _____ ?

2 He shouldn't eat so much, _____ ?

3 We would love to go to your party, _____ ?

4 You could help me, _____ ?

5 She could stay with you, _____ ?

6 We should save some money, _____ ?

7 You wouldn't tell her, _____ ?

8 She shouldn't work so hard, _____ ?

9 You would like a snack, _____ ?

46.8 LISTEN TO THE AUDIO AND ANSWER THE QUESTIONS

 Aman and Leta are packing for their vacation.

Aman forgot to pack the sun cream.
True ☐ **False** ☑

1 Leta packed their swimming things.
True ☐ **False** ☐

2 Aman thinks they need to take a gift.
True ☐ **False** ☐

3 Leta thinks Aman enjoys golf.
True ☐ **False** ☐

4 Aman doesn't want Leta to go hiking.
True ☐ **False** ☐

46.9 SAY THE SENTENCES OUT LOUD, ADDING QUESTION TAGS

It's raining outside, _isn't it_ ?

1 He would enjoy this book, _____ ?

2 He wouldn't let me try, _____ ?

3 They should buy the house, _____ ?

4 It isn't too cold here, _____ ?

5 She did tell you, _____ ?

---

46 ✓ CHECKLIST

⚙ Question tags ☐   **Aa** Travel and leisure plans ☐   🧩 Checking information ☐

↻ REVIEW THE ENGLISH YOU HAVE LEARNED IN UNITS 42–46

NEW LANGUAGE	SAMPLE SENTENCE	☑	UNIT
"MUST" AND "HAVE TO"	You must rest, or your leg won't heal. You have to rest, or your leg won't heal.	☐	42.1
"MUST NOT" AND "DON'T HAVE TO"	You must not get your bandage wet. You don't have to come here again.	☐	42.1
"MIGHT" AND "COULD"	John has a sore ankle. It might be broken. John has a sore ankle. It could be broken.	☐	43.1
"MIGHT NOT" AND "COULD NOT"	It might not be a serious injury. His ankle was so sore that he could not walk.	☐	43.1
"CAN," "COULD," AND "MAY"	Can I have some popcorn? / Could I sit here, please? May I take your coat?	☐	44.1
THREE-WORD PHRASAL VERBS	He looks up to his brother.	☐	45.1
QUESTION TAGS	Mel plays the violin, doesn't she?	☐	46.1
QUESTION TAGS WITH MODAL VERBS	Tim should be here by now, shouldn't he?	☐	46.5

47.1 SCIENCE

chemicals · solid · liquid · gas · crystals

hypothesis · to record · to observe · experiment · results

to pour · to mix · reaction · to stir · to dissolve

to heat · to burn · to boil · steam · to evaporate

to cool · to freeze · to melt · to float · to sink

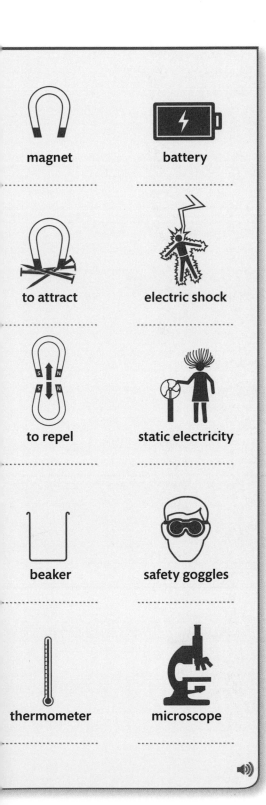

magnet

battery

to attract

electric shock

to repel

static electricity

beaker

safety goggles

thermometer

microscope

47.2 TOOLS

saw

hacksaw

file

hammer

screwdriver

wrench (US)
spanner (UK)

nail

screw

bolt

drill

pliers

nut

level (US)
spirit level (UK)

vice

tape measure

48 Things that are always true

English uses the zero conditional to talk about actions that always have the same results. This is useful for talking about scientific facts.

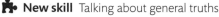
- ⚙ **New language** Zero conditional
- **Aa Vocabulary** Scientific facts
- 🧩 **New skill** Talking about general truths

48.1 KEY LANGUAGE THE ZERO CONDITIONAL

The zero conditional uses "if" or "when" with the present simple, followed by the present simple in the main clause.

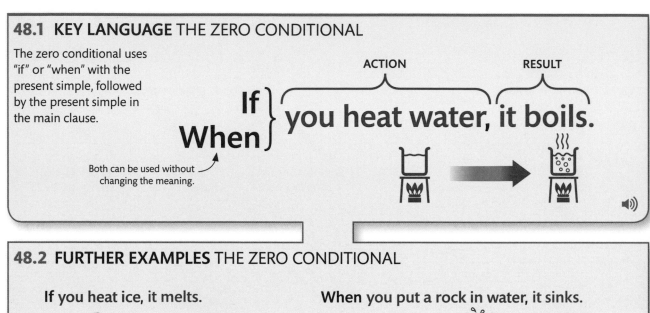

ACTION **RESULT**

If / When **you heat water, it boils.**

Both can be used without changing the meaning.

48.2 FURTHER EXAMPLES THE ZERO CONDITIONAL

If you heat ice, it melts.

If you drop an apple, it falls.

When you put a rock in water, it sinks.

When you pour oil onto water, it floats.

48.3 HOW TO FORM THE ZERO CONDITIONAL

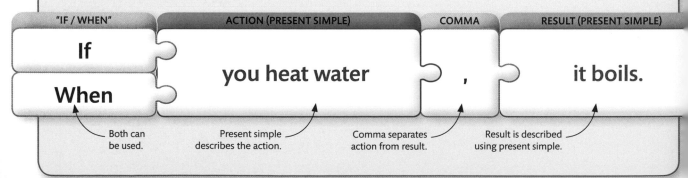

"IF / WHEN"	ACTION (PRESENT SIMPLE)	COMMA	RESULT (PRESENT SIMPLE)
If / **When**	**you heat water**	**,**	**it boils.**

- Both can be used.
- Present simple describes the action.
- Comma separates action from result.
- Result is described using present simple.

48.4 MATCH THE BEGINNINGS OF THE SENTENCES TO THE CORRECT ENDINGS

When carbon reacts with oxygen, ——→ you get carbon dioxide.

1. If you throw a ball up,
2. If you mix blue and yellow paint,
3. When you freeze water,
4. If you put sugar in water,
5. If you set fire to paper,
6. If you don't water plants,
7. When you boil water,

it falls down again.

it turns to ice.

it burns.

you get carbon dioxide.

you make green paint.

you produce steam.

it dissolves.

they die.

48.5 READ THE ARTICLE AND ANSWER THE QUESTIONS

Static electricity can make your hair stick out.
True ✓ **False** ☐ **Not given** ☐

1. Static electricity can't make a can move on its own.
True ☐ **False** ☐ **Not given** ☐

2. Static electricity can power a light bulb.
True ☐ **False** ☐ **Not given** ☐

3. Static electricity can make water move away.
True ☐ **False** ☐ **Not given** ☐

4. Static electricity doesn't make things stick to walls.
True ☐ **False** ☐ **Not given** ☐

5. Static electricity can give you an electric shock.
True ☐ **False** ☐ **Not given** ☐

FUN SCIENCE: Static Electricity

⚡ When you rub a balloon against your hair, it makes your hair stick out. This is because you've generated static electricity.

⚡ Static electricity can also move an empty soda can. Rub the balloon against your hair, then put the balloon near the can. The can rolls away by itself.

⚡ Static electricity can also move water. Turn on a faucet, so that water is dripping. If you rub the balloon on your hair again and put the balloon near the water, the water moves away from the balloon.

⚡ Static electricity can make things stick. If you rub the balloon on your hair then put the balloon on a wall, it sticks to the wall.

163

48.6 LISTEN TO THE AUDIO, THEN NUMBER THE SENTENCES IN THE ORDER YOU HEAR THEM

Ayida is giving her class a science lesson.

① Water in the form of a gas is called steam ☐
② Water can be a solid, a liquid, or a gas. [1]
③ Water becomes ice if we cool it to 32°F. ☐
④ Steam becomes liquid again when it cools. ☐
⑤ When water boils, it changes to a gas. ☐
⑥ If we heat water, it boils. ☐

Aa 48.7 LOOK AT THE PICTURES AND FILL IN THE GAPS USING THE WORDS IN THE PANEL

When you ___*heat*___ butter, it ___*melts*___ .

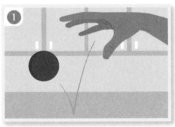

① If you _____ a ball, it _____ .

② If you _____ red and blue, you _____ purple.

③ When you _____ salt in water, it _____ .

④ If you _____ water, it _____ steam.

⑤ When you _____ a match, it _____ .

get	bounces	strike	boil	dissolves	mix
~~heat~~	put	burns	~~melts~~	drop	becomes

48.8 ANOTHER WAY TO SAY THE ZERO CONDITIONAL

Sentences using the zero conditional can be
reversed, so the result comes before the action.

Use a comma if the action comes first.

When you freeze water, ice forms.

Ice forms when you freeze water.

The result can come at the
beginning of the sentence.

"If" or "when" can sit between the action
and result, without a comma.

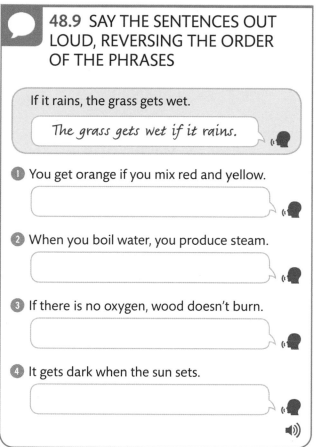

48.9 SAY THE SENTENCES OUT LOUD, REVERSING THE ORDER OF THE PHRASES

If it rains, the grass gets wet.

The grass gets wet if it rains.

① You get orange if you mix red and yellow.

② When you boil water, you produce steam.

③ If there is no oxygen, wood doesn't burn.

④ It gets dark when the sun sets.

48.10 REWRITE THE SENTENCES, PUTTING THE WORDS IN THE CORRECT ORDER

| a | drop | If | falls. | it | rock, | you |

If you drop a rock, it falls.

① | when | it. | melts | Ice | you | heat |

_____

② | ball, | moves. | If | kick | it | you | a |

_____

③ | water | grow | you | Plants | them. | if |

_____

④ | sun | rises, | light. | it | When | gets | the |

_____

48 ✓ CHECKLIST

⚙ Zero conditional ☐   Aa Scientific facts ☐   🧩 Talking about general truths ☐

49 Describing a process

When the thing receiving the action is more important that the person or thing doing the action, you can emphasize it using the present simple passive.

⚙ **New language** Present simple passive
Aa Vocabulary Science experiments
🧩 **New skill** Describing a process

49.1 KEY LANGUAGE THE PRESENT SIMPLE PASSIVE

When it is unimportant, or not known, who or what does an action, English uses the present simple passive. The passive also has the effect of emphasizing the action.

In the experiment, water **is heated** until it boils.

It is not known or not important who heats the water.

🔊

49.2 FURTHER EXAMPLES THE PRESENT SIMPLE PASSIVE

The water **is not stirred** in this experiment.

Use "not" to form negatives of the present simple passive.

A thermometer **is suspended** above the water.

After two minutes, the temperature **is taken.**

The results **are recorded** on the chart.

🔊

49.3 HOW TO FORM THE PRESENT SIMPLE PASSIVE

SUBJECT	"IS / ARE"	PAST PARTICIPLE	REST OF SENTENCE
Water	**is**	**heated**	**until it boils.**

The thing that receives the action.

Present simple of verb "to be."

The past participle describes what happens to the subject.

49.4 FILL IN THE GAPS BY PUTTING THE VERBS IN THE PRESENT SIMPLE PASSIVE

The water _____ *is frozen* _____ (freeze) to make ice to use in the experiment.

1. The liquid _____ (heat) for several minutes until it starts to boil.

2. The plant cells _____ (observe) using a state-of-the art microscope.

3. Static electricity _____ (generate) when you rub a balloon against your hair.

4. The chemicals _____ (add) slowly to the water to start the reaction.

5. The temperature of the salt water _____ (take) using a thermometer.

6. Two beakers _____ (fill) almost to the top with a mixture of oil and water.

49.5 REWRITE THE SENTENCES USING THE PRESENT SIMPLE PASSIVE

We heat the liquid for 10 minutes.
The liquid is heated for 10 minutes.

1. We do not remove the liquid from the heat.
_____

2. We leave the liquid to cool in a glass jar.
_____

3. We observe crystals forming in the jar.
_____

4. We measure the size of the crystals.
_____

5. We do not pour oil into the water.
_____

6. We boil the water to make steam.
_____

7. We dissolve salt in the water.
_____

8. We do not mix the oil and water together.
_____

9. We record the results of the experiment.
_____

49.6 SAY FULL SENTENCES OUT LOUD, FILLING IN THE GAPS BY PUTTING THE VERBS IN THE PRESENT SIMPLE PASSIVE

The temperature of the water _____ *is recorded* _____ (record) every five minutes.

① The water _____ (remove) from the heat once it has boiled.

② The chemicals _____ (pour) into a test tube to start the reaction.

③ When the substance _____ (mix) with water, it changes color.

④ The reaction between the chemicals and the water _____ (observe).

⑤ The mixture _____ (cool) for approximately one hour until it sets.

⑥ The water _____ (stir) for 5 minutes until all the salt dissolves.

⑦ The two substances _____ (place) in a test tube together.

⑧ The results _____ (estimate) before the experiment takes place.

49.7 LISTEN TO THE AUDIO AND MARK WHETHER EACH ACTIVITY IS DESCRIBED IN THE ACTIVE OR PASSIVE VOICE

A ACTIVE   B PASSIVE

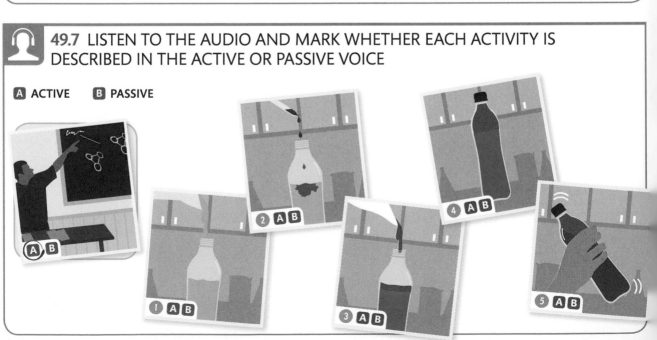

Chemistry Now

The Scientific Method is used to help us answer questions or solve problems. It has six stages:

Stage 1 **Asking a question:** A question is posed. For example, does grass grow quicker under green or red light?

Stage 2 **Research:** Research is carried out, for example using books, journals, and articles.

Stage 3 **Hypothesis:** The results of the research are used to predict the answer to the question. This prediction is called a hypothesis.

Stage 4 **Experiment:** Now a test or process is designed so that the hypothesis can be tested. For example, grass seeds are grown under red light and under green light. The growth is observed and noted. In this way, the growth rates of the grass under different conditions can be compared.

Stage 5 **Analysis of the results:** The results of the experiment are recorded and analyzed.

Stage 6 **Conclusion:** The results are reviewed to check whether or not they support the original hypothesis.

What is the first stage of the Scientific Method?

Asking a question ☑
Solving a problem ☐
Answering a question ☐

① What are scientists least likely to use when carrying out their research?

Books ☐
Articles ☐
Newspapers ☐

② What do scientists generally use to form a hypothesis?

A test or process ☐
Results of their research ☐
A questionnaire ☐

③ How do scientists test whether or not a hypothesis is correct?

They research the hypothesis ☐
They grow grass seeds ☐
They design an experiment ☐

④ What stage of the Scientific Method comes after the experiment?

Analyzing the results ☐
Checking the results ☐
Recording the hypothesis ☐

⑤ What do scientists do in the final stage of the Scientific Method?

Prove the original hypothesis ☐
Review the results ☐
Disprove the hypothesis ☐

---

49 ✓ CHECKLIST

⚙ Present simple passive ☐   **Aa** Science experiments ☐   🧩 Describing a process ☐

50 Things that might happen

English uses conditional verbs to describe the future results of a proposed action. This is useful for suggesting plans and giving advice.

🔧 **New language** First conditional
Aa Vocabulary Tools and making things
🧩 **New skill** Giving advice and instructions

50.1 KEY LANGUAGE THE FIRST CONDITIONAL

The first conditional expresses a suggested action that might lead to a future result.

SUGGESTED ACTION · · · · · · · · · · · · · · · FUTURE RESULT

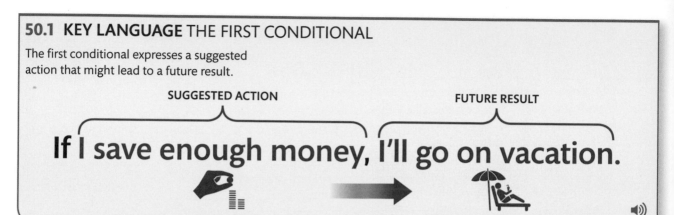

If I save enough money, I'll go on vacation.

50.2 FURTHER EXAMPLES THE FIRST CONDITIONAL

First conditional sentences can start with the result. There is no comma before "if."

If I go jogging, I'll lose weight.

If it snows, I'll go skiing.

I won't go outside if it rains.

If I cook, will you do the dishes?

50.3 HOW TO FORM THE FIRST CONDITIONAL

The first conditional is usually introduced by "if" followed by the present simple. The future with "will" expresses the result.

"IF"	PRESENT SIMPLE	COMMA	FUTURE WITH "WILL"
If	**I save enough money**	**,**	**I'll go on vacation.**

"If" shows that the sentence is conditional.

Present simple tense describes suggested action.

Comma separates action from result.

Future with "will" describes the result.

50.4 FILL IN THE GAPS BY PUTTING THE VERBS IN THE CORRECT TENSES

If you __hold__ (hold) the ladder, I __will paint__ (paint) the wall.

1 If I _____ (eat) healthily, I _____ (lose) weight.

2 We _____ (dance) if the band _____ (play) good music.

3 If we _____ (go) shopping, I _____ (buy) you something nice.

4 I _____ (build) the cupboard if you _____ (read) the instructions.

50.5 LISTEN TO THE AUDIO AND ANSWER THE QUESTIONS

Gilly is building a cupboard and Colin is trying to help.

Colin knows what Gilly is doing.
True ☐ **False** ☑

1 Gilly wants to protect the floor.
True ☐ **False** ☐

2 Gilly is organizing her materials and tools.
True ☐ **False** ☐

3 Gilly has her own electric screwdriver.
True ☐ **False** ☐

4 Gilly wants Colin to read the instructions.
True ☐ **False** ☐

5 The cupboard won't fit through the door.
True ☐ **False** ☐

50.6 SAY THE SENTENCES OUT LOUD, REVERSING THE ORDER OF THE PHRASES

If it rains, you'll get wet.

You'll get wet if it rains.

1 He'll find it if he looks for it.

2 If she's hungry, I'll cook dinner.

3 If it's broken, will they fix it?

4 I'll tell him to call you if I see him.

50.7 KEY LANGUAGE FIRST CONDITIONAL WITH "UNLESS"

You can use "unless" instead of "if" in conditional sentences.
"Unless" means "if...not," so the future result depends
on the suggested action not happening.

If you don't
Unless you } study hard, you will fail your exams.

50.8 FURTHER EXAMPLES FIRST CONDITIONAL WITH "UNLESS"

If you don't
Unless you } get up now, you'll be late for work.

I'll be angry if he doesn't turn
I'll be angry unless he turns } that music down.

50.9 REWRITE THE SENTENCES USING "UNLESS"

If they don't listen, they'll get it wrong.
Unless they listen, they'll get it wrong.

1 You'll damage the floor if you don't cover it.
_____

2 If you don't go to bed, you'll be tired tomorrow.
_____

3 He'll get annoyed if you don't speak politely.
_____

4 The cat won't run away if she's not frightened.
_____

5 She'll arrive on time if her train isn't delayed.
_____

6 If you don't attach it securely, it will break.
_____

7 We'll do the job if it's not too difficult.
_____

50.10 READ THE INSTRUCTION MANUAL AND WRITE ANSWERS TO THE QUESTIONS AS FULL SENTENCES

1. Use wood glue carefully unless you want your new furniture to be stained. Leave the glue to set for 24 hours.

2. If you use an electric screwdriver to join parts together, there's a risk that the screws will be too tight. Unless you finish the process by hand, you could damage your new furniture.

3. Make sure all pieces are in the right place and fit perfectly before you try to fasten them.

4. If you check that the doors fit before you tighten the hinges, your doors will open smoothly. If you don't check that the doors fit, they will stick and look uneven.

What will happen if you don't use wood glue carefully?

Your new furniture will be stained.

❸ What must you check before you try to fasten all the pieces?

_____

❶ What might happen if you use an electric screwdriver to join parts together?

_____

❹ What must you do to make sure your doors open smoothly?

_____

❷ How can you make sure you don't damage your new furniture?

_____

❺ What will happen unless you check that the doors fit properly?

_____

50 ✅ **CHECKLIST**

⚙️ First conditional ☐   **Aa** Tools and making things ☐   🧩 Giving advice and instructions ☐

You can use the first conditional with an imperative to give people practical instructions or advice, such as how to solve problems or improve their lifestyle.

New language First conditional with imperative
Aa Vocabulary Health and wellbeing
New skill Giving advice and instructions

51.1 KEY LANGUAGE FIRST CONDITIONAL WITH IMPERATIVE

In first conditional sentences, you can use an imperative instead of the future with "will."
This makes the sentence an instruction or a suggestion instead of a prediction about the future.

PROBLEM   SOLUTION

If you're cold, put on a coat.

51.2 FURTHER EXAMPLES FIRST CONDITIONAL WITH IMPERATIVE

If you feel sick, call a doctor.

If the traffic is bad, cycle to work.

Don't stay up late if you're tired.

Leave the comma out of sentences that start with the imperative.

51.3 HOW TO FORM FIRST CONDITIONAL WITH IMPERATIVE

Use "if" followed by the present simple to describe a problem.
The imperative gives the solution to the problem.

"IF"	PRESENT SIMPLE	COMMA	IMPERATIVE
If	you're cold	,	put on a coat.

"If" shows that the sentence is conditional.

Present simple tense describes the problem.

Comma separates problem from solution.

The imperative gives the solution to the problem.

51.4 MATCH THE BEGINNINGS OF THE SENTENCES TO THE CORRECT ENDINGS

If you get lost, → ask someone for directions.

if you need some fresh air.

1. Open the window

tell him I tried to call him.

2. If you get too cold,

if you go out this afternoon.

3. If you see Malik,

ask someone for directions.

4. Remember to lock the door

turn on the heating.

51.5 REWRITE THE SENTENCES, CORRECTING THE ERRORS

If you'll be thirsty, drink more water.
If you're thirsty, drink more water.

1. You don't like your job, look for a new one.

_____

2. If you like those shoes, to buy them.

_____

3. Help yourself if you wanted some more food.

_____

4. If you need to talk to someone call me.

_____

5. Take a break you feel stressed.

_____

51.6 LISTEN TO THE AUDIO AND ANSWER THE QUESTIONS

Tanya is talking to her father about selling her house.

Tanya's father offers to give her money.
True ✓ **False** ☐

1. Tanya says her plan will make her happy.
True ☐ **False** ☐

2. Tanya will sell all her furniture.
True ☐ **False** ☐

3. Tanya doesn't offer her father her furniture.
True ☐ **False** ☐

4. Tanya doesn't want a simpler life.
True ☐ **False** ☐

5. Tanya's father supports her plan.
True ☐ **False** ☐

175

YOUR HEALTH

How to Live a Simpler Life

Do you work too hard in order to maintain your lifestyle? Read this guide!

1 If you are always working, take some time off to think, reflect, and enjoy your surroundings.

2 If you can't take time off and you're stressed at work, think about what tasks you can delegate to your colleagues. You don't have to do all the work yourself.

3 If you want to feel calmer, slow your pace! Plan your day carefully and don't do too much.

4 If you're constantly checking your emails or smartphone when you're at home, stop it. You'll feel much more relaxed if you read a book or listen to some music instead.

5 If you have too many possessions, sell them or give them away. You won't notice that they have gone!

6 If you live in a large house and don't really need to, consider downsizing and buying a smaller one.

What should you do if you work all the time?

Go on vacation ☐
Take some time off ☑
Leave your job ☐

① What should you do if you're stressed and can't take time off work?

Talk to your boss ☐
Call in sick ☐
Ask your colleagues to help you ☐

② What should you do if you want to feel calmer?

Plan your day carefully ☐
Go running ☐
Try to keep busy ☐

③ What should you do if you're always checking your smartphone?

Throw it away ☐
Read a book ☐
Email a friend ☐

④ What should you do if you have too many possessions?

Get rid of some of them ☐
Buy extra storage ☐
Move to a bigger house ☐

⑤ What should you do if you have a bigger house than you need?

Rent it to someone ☐
Buy more things ☐
Buy a smaller house ☐

Aa 51.8 MATCH THE DEFINITIONS TO THE WORDS AND PHRASES

to do things more slowly ——————→ to slow your pace

your surroundings

1 the things you own

to delegate tasks

2 the area around you

constantly

3 to move to a smaller home

to slow your pace

4 to give work to other people

possessions

5 all the time

to downsize

51.9 USE THE FIRST CONDITIONAL WITH AN IMPERATIVE TO GIVE ADVICE FOR EACH SITUATION, SPEAKING OUT LOUD

Nadia says she's always tired in the morning. Tell her to go to bed earlier.

If you're always tired in the morning, go to bed earlier.

1 Fred is stressed at work. Tell him to go for a walk during his lunch break.

2 Jeremy is always checking his emails. Tell him to turn off his smartphone.

3 Rima sees a new car that she likes. Tell her to buy it.

4 Sandra says she's lonely. Tell her to visit you this weekend.

51 ✓ CHECKLIST

⚙ First conditional with imperative ☐   **Aa** Health and wellbeing ☐   🧩 Giving advice and instructions ☐

52 Planning activities

You can use subordinate time clauses to talk about sequences of events, where one thing must happen before another thing can happen.

⚙ **New language** Subordinate time clauses
Aa Vocabulary Building works
🧩 **New skill** Describing sequences of events

52.1 KEY LANGUAGE SUBORDINATE TIME CLAUSES

English uses "when" and "as soon as" to talk about events or actions in the future that happen before another event or action can take place. These phrases are called subordinate time clauses.

FIRST EVENT   SECOND EVENT

{ **When**
As soon as } **it gets dark, he'll light the fire.**

These phrases indicate that the first event has not happened yet.

52.2 FURTHER EXAMPLES SUBORDINATE TIME CLAUSES

You can also use subordinate time clauses to ask about future events.

When I finish my report, I'll call you.

When you get home, will you make dinner?

I'll put up shelves when the paint dries.

As soon as it stops raining, I'll go out.

52.3 HOW TO FORM SUBORDINATE TIME CLAUSES

"WHEN / AS SOON AS"	PRESENT SIMPLE	COMMA	FUTURE WITH "WILL"
When / **As soon as**	**it gets dark**	**,**	**he'll light the fire.**

The present simple describes the first event, even though it is a future event.

The future with "will" describes the second event.

52.4 FILL IN THE GAPS BY PUTTING THE VERBS IN THE PRESENT SIMPLE OR FUTURE WITH "WILL"

As soon as this TV show ___ends___ (end), I ___will go___ (go) to bed.

1. We _____ (sing) "Happy Birthday" as soon as she _____ (come) in.

2. When I _____ (finish) fixing the car, I _____ (drive) you to the station.

3. As soon as she _____ (get) to the beach, she _____ (go) swimming.

4. I _____ (call) him when I _____ (arrive) at the hotel.

5. As soon as I _____ (find) my keys, I _____ (lock) the door.

52.5 READ THE EMAIL AND ANSWER THE QUESTIONS

To: Jamal

Subject: Building work

Hi Jamal,

I got your email; please don't worry. I know it's difficult to wait for the builders to finish our house. The problem is, they are all dependent on each other. So the plasterer will plaster the wall when the electrician finishes the wiring. The painter will only paint the walls when the plaster is dry. They'll install the kitchen as soon as they finish all the other jobs. Try not to worry about the patio. We'll do it together as soon as I get home. Remember that when I finish this work contract, I'll be home for eight weeks.

Love, Tia

The builders are behind schedule.
True ☐ **False** ☐ **Not given** ☑

1. The plastering comes before the wiring.
True ☐ **False** ☐ **Not given** ☐

2. The kitchen will be the builders' last job.
True ☐ **False** ☐ **Not given** ☐

3. Jamal can work on the patio immediately.
True ☐ **False** ☐ **Not given** ☐

4. Tia will fix the garage.
True ☐ **False** ☐ **Not given** ☐

5. Tia has finished her work contract.
True ☐ **False** ☐ **Not given** ☐

52.6 ANOTHER WAY TO SAY SUBORDINATE TIME CLAUSES

UK English sometimes uses the present perfect instead
of the present simple in subordinate time clauses.

When it has stopped raining, we'll go outside.

We'll go outside when it has stopped raining.

The present perfect still describes a future event. ⟋

 52.7 LISTEN TO THE AUDIO, THEN NUMBER THE PICTURES IN THE ORDER THEY ARE DESCRIBED

A ☐

B ☐

C ☐ 1

D ☐

E ☐

 52.8 SAY THE SENTENCES OUT LOUD, REVERSING THE ORDER OF THE PHRASES

When I get home, I'll call you.

> *I'll call you when I get home.*

① I'll buy a car when I've saved enough money.

② You'll feel better when you've had a rest.

③ As soon as I finish work, we'll meet up.

④ When the weather's better, I'll go out.

⑤ They'll put up pictures when the paint dries.

52.9 MATCH THE BEGINNINGS OF THE SENTENCES TO THE CORRECT ENDINGS

As soon as I've finished this book, → I'll lend it to you.

1 They'll buy new furniture — when they've finished redecorating.

2 When we've built a fire, — when the sun comes out.

3 We'll go and sit outside — we'll visit the Statue of Liberty.

4 She'll look for a job — we'll cook some food.

5 When we go to New York, — I'll buy that expensive dress.

6 As soon as I get paid, — as soon as she finishes college.

🔊

---

52 ✓ CHECKLIST

⚙ Subordinate time clauses ☐ **Aa** Building works ☐ 🧩 Describing sequences of events ☐

♻ REVIEW THE ENGLISH YOU HAVE LEARNED IN UNITS 48–52

NEW LANGUAGE	SAMPLE SENTENCE	☑	UNIT
ZERO CONDITIONAL	When you pour **oil onto water**, it floats.	☐	48.2
PRESENT SIMPLE PASSIVE	**In the experiment**, water is heated **until it boils**.	☐	49.1
FIRST CONDITIONAL WITH "IF"	If we save **enough money**, we'll go **on vacation**.	☐	50.1
FIRST CONDITIONAL WITH "UNLESS"	Unless you study **hard**, you won't pass **your exams**.	☐	50.7
FIRST CONDITIONAL PLUS IMPERATIVE	If you're **cold**, put on **a coat**.	☐	51.1
SUBORDINATE TIME CLAUSES WITH PRESENT SIMPLE	As soon as it gets **dark**, he'll light **the fire**.	☐	52.1
SUBORDINATE TIME CLAUSES WITH PRESENT PERFECT	When it has stopped **raining**, we'll go **outside**.	☐	52.6

53 Unlikely situations

English uses the second conditional to describe the result of an unlikely or impossible event. Because the event is unlikely, the result is also unlikely.

⚙ **New language** Second conditional
Aa Vocabulary Collocations with "make" and "do"
🧩 **New skill** Talking about future dreams

53.1 KEY LANGUAGE THE SECOND CONDITIONAL

Like the first conditional, the second conditional uses "if" to describe an action. The result is described using "would."

UNLIKELY ACTION   **UNLIKELY RESULT**

If I won the lottery, I would leave my job.

 🔊

53.2 FURTHER EXAMPLES THE SECOND CONDITIONAL

"He would" can be shortened to "he'd."

 # If he wasn't so busy, he'd go on vacation.

The action can come after the result in second conditional sentences. There is no comma before "if."

0123...? # I'd call her if I knew her number. 🔊

53.3 HOW TO FORM THE SECOND CONDITIONAL

"IF"	PAST SIMPLE	COMMA	"WOULD" + BASE FORM OF VERB
If	**I won the lottery**	**,**	**I would leave my job.**

"If" shows that the sentence is conditional.

Past simple tense describes the action.

Comma separates action from result.

Result is described using "would" + verb.

53.4 FILL IN THE GAPS TO FORM SECOND CONDITIONAL SENTENCES USING THE VERBS IN BRACKETS

If she _____applied_____ (apply) for the job, we _____would offer_____ (offer) it to her.

1 If my job _____ (be) better paid, I _____ (buy) my own apartment.

2 We _____ (employ) many more staff if we _____ (have) more office space.

3 If they _____ (raise) enough money, they _____ (start) their own business.

4 We _____ (increase) our profits if we _____ (advertise) on national TV.

🔊

53.5 LISTEN TO THE AUDIO AND ANSWER THE QUESTIONS

Gavin tells Sara about his new business idea.

Gavin wants to run a hotel.
True ✓ False ☐

1 Gavin needs to raise money to buy the house.
True ☐ False ☐

2 Gavin says they wouldn't need much money.
True ☐ False ☐

3 Gavin says there's no need to sell their house.
True ☐ False ☐

4 Sara doesn't take Gavin's idea seriously.
True ☐ False ☐

5 Gavin thinks he could make a lot of money.
True ☐ False ☐

6 Sara thinks they should make a quick decision.
True ☐ False ☐

53.6 MATCH THE BEGINNINGS OF THE SENTENCES TO THE CORRECT ENDINGS

If I had the money, ——→ I'd invest in your business.

1 If he sold his apartment,   he'd buy a villa in Spain.

2 If she invested her money wisely,   she'd be very rich.

3 If he took his work seriously,   we'd increase productivity.

4 If we modernized the factory,   he'd be offered a promotion.

🔊

183

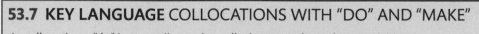

53.7 KEY LANGUAGE COLLOCATIONS WITH "DO" AND "MAKE"

In collocations, "do" is generally used to talk about regular tasks or activities.
"Make" generally expresses a single action or the creation of something new.

Use "do" for ongoing activities.

I do the paperwork on Tuesday afternoons.

Use "make" for single actions.

He always makes decisions very quickly.

Aa 53.8 READ THE EMAIL AND MATCH THE COLLOCATIONS TO THEIR DEFINITIONS

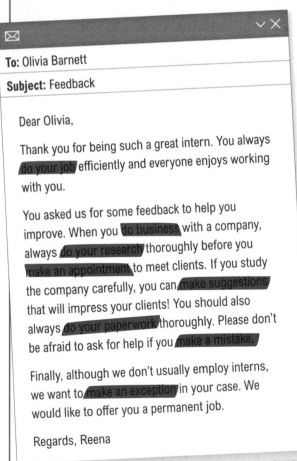

To: Olivia Barnett

Subject: Feedback

Dear Olivia,

Thank you for being such a great intern. You always do your job efficiently and everyone enjoys working with you.

You asked us for some feedback to help you improve. When you do business with a company, always do your research thoroughly before you make an appointment to meet clients. If you study the company carefully, you can make suggestions that will impress your clients! You should also always do your paperwork thoroughly. Please don't be afraid to ask for help if you make a mistake.

Finally, although we don't usually employ interns, we want to make an exception in your case. We would like to offer you a permanent job.

Regards, Reena

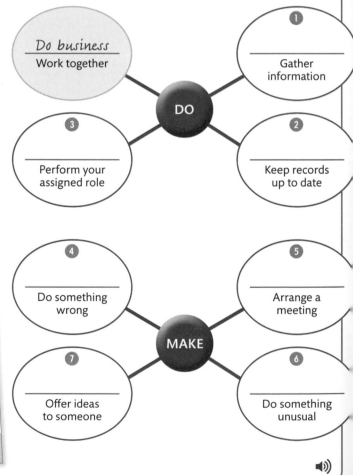

Do business
Work together

DO

① Gather information

② Keep records up to date

③ Perform your assigned role

MAKE

④ Do something wrong

⑤ Arrange a meeting

⑥ Do something unusual

⑦ Offer ideas to someone

Aa 53.9 REWRITE THE SENTENCES, CORRECTING THE ERRORS

I'll do mistakes if I rush my work.
I'll make mistakes if I rush my work.

1 I think I've done the right decision.

_____

2 Levi can help you make the paperwork.

_____

3 I enjoy making business with new clients.

_____

4 If you worked harder, you'd make a better job.

_____

5 Selma always does great suggestions.

_____

6 I need to do an important call.

_____

7 Have you made your research properly?

_____

8 Can you do an exception for me?

_____

9 I've done an appointment to see Mr. Cox.

_____

◀))

53.10 SAY THE SENTENCES OUT LOUD, FILLING IN THE GAPS

Have you ___*made*___ that phone call yet?

1 He _____ mistakes all the time.

2 It was great to _____ business with you.

3 Can I _____ a suggestion?

4 I'm afraid we can't _____ an exception.

5 You've _____ a great job this week.

6 It's important to _____ your research.

7 I hate _____ the paperwork.

◀))

54.1 EMOTIONS

 calm

 relaxed

 happy

 confident

 proud

 excited

 surprised

 pleased

 cheerful

 thrilled

 interested

 amazed

 amused

 delighted

 ecstatic

 angry / mad

 annoyed

 irritated

 furious

 frustrated

 disgusted

 sad

 unhappy

 upset

 lonely

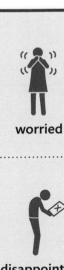 worried

 miserable

 depressed

 stressed

 jealous

 disappointed

 unimpressed

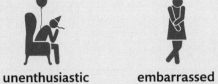 unenthusiastic

 embarrassed

 scared

 shocked

 frightened

 terrified

 nervous

 anxious

 tired

 exhausted

 bored

 distracted

 confused

 curious

 intrigued

 grateful

 lucky

 serious

187

55 Giving advice

The phrase "If I were you" is often used to give advice in English. By saying it, you imagine that you are in the same position as the person you are talking to.

- ⚙ **New language** "If I were you"
- **Aa Vocabulary** Phrases for giving advice
- 🧩 **New skill** Making suggestions

55.1 KEY LANGUAGE "IF I WERE YOU"

English uses "if I were you" to give advice in second conditional sentences. The advice is expressed using "I would."

I don't know if I should take this job.

English uses "were," not "was," in this context.

If I were you, I would take it.

The advice comes after "I would."

55.2 FURTHER EXAMPLES "IF I WERE YOU"

I'm going to the concert tonight.

If I were you, I'd set off early. The traffic is awful.

I think I'll buy this shirt.

The suggestion can come first without changing the meaning.

I wouldn't buy it if I were you. I don't like the pattern.

There is no comma before "if."

55.3 REWRITE THE SENTENCES, REVERSING THE ORDER OF THE PHRASES

If I were you, I wouldn't leave my job.
I wouldn't leave my job if I were you.

1 I'd apply for a promotion if I were you.

_____

2 If I were you, I'd invest some of my money.

_____

3 I wouldn't buy that car if I were you.

_____

4 If I were you, I'd take a long vacation.

_____

5 I'd start my own company if I were you.

_____

55.4 MARK THE SENTENCES THAT ARE CORRECT

If I were you, I'd buy that house. ✓
If I were you, I'll buy that house. ☐

① I'd call a doctor if I was you. ☐
I'd call a doctor if I were you. ☐

② If I were you, I'd study harder. ☐
If I were you, study harder. ☐

③ I wouldn't go out if I were you. ☐
I won't go out if I were you. ☐

④ If I were you, I join a choir. ☐
If I were you, I'd join a choir. ☐

⑤ If I were you, I wouldn't tell him. ☐
If I were you, don't tell him. ☐

55.5 USE "IF I WERE YOU" TO GIVE ADVICE, SPEAKING OUT LOUD

There is a boat for sale that Javid likes.

If I were you, I'd buy the boat.

① The car Ava wants to drive has a flat tire.

_____ change the tire.

② Mia has been offered a promotion at work.

_____ take the promotion.

③ André wants to go outside in the rain.

_____ go outside.

④ Lily has been invited to a great party.

_____ go to the party.

55.6 LISTEN TO THE AUDIO AND ANSWER THE QUESTIONS

Connor asks his colleague Isobel for some advice at work.

How does Connor feel about the work presentation he was asked to do?
Excited ☐
Scared ✓
Bored ☐

① How does Isobel think Connor should feel?
Happy ☐
Angry ☐
Nervous ☐

② What does Connor think he is bad at?
Meeting clients ☐
Coming up with ideas ☐
Talking to large groups of people ☐

③ What has Connor done at work in the past?
Won prizes ☐
Made lots of money ☐
Been promoted ☐

④ What doesn't Isobel say Connor should do?
Practice the presentation ☐
Call in sick ☐
Talk to Jamila ☐

55.7 KEY LANGUAGE QUESTION PHRASES WITH GERUNDS

To make suggestions, you can use a variety of opening
question phrases. These are always followed by a gerund.

What should
we do tonight?

Question
phrase.   Gerund.

How about eating **in that new restaurant?**

I need to tell
you something.

What about having **a chat over dinner?**

I'm so bored!

Have you tried doing **something new?**

I love pizza, but
it's expensive.

Have you thought of making **it yourself?**

55.8 REWRITE THE SENTENCES USING QUESTION PHRASES WITH GERUNDS

You should make a list of the advantages and disadvantages of the situation.
How about _making a list of the advantages and disadvantages of the situation?_

1 You should discuss the idea with your colleagues and see what they think of it.
Have you tried _____

2 We should meet our new clients for dinner at a nice restaurant.
How about _____

3 You should plan a marketing strategy with your team before you present it to your boss.
What about _____

4 You should invest in property and buy some apartments to rent out.
Have you thought of _____

55.9 USE THE CHART TO CREATE 12 CORRECT SENTENCES AND SAY THEM OUT LOUD

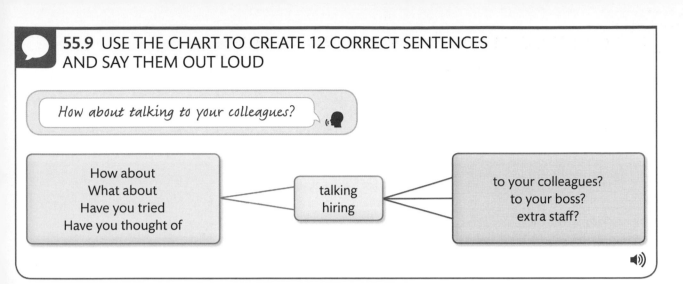

How about talking to your colleagues?

How about		to your colleagues?
How about	talking	to your colleagues?
What about	hiring	to your boss?
Have you tried		extra staff?
Have you thought of		

55.10 READ THE ARTICLE AND ANSWER THE QUESTIONS

LIFESTYLE

Digital detox

by lifestyle expert Alison Grant

- How about turning off your phone and computer at night? You will sleep much better.

- Have you tried using an alarm clock instead of your phone? You won't be tempted to surf the net in bed with an alarm clock.

- If you're lost, have you thought of asking a real person for directions instead of looking at your smartphone? You might even make a new friend.

- In the evenings, how about doing something creative like baking a cake? The sense of achievement will feel great!

- Finally, what about having a gadget-free day, so you can really connect with the people you love?

Turning off gadgets at night will stop you sleeping.
True ☐ **False** ☐ **Not given** ☑

1 You can't go online with an ordinary alarm clock.
True ☐ **False** ☐ **Not given** ☐

2 Smartphones don't give accurate directions.
True ☐ **False** ☐ **Not given** ☐

3 Alison Grant thinks you shouldn't talk to strangers.
True ☐ **False** ☐ **Not given** ☐

4 Doing creative things will make you feel positive.
True ☐ **False** ☐ **Not given** ☐

5 Alison Grant thinks you should always use gadgets.
True ☐ **False** ☐ **Not given** ☐

6 People who never use gadgets have more friends.
True ☐ **False** ☐ **Not given** ☐

55 ✓ CHECKLIST

⚙ "If I were you" ☐　　**Aa** Phrases for giving advice ☐　　🧩 Making suggestions ☐

56 Real and unreal situations

English uses conditional sentences to talk about possibilities. Use the first conditional or the second conditional depending on how likely the situation is.

⚙ **New language** First and second conditional
Aa Vocabulary Collocations for business meetings
🧩 **New skill** Talking about possibilities

56.1 KEY LANGUAGE FIRST AND SECOND CONDITIONAL

FIRST CONDITIONAL

Use the first conditional to describe the result of a likely situation.

LIKELY SITUATION (PRESENT SIMPLE)

RESULT ("WILL" + BASE VERB)

If I see Katherine, I'll invite her to the meeting.

SECOND CONDITIONAL

Use the second conditional to describe the result of an unlikely situation.

UNLIKELY SITUATION (PAST SIMPLE)

RESULT ("WOULD" + BASE VERB)

If I ran the company, I'd give all my staff a bonus.

56.2 MATCH THE BEGINNINGS OF THE SENTENCES TO THE CORRECT ENDINGS

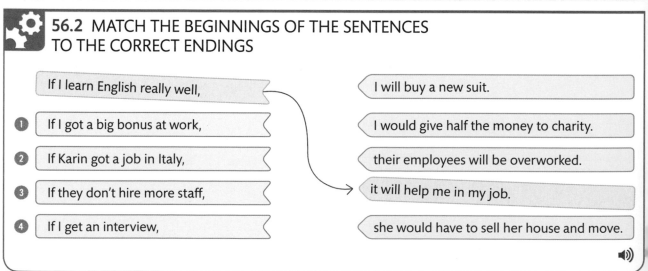

If I learn English really well,

1 If I got a big bonus at work,

2 If Karin got a job in Italy,

3 If they don't hire more staff,

4 If I get an interview,

I will buy a new suit.

I would give half the money to charity.

their employees will be overworked.

it will help me in my job.

she would have to sell her house and move.

56.3 REWRITE THE SENTENCES, CORRECTING THE ERRORS

> If you're letting me know that you want to come, I book tickets today.
>
> _If you let me know that you want to come, I'll book tickets today._

1 If I am you, I'll stop eating so much junk food and join a gym.

_____

2 If he is a better listener, he realizes that I'm not happy in my job.

_____

3 If I'll feel lonely or bored, I video call my brother in New Zealand.

_____

4 If we are very rich, we go on a round-the-world trip.

_____

5 If they're having time to spare before the train leaves, they're going shopping.

_____

56.4 LISTEN TO THE AUDIO AND ANSWER THE QUESTIONS

Carlos is at a job interview.
The interviewer asks him what he
would do in different situations.

	True	False
The interviewer asks Carlos what he would do if he worked with a rude person.	✓	☐
1 If someone was rude to Carlos, he would be rude back.	☐	☐
2 If someone was aggressive to Carlos, he would still listen to them.	☐	☐
3 Carlos would send an aggressive person an email, rather than try to talk to them.	☐	☐
4 If someone was aggressive toward Carlos, he would always report it to his boss.	☐	☐
5 Carlos would never contact a colleague who was on vacation.	☐	☐

56.5 KEY LANGUAGE COLLOCATIONS WITH "GIVE," "HOLD," AND "SET"

The verbs "give," "hold," and "set" are often used in English collocations in a business context.

I'll **give some thought to** the new proposal.

They **held a meeting** to discuss the committee's decision.

He **set the goals** for his team to meet this week.

Aa 56.6 READ THE EMAIL AND MATCH THE COLLOCATIONS TO THEIR DEFINITIONS

To: All staff

Subject: New store opening in Lakewood

At the beginning of the financial year, the company held discussions to decide on our plans for the year. It was agreed that we would give priority to opening a new store in Lakewood.

The store needs significant renovation. I have contacted three building companies about this. We will need to set limits on how much the renovation costs, and hold off on starting the works until we have planned our budget.

We have also hired a new manager for the store, Aimee Turner. Staff from headquarters will join her in the first few weeks after opening to train her and give some help.

The process has gone extremely smoothly so far, and we hope this will set a precedent for all new stores we open in the future.

Regards, Jack Milton

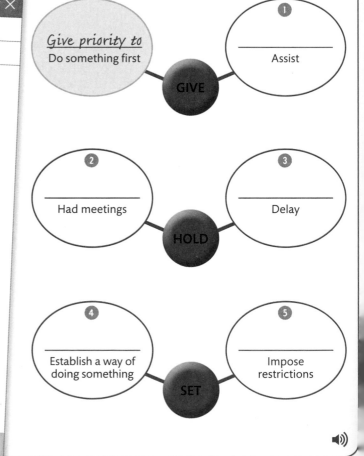

Give priority to
Do something first

GIVE

① _____ Assist

② _____ Had meetings

③ _____ Delay

HOLD

④ _____ Establish a way of doing something

⑤ _____ Impose restrictions

SET

56.7 FILL IN THE GAPS USING THE PHRASES IN THE PANEL

The two governments will hold _____ *talks* _____ in the spring.

1 I've never really given _____ working overseas, but I wouldn't mind.

2 I'm sorry, I can't give you extra time off. It would set _____ .

3 Let's think about what we want to achieve this year and set _____ .

4 I think we should hold _____ with our supplier to talk about prices.

5 Janice, please could you give _____ Hakim? It's his first day today.

6 Let's hold _____ making big decisions until we have all the facts.

7 We've _____ limits on the number of new people we can hire this year.

8 This year, we need to give _____ to boosting sales in all our markets.

a meeting	a precedent	off on	much thought to
priority	set	some goals	some help to	~~talks~~

🔊

56.8 USE THE CHART TO CREATE 6 CORRECT SENTENCES AND SAY THEM OUT LOUD

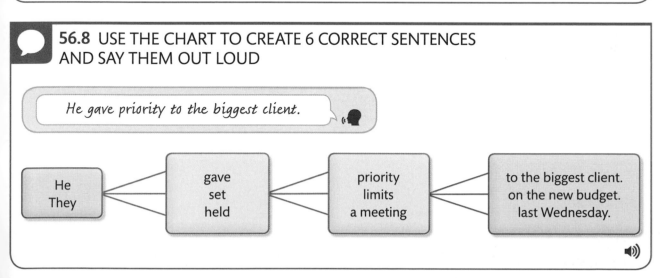

He gave priority to the biggest client.

| He / They | gave / set / held | priority / limits / a meeting | to the biggest client. / on the new budget. / last Wednesday. |

🔊

56 ✓ CHECKLIST

⚙ First and second conditionals ☐   **Aa** Collocations for business meetings ☐   🧩 Talking about possibilities ☐

57 Being specific

A relative clause is a part of a sentence that provides more information about the subject. A defining relative clause identifies the subject we are talking about.

⚙ **New language** Defining relative clauses
Aa Vocabulary Personal characteristics
🧩 **New skill** Describing people and jobs

57.1 KEY LANGUAGE DEFINING RELATIVE CLAUSES

Defining relative clauses are used to describe exactly which person or thing we are referring to. Without this information, the meaning of the sentence changes.

Here the defining clause gives essential information about a person.

MAIN CLAUSE   DEFINING RELATIVE CLAUSE

She'd like to meet someone who is kind.

Relative pronoun for people.

Here the defining clause gives essential information about a thing.

MAIN CLAUSE   DEFINING RELATIVE CLAUSE

I'm looking for a job that I'll enjoy.

Relative pronoun for things.

The defining clause can also go in the middle of the main clause.

MAIN CLAUSE   DEFINING RELATIVE CLAUSE   MAIN CLAUSE CONTINUED

The job that I heard about is interesting.

Relative pronoun for things.

57.2 HOW TO FORM DEFINING RELATIVE CLAUSES

Defining relative clauses begin with a relative pronoun.
English uses different relative pronouns to talk about
people and things.

TIP
"That" is sometimes used as a relative pronoun for a person. While this is commonly used, it is not correct.

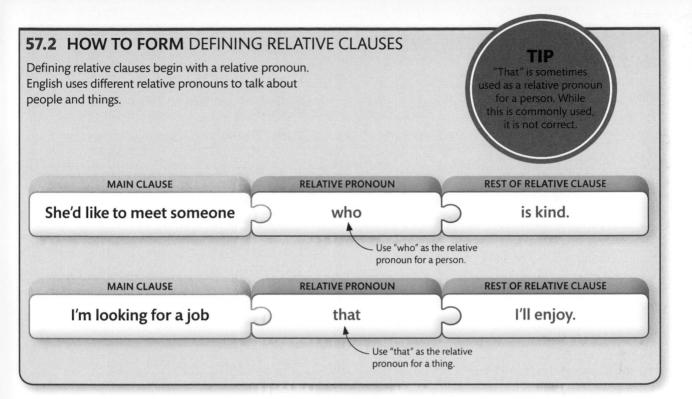

MAIN CLAUSE	RELATIVE PRONOUN	REST OF RELATIVE CLAUSE
She'd like to meet someone	who	is kind.

Use "who" as the relative pronoun for a person.

MAIN CLAUSE	RELATIVE PRONOUN	REST OF RELATIVE CLAUSE
I'm looking for a job	that	I'll enjoy.

Use "that" as the relative pronoun for a thing.

57.3 REWRITE THE SENTENCES USING DEFINING RELATIVE CLAUSES

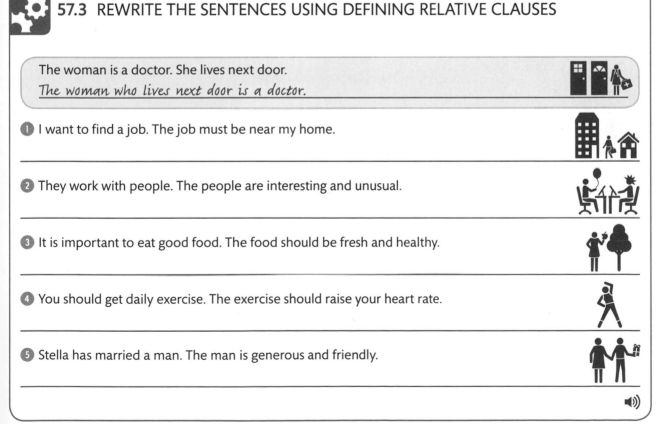

The woman is a doctor. She lives next door.
The woman who lives next door is a doctor.

1 I want to find a job. The job must be near my home.
_____

2 They work with people. The people are interesting and unusual.
_____

3 It is important to eat good food. The food should be fresh and healthy.
_____

4 You should get daily exercise. The exercise should raise your heart rate.
_____

5 Stella has married a man. The man is generous and friendly.
_____

57.4 READ THE JOB DESCRIPTIONS AND ANSWER THE QUESTIONS

NURSE: FULL TIME
Rocklands Hospital

We are looking for a confident, qualified nurse who is efficient and caring to work in our busy medical team. The ideal candidate will be someone who enjoys working with the public. We particularly want someone who is cheerful and calm, even in difficult situations.

CHILDREN'S ENTERTAINER: PART TIME
Binghams Entertainment

Wanted: an outgoing and fun-loving person with a good sense of humor to join our team of children's entertainers. We are looking for someone who is reliable and enjoys being around children. We will provide all the training for the right candidate.

Rocklands needs a nurse who is unqualified.
True ☐ **False** ☑

① The nurse should manage difficult situations well.
True ☐ **False** ☐

② Rocklands need a nurse who is cheerful.
True ☐ **False** ☐

③ Binghams want an entertainer who is calm.
True ☐ **False** ☐

④ The entertainer must enjoy working with children.
True ☐ **False** ☐

⑤ Binghams wants an entertainer who is efficient.
True ☐ **False** ☐

Aa 57.5 READ THE JOB DESCRIPTIONS AGAIN AND MATCH THE DEFINITIONS TO THE WORDS AND PHRASES

	Definitions	Words
	Not excited or nervous	Caring
①	Of a happy disposition	Confident
②	Good at looking after people	Cheerful
③	Sure about your abilities	Calm
④	Works in an organized way	Outgoing
⑤	Someone you can trust	Efficient
⑥	Friendly and communicative	Reliable
⑦	Likes having a good time	Good sense of humor
⑧	Appreciates funny things	Fun-loving

57.6 LISTEN TO THE AUDIO, THEN NUMBER THE SENTENCES IN THE ORDER YOU HEAR THEM

George is lonely. He's having coffee with his friend Tina, who has a solution.

A I'd love to meet some people who are fun to be with. ☐

B I can introduce you to some people who will absolutely love you! ☐

C I have a job that is challenging and very interesting. [1]

D Yes, it's tough moving to a new place where you don't know many people. ☐

E There are lots of amazing people who live in this area. ☐

F I'll invite a group of people who I think you'll find both interesting and great fun. ☐

57.7 USE A DEFINING RELATIVE CLAUSE TO COMBINE THE SENTENCES, THEN SAY THEM OUT LOUD

> I enjoy working with people. At work people should be efficient and cheerful.
>
> *I enjoy working with people who are efficient and cheerful.*

1 It's important to have a good boss. A good boss is confident and reliable.

2 It's good to have interesting work. The work should be challenging.

3 We are looking for a new secretary. The secretary should be calm and efficient.

4 I'm working on a project. The project is new and exciting.

---

57 ✓ CHECKLIST

⚙ Defining relative clauses ☐   **Aa** Personal characteristics ☐   🧩 Describing people and jobs ☐

Like defining relative clauses, non-defining relative clauses add extra information about something. However, the information is not essential, but gives extra detail.

⚙ **New language** Non-defining relative clauses
Aa Vocabulary Personal characteristics
🧩 **New skill** Describing people, places, and things

58.1 KEY LANGUAGE NON-DEFINING RELATIVE CLAUSES

The non-defining clause in this sentence gives secondary information about a person.

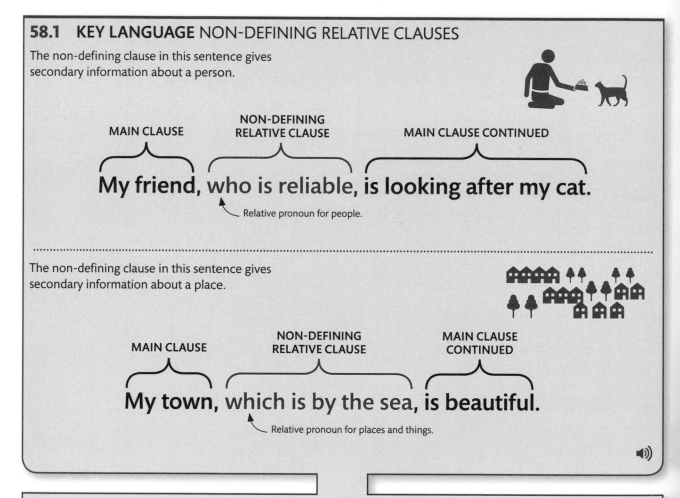

MAIN CLAUSE | NON-DEFINING RELATIVE CLAUSE | MAIN CLAUSE CONTINUED

My friend, who is reliable, is looking after my cat.

Relative pronoun for people.

The non-defining clause in this sentence gives secondary information about a place.

MAIN CLAUSE | NON-DEFINING RELATIVE CLAUSE | MAIN CLAUSE CONTINUED

My town, which is by the sea, is beautiful.

Relative pronoun for places and things.

58.2 FURTHER EXAMPLES NON-DEFINING RELATIVE CLAUSES

 Our teacher, who comes from Paris, **is wonderful.**

 The doctor, who was very nice, **looked after my mother.**

 Our local concert hall, which is very old, **is a beautiful building.**

58.3 HOW TO FORM NON-DEFINING RELATIVE CLAUSES

Non-defining relative clauses come in the middle of a sentence,
after the subject and before the main verb.

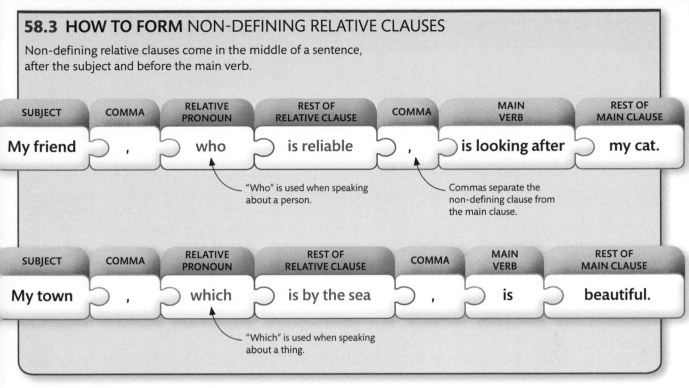

SUBJECT	COMMA	RELATIVE PRONOUN	REST OF RELATIVE CLAUSE	COMMA	MAIN VERB	REST OF MAIN CLAUSE
My friend	,	who	is reliable	,	is looking after	my cat.

"Who" is used when speaking about a person.

Commas separate the non-defining clause from the main clause.

SUBJECT	COMMA	RELATIVE PRONOUN	REST OF RELATIVE CLAUSE	COMMA	MAIN VERB	REST OF MAIN CLAUSE
My town	,	which	is by the sea	,	is	beautiful.

"Which" is used when speaking about a thing.

58.4 FILL IN THE GAPS USING THE NON-DEFINING RELATIVE CLAUSES IN THE PANEL

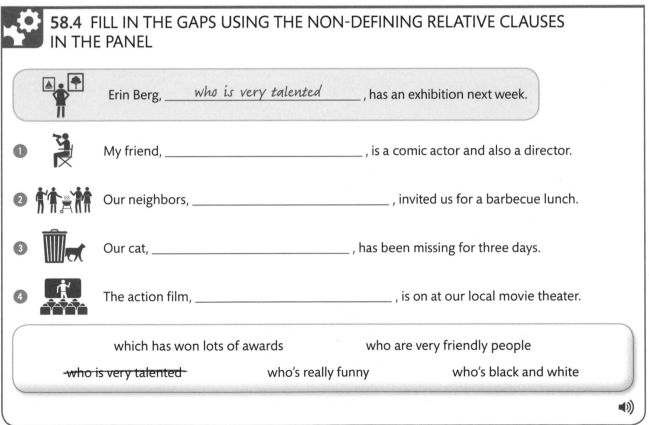

Erin Berg, _who is very talented_ , has an exhibition next week.

1. My friend, _____ , is a comic actor and also a director.

2. Our neighbors, _____ , invited us for a barbecue lunch.

3. Our cat, _____ , has been missing for three days.

4. The action film, _____ , is on at our local movie theater.

which has won lots of awards   who are very friendly people

~~who is very talented~~   who's really funny   who's black and white

58.5 REWRITE THE SENTENCES, CORRECTING THE ERRORS

> The statue, who is very old, is next to Lilydale Park.
> *The statue, which is very old, is next to Lilydale Park.*

① My brother, which is very talented, is an opera singer.

_____

② My house, who is very old, is located in a quiet street in Ringwood.

_____

③ The teacher, what is very outgoing, loves soccer.

_____

④ This fashion magazine, who is very expensive, is extremely boring.

_____

⑤ My dog what is very energetic, likes to go running in the park.

_____

58.6 LISTEN TO THE AUDIO, THEN NUMBER THE PICTURES IN THE ORDER THEY ARE DESCRIBED

58.7 USE THE CHART TO CREATE 16 CORRECT SENTENCES AND SAY THEM OUT LOUD

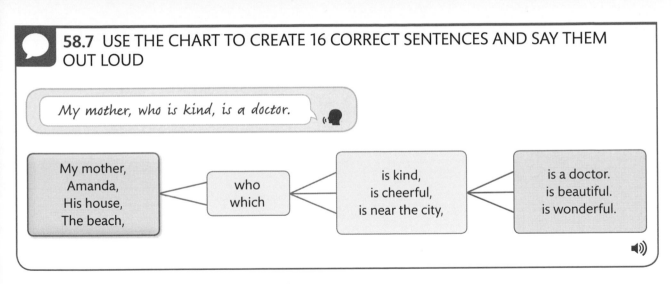

My mother, who is kind, is a doctor.

| My mother, Amanda, His house, The beach, | who which | is kind, is cheerful, is near the city, | is a doctor. is beautiful. is wonderful. |

58 ✓ CHECKLIST

⚙ Non-defining relative clauses ☐   **Aa** Personal characteristics ☐   🧩 Describing people, places and things ☐

♲ REVIEW THE ENGLISH YOU HAVE LEARNED IN UNITS 53–58

NEW LANGUAGE	SAMPLE SENTENCE	☑	UNIT
THE SECOND CONDITIONAL	If I won the lottery, I would leave my job.	☐	53.1
COLLOCATIONS WITH "DO" AND "MAKE"	I do the paperwork **on Tuesday afternoons.** He makes a call **before each weekly meeting.**	☐	53.7
"IF I WERE YOU"	If I were you, I would be careful on the ice.	☐	55.1
QUESTION PHRASES WITH GERUNDS	How about eating **in that new Italian restaurant tonight?**	☐	55.8
FIRST AND SECOND CONDITIONALS	If I see Katherine, I'll invite her to the meeting. If I ran the company, I'd give my staff a bonus.	☐	56.1
COLLOCATIONS WITH "GIVE" AND "HOLD"	I'll give some thought to **the new proposal.** They held a meeting **to discuss the decision.**	☐	56.5
COLLOCATIONS WITH "SET"	He set the goals **for his team this week.**	☐	56.5
DEFINING RELATIVE CLAUSES	**She'd like to meet someone** who is kind. **The job** that I heard about **is interesting.**	☐	57.1
NON-DEFINING RELATIVE CLAUSES	**My friend,** who is reliable, **looks after my cat.** **My town,** which is by the sea, **is beautiful.**	☐	58.1

What was happening when?

To report on past events, such as a crime or accident, you often need to explain what else was happening at the time. Use the past continuous to do this.

🔧 **New language** Past continuous
Aa **Vocabulary** Verb / noun collocations
🧩 **New skill** Talking about events at given times

59.1 KEY LANGUAGE THE PAST CONTINUOUS

English uses the past continuous to talk about actions that were in progress at a certain time in the past.

I knocked on your door at noon but you weren't at home. What were you doing?

Past simple

11:30AM   12:00PM   12:30PM

Past continuous

I was having lunch with a friend.

🔊

59.2 FURTHER EXAMPLES THE PAST CONTINUOUS

Sorry I missed your call. I was mowing the lawn.

He didn't go to the party because he was working late.

This time last week, we were hiking in Peru.

🔊

59.3 HOW TO FORM THE PAST CONTINUOUS

Use "was" or "were" followed by the verb with "-ing" to form the past continuous.

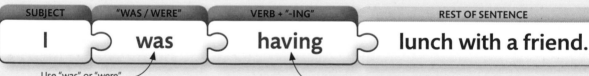

SUBJECT	"WAS / WERE"	VERB + "-ING"	REST OF SENTENCE
I	was	having	lunch with a friend.

Use "was" or "were" depending on the subject.

Add "-ing" to the main verb.

59.4 FILL IN THE GAPS BY PUTTING THE VERBS IN THE PAST CONTINUOUS

The children _____ were playing _____ (play) outside yesterday afternoon.

1 They _____ (sing) in the choir last night. It was a very good concert.

2 You _____ (talk) on the phone at lunchtime today. I didn't want to interrupt your call.

3 Sorry I didn't answer the phone. I _____ (eat) my dinner when you called.

4 She _____ (drive) down my road earlier today. I waved, but she didn't see me.

5 He _____ (do) his homework when his friend arrived. So he still has lots to do.

6 Ethan _____ (pick) apples outside this morning. They look absolutely delicious!

◀))

59.5 LISTEN TO THE AUDIO, THEN NUMBER THE PICTURES IN THE ORDER THEY ARE DESCRIBED

A police officer is interviewing the owner of a house where a burglary has taken place.

59.6 READ THE NOTES AND FILL IN THE GAPS IN THE SUMMARY USING THE PAST CONTINUOUS

At 10:30, Mr. Black __was gardening__ when he saw a man get into a car. The man _____ jeans and a black t-shirt. At 10:37, Mrs. Gomez _____ back from the stores. Ten minutes later, she saw the same man in a car. He _____ very fast. Mr. Chandra _____ his car at 10:30. At 10:38, he also saw the same man. The suspect _____ up and down the road, and _____ at all the houses. Mr. Chandra saw him again at 10:45. This time, he _____ the house next door, and_____ a big, heavy-looking bag.

Time	Name	Activity
10:30	Mr. Black	Gardening.
10:30	Mr. Chandra	Wash car.
10:35	Mr. Black	Saw man in jeans and black t-shirt get into car.
10:37	Mrs. Gomez	Walk back from stores.
10:38	Mr. Chandra	Saw same man walk up and down road, looking at houses.
10:45	Mr. Chandra	Saw man leave next door, carrying big bag.
10:47	Mrs. Gomez	Saw same man driving fast car.

59.7 SAY THE SENTENCES OUT LOUD, FILLING IN THE GAPS BY PUTTING THE VERBS IN THE PAST CONTINUOUS

I ___was cleaning___ (clean) the kitchen.

1 You _____ (vacuum) the living room.

2 She _____ (work) outside.

3 They _____ (wash) the car.

4 We _____ (walk) home.

5 He _____ (look) at houses.

Aa 59.8 READ THE LEAFLET AND WRITE THE HIGHLIGHTED COLLOCATIONS NEXT TO THEIR DEFINITIONS

NEIGHBORHOOD WATCH

Thank you for joining the fight against crime!

REMEMBER: It takes time to build a good team, so it's worth having a discussion with your neighbors in order to take a view on who does what, and decide who should take charge.

It's best to have two people "on watch" at the same time. This means that, if you make a discovery, you should make an effort to discuss it with your neighbor in order to make sense of what you've seen.

Once you are sure the activity is suspicious, you need to have a plan about what to do. It's tempting to rush things if you want to make progress, but don't approach a suspect, unless you are certain it's safe to do so. Criminals will take advantage of any situation if they have the chance to do so and you may put yourself in danger.

Lead a team	=	_take charge_
① Put work into something	=	_____
② Understand	=	_____
③ Know what to do	=	_____
④ Happen slowly	=	_____
⑤ Talk about things	=	_____
⑥ Have an opportunity	=	_____
⑦ Form an opinion	=	_____
⑧ Benefit from a situation	=	_____
⑨ Find something out	=	_____
⑩ Achieve something	=	_____

Aa 59.9 FILL IN THE GAPS USING THE PHRASES IN THE PANEL

You need to ____*make an effort*____ if you want to succeed.

① This project will _____ , but I must get it right.

② Thanks for helping me _____ my homework.

③ It's good to _____ to solve problems.

④ Let's meet up next week if we _____ .

⑤ You must not let people _____ of you.

take time
~~make an effort~~
take advantage
have a discussion
have the chance
make sense of

59 ✓ CHECKLIST

⚙ Past continuous ☐   Aa Verb / noun collocations ☐   Talking about events at given times ☐

207

60 Vocabulary

60.1 THE NATURAL WORLD

star

Sun

planet

Earth

Moon

stream

river

sea

farmland

wave

beach

high tide

low tide

desert

polar region

jungle

forest

tree

branch / twig

leaf

plant

grass

bird

eagle

seagull

owl

parrot

insect

butterfly

bee

fly

mosquito

bear

camel

lion

tiger

elephant

rhino

giraffe

kangaroo

buffalo

cow

monkey

mouse

rat

snake

spider

frog

crocodile

lizard

turtle

crab

whale

dolphin

shark

fish

octopus

61 Setting the scene

To set the scene in a story, English uses the past continuous to describe the background situation, and descriptive adjectives to say what a place is like.

⚙ **New language** Past continuous
Aa Vocabulary Adjectives to describe places
🧩 **New skill** Setting the scene for a story

61.1 KEY LANGUAGE PAST CONTINUOUS FOR SCENE-SETTING

The past continuous is formed the same way when setting a scene as for describing past actions in progress.

It was a beautiful day.
The sun was shining and the birds were singing.
Children were laughing and playing in the street.

🔊

61.2 READ THE STORY AND WRITE ANSWERS TO THE QUESTIONS AS FULL SENTENCES

On a busy morning in Georgetown, Special Agent Zoe Gordon was sitting in her car. The picturesque, peaceful little town was looking charming today, surrounded by the magnificent, open country, where colorful wild flowers were blooming. All was well in this magical, rural town… or was it?

People were shopping and chatting on Main Street. Teenagers were skateboarding along the sidewalk, but Zoe was watching the alleyway between two stores. On the other side of the street, two more agents were in position, waiting for someone to appear.

At 11:00, a suspicious-looking man came out of the alleyway, carrying a large bag. The two agents followed him, and Zoe started her car.

> Where was Agent Zoe Gordon sitting?
> _She was sitting in her car._

❶ What were people doing on Main Street?
_____

❷ Where were teenagers skateboarding?
_____

❸ What was Zoe watching?
_____

❹ What were the two other agents doing?
_____

❺ What was the suspect carrying?
_____

Aa 61.3 MATCH THE DEFINITIONS TO THE WORDS

Very impressive and beautiful	Picturesque
❶ Brightly colored	Peaceful
❷ Quiet and calm	Magnificent
❸ Pretty or charming	Open
❹ In the country	Colorful
❺ Not enclosed or fenced	Magical
❻ Mysterious or wonderful	Rural

🔊

61.4 LISTEN TO THE AUDIO AND ANSWER THE QUESTIONS

You will hear the beginning of a short story.

Sam's face was getting very cold.
True ✓   False ☐   Not given ☐

❶ People were walking slowly down the street.
True ☐   False ☐   Not given ☐

❷ The waitress was wearing colorful clothes.
True ☐   False ☐   Not given ☐

❸ Sam was eating a cheese sandwich.
True ☐   False ☐   Not given ☐

❹ Sam didn't know what the boy was carrying.
True ☐   False ☐   Not given ☐

Aa 61.5 READ THE DIARY AND FILL IN THE GAPS USING THE WORDS IN THE PANEL

September 2013

21 SATURDAY

Today we were ___walking___ in the country. The mountains were looking _____ against the blue sky. There were _____ flowers everywhere, and the children were _____ bunches of them to take home. We stopped for coffee in a _____ little village and we sat in the sunshine while the children played in the playground. It was a really _____ day.

walking
picturesque
colorful
magical
magnificent
picking

61 ✔ CHECKLIST

⚙️ Past continuous ☐   Aa Adjectives to describe places ☐   🧩 Setting the scene for a story ☐

62 Interrupted actions

English often uses the past continuous and the past simple together to tell stories, especially when one event interrupts another.

⚙ **New language** Past continuous and past simple
Aa Vocabulary Travel and leisure
🧩 **New skill** Describing interrupted actions

62.1 KEY LANGUAGE PAST CONTINUOUS AND PAST SIMPLE

When English uses the past continuous and past simple together, the past continuous describes a longer, background action, and the past simple describes a shorter action that interrupts the background action.

LONGER BACKGROUND ACTION   **SHORTER MAIN ACTION**

I was taking a photo when a monkey grabbed my camera.

62.2 FURTHER EXAMPLES PAST CONTINUOUS AND PAST SIMPLE

He was sunbathing **when it started to rain.**   She was sleeping **when the phone rang.**

62.3 LISTEN TO THE AUDIO AND MARK WHICH TENSE DESCRIBES THE ACTIVITY IN EACH PICTURE

Past continuous ☑
Past simple ☐

① Past continuous ☐
Past simple ☐

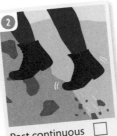

② Past continuous ☐
Past simple ☐

③ Past continuous ☐
Past simple ☐

④ Past continuous ☐
Past simple ☐

62.4 FILL IN THE GAPS BY PUTTING THE VERBS IN THE CORRECT TENSES

When I ___got back___ (🚪 get back) to my room, a cleaner ___was vacuuming___ (🧹 vacuum) it.

1 When I _____ (🌲 enter) the forest, a monkey _____ (🌲 swing) through the trees.

2 The next day, Chloe _____ (📖 read) a book when Russell _____ (☕ walk) into the café.

3 Kelly and Dean _____ (🏄 surf) when Dean _____ (fall) off his board.

4 We _____ (see) some baby turtles while we _____ (🏃 jog) along the beach.

🔊

62.5 READ THE EMAIL AND ANSWER THE QUESTIONS

Caleb met Owen in a café.
True ✓ **False** ☐ **Not given** ☐

1 Caleb and Owen were sunbathing
when Owen saw a shark.
True ☐ **False** ☐ **Not given** ☐

2 Caleb and Owen stopped sunbathing
because they got too hot.
True ☐ **False** ☐ **Not given** ☐

3 Caleb hurt his ankle because he was
rushing back to the hotel.
True ☐ **False** ☐ **Not given** ☐

4 Owen enjoyed the party.
True ☐ **False** ☐ **Not given** ☐

5 Caleb missed his plane home.
True ☐ **False** ☐ **Not given** ☐

✉
To: Frances Smith

Subject: Bali

I'm having a fantastic time here in Bali.

Last week I met my old friend Owen. I was just having a drink in a café when he turned up. We had a few adventures after that!

On Saturday, we were swimming in the sea when Owen saw a shark, so we got out quickly. Later we were sunbathing when it started raining hard. We were running back to the hotel when I fell over. I hurt my ankle, so I missed a party we were supposed to go to that night. Owen went, but he stayed too long and missed his plane. He's so disorganized!

We should meet up when I'm back from Bali.

See you soon,
Caleb

Aa 62.6 READ THE EMAIL AND MATCH THE ADJECTIVES THAT HAVE SIMILAR MEANINGS

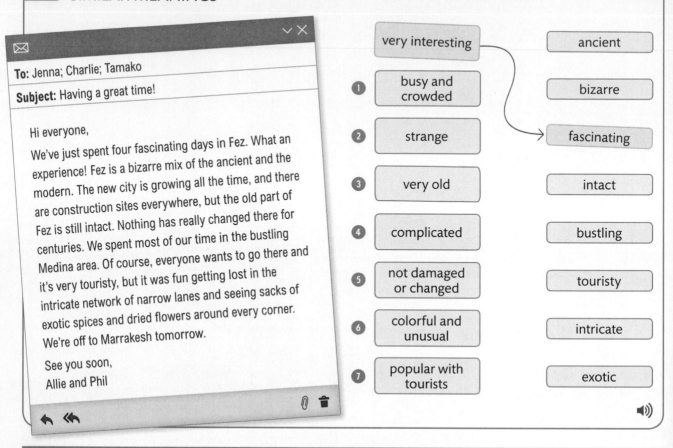

To: Jenna; Charlie; Tamako
Subject: Having a great time!

Hi everyone,

We've just spent four fascinating days in Fez. What an experience! Fez is a bizarre mix of the ancient and the modern. The new city is growing all the time, and there are construction sites everywhere, but the old part of Fez is still intact. Nothing has really changed there for centuries. We spent most of our time in the bustling Medina area. Of course, everyone wants to go there and it's very touristy, but it was fun getting lost in the intricate network of narrow lanes and seeing sacks of exotic spices and dried flowers around every corner. We're off to Marrakesh tomorrow.

See you soon,
Allie and Phil

very interesting	→	fascinating
1 busy and crowded		ancient
2 strange		bizarre
3 very old		intact
4 complicated		bustling
5 not damaged or changed		touristy
6 colorful and unusual		intricate
7 popular with tourists		exotic

62.7 SAY THE SENTENCES OUT LOUD, FILLING IN THE GAPS

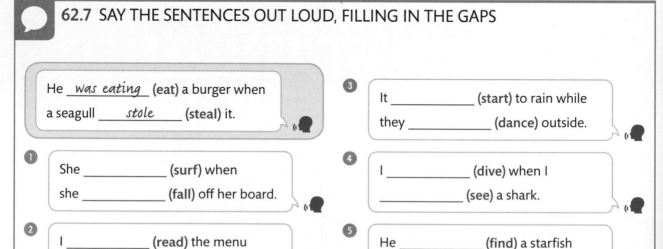

He _was eating_ (eat) a burger when a seagull ___stole___ (steal) it.

1 She _____ (surf) when she _____ (fall) off her board.

2 I _____ (read) the menu when the waiter _____ (arrive).

3 It _____ (start) to rain while they _____ (dance) outside.

4 I _____ (dive) when I _____ (see) a shark.

5 He _____ (find) a starfish while he _____ (lie) in the sun.

62.8 CROSS OUT THE INCORRECT WORDS IN EACH SENTENCE

I ~~watched~~ / was watching a great movie on TV when the phone rang / ~~was ringing~~.

1. Felipe **took** / **was taking** a long bath when someone **knocked** / **was knocking** on his door.

2. Karen **met** / **was meeting** her old friend Madeleine while she **traveled** / **was traveling** in Australia.

3. Christopher **cooked** / **was cooking** dinner when his party guests **arrived** / **were arriving** early.

4. We **learned** / **were learning** to speak Thai while we **stayed** / **were staying** in Bangkok.

5. I **wrote** / **was writing** a report when my boss **asked** / **was asking** me to come to her office.

Aa 62.9 FILL IN THE GAPS USING THE WORDS IN THE PANEL

Hi Emily,

Paul and I are having a great time in Marrakesh. Today we were ___walking___ in the old part of the city when we saw an old man. Actually, he looked _____ ! He was _____ a large, heavy basket, so I offered to carry it for him. The old man was _____ at me but I _____ nervous, so I gave the basket to Paul. Suddenly we arrived in a _____ square with market stalls and people everywhere. I looked for the old man. He was sitting with the basket open. He was _____ the flute and out of the basket came two enormous snakes. I'd never seen anything like it in my life: it was _____ . They were moving to the music he was playing. It was _____ to watch, but I didn't offer to carry his basket again.

Love Hania

carrying
bustling
~~walking~~
playing
fascinating
smiling
ancient
felt
bizarre

62 ✓ CHECKLIST

⚙ Past continuous and past simple ☐   **Aa** Travel and leisure ☐   🧩 Describing interrupted actions ☐

215

63 Events in the past

English uses the past simple passive to talk about events in the past when it is the effect of an action that is important, rather than the cause of the action.

⚙ **New language** Past simple passive
Aa Vocabulary Environmental disasters
🧩 **New skill** Talking about important events

63.1 KEY LANGUAGE THE PAST SIMPLE PASSIVE

You can use the past simple passive to emphasize the importance of actions and events in the past and to draw attention to the things or people that were affected by the events.

PAST SIMPLE PASSIVE

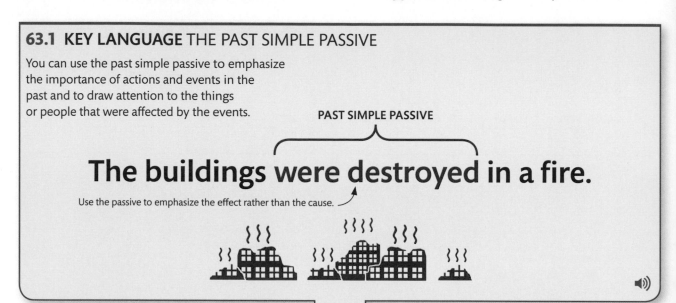

The buildings were destroyed in a fire.

Use the passive to emphasize the effect rather than the cause.

63.2 FURTHER EXAMPLES THE PAST SIMPLE PASSIVE

The trees were cut down last year.

The railway line was damaged during the storm.

Two people were injured in the accident.

63.3 HOW TO FORM THE PAST SIMPLE PASSIVE

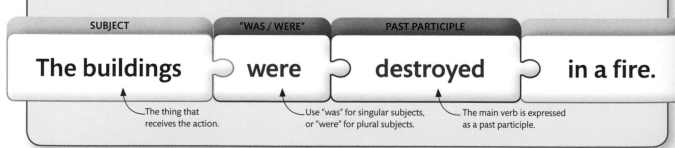

SUBJECT	"WAS / WERE"	PAST PARTICIPLE	
The buildings	**were**	**destroyed**	**in a fire.**

The thing that receives the action.

Use "was" for singular subjects, or "were" for plural subjects.

The main verb is expressed as a past participle.

63.4 FILL IN THE GAPS BY PUTTING THE VERBS IN THE PAST SIMPLE PASSIVE

Many trees _____were burned_____ (burn) in a forest fire last night.

1. Several buildings _____ (destroy) after a powerful earthquake.

2. The factory _____ (demolish) because it was unsafe.

3. Many homes _____ (flood) after the river burst its banks.

4. The explorer _____ (rescue) after she got lost in the mountains.

5. The beaches _____ (cover) in oil this morning.

6. My train _____ (delay) because a tree fell onto the line.

63.5 SAY THE SENTENCES OUT LOUD, CHANGING THEM FROM THE PAST SIMPLE ACTIVE TO THE PAST SIMPLE PASSIVE

Someone burned down the building.

The building was burned down.

1. Something destroyed the factory.

2. Someone spilled the oil into the ocean.

3. Something polluted the lake.

4. Someone hurt the animals.

5. Something damaged many people's homes.

63.6 VOCABULARY DISASTERS AND ENVIRONMENTAL ISSUES

oil spill

deforestation

air pollution

global warming

smog

flood

shipwreck

overpopulation

63.7 READ THE ARTICLE AND WRITE ANSWERS TO THE QUESTIONS AS FULL SENTENCES

26 DAILY NEWS

CHEMICAL SPILL TURNS LAKE RED

Following an explosion at Bander Chemical Factory last night, toxic chemicals were released into the air. Lake Bander, which provides water for the factory, was turned red by the chemicals, which were carried into the lake by last night's rain.

Thousands of fish were killed, local farmers' crops were destroyed, and this morning the entire Bander area was declared a disaster area. The CEO of Bander Chemicals apologized for the leak and said the company was doing everything possible to clean the lake and surrounding countryside. Local farmer John Hawkins said, "My business was ruined last night. I just hope Bander Chemicals will help us now."

> What happened to the chemicals last night?
> _The chemicals were released into the air._

1 What happened to Lake Bander?

_____

2 How did the chemicals get into the lake?

_____

3 What happened to thousands of fish?

_____

4 What happened to local farmers' crops?

_____

5 What happened to the Bander area?

_____

6 What happened to John Hawkins' business?

_____

63.8 LISTEN TO THE AUDIO AND ANSWER THE QUESTIONS

A news reporter interviews Rosie, an eyewitness, and José, a vet, about an oil spill.

The birds were covered in oil.
True ☑ **False** ☐ **Not given** ☐

1 Rosie thought there had been an oil spill.
True ☐ **False** ☐ **Not given** ☐

2 The emergency services were not called.
True ☐ **False** ☐ **Not given** ☐

3 The birds were cleaned on the beach.
True ☐ **False** ☐ **Not given** ☐

4 Many of the birds were killed.
True ☐ **False** ☐ **Not given** ☐

5 The oil spill happened after a shipwreck.
True ☐ **False** ☐ **Not given** ☐

6 The ship ran into some rocks.
True ☐ **False** ☐ **Not given** ☐

7 The public were not allowed on the beach.
True ☐ **False** ☐ **Not given** ☐

63 ✓ CHECKLIST

⚙ Past simple passive ☐   **Aa** Environmental disasters ☐   🧩 Talking about important events ☐

♺ REVIEW THE ENGLISH YOU HAVE LEARNED IN UNITS 59–63

NEW LANGUAGE	SAMPLE SENTENCE	☑	UNIT
PAST CONTINUOUS	I was having lunch **with a friend**.	☐	59.1
COLLOCATIONS WITH "TAKE"	It takes time **to build a good team**.	☐	59.8
COLLOCATIONS WITH "MAKE"	It's tempting to rush things if you want to make progress.	☐	59.8
COLLOCATIONS WITH "HAVE"	It's worth having a discussion with your neighbors.	☐	59.8
PAST CONTINUOUS FOR SCENE-SETTING	The sun was shining and the birds were singing.	☐	61.1
PAST CONTINUOUS AND PAST SIMPLE	I was taking a photo when a monkey grabbed my camera.	☐	62.1
PAST SIMPLE PASSIVE	The buildings were destroyed in a fire.	☐	63.1

64 Before and after

English uses the past perfect with the past simple to talk about two or more events that happened at different times in the past.

⚙ **New language** Past perfect and past simple
Aa **Vocabulary** Visual arts
🧩 **New skill** Describing sequences of past events

64.1 KEY LANGUAGE PAST PERFECT AND PAST SIMPLE

The past simple describes the event that is closest to the time of speaking.
The past perfect describes an event further back in the past.

PAST PERFECT   PAST SIMPLE

The train had left before we arrived at the station.

8:10PM   8:20PM   NOW

64.2 FURTHER EXAMPLES PAST PERFECT AND PAST SIMPLE

I knocked on Pablo's door, but he had already gone to work.

7:00AM   7:30AM   NOW

The traffic was bad because a car had broken down on the road.

2:30PM   3:00PM   NOW

64.3 HOW TO FORM THE PAST PERFECT

Use "had" followed by the past participle to form the past perfect.

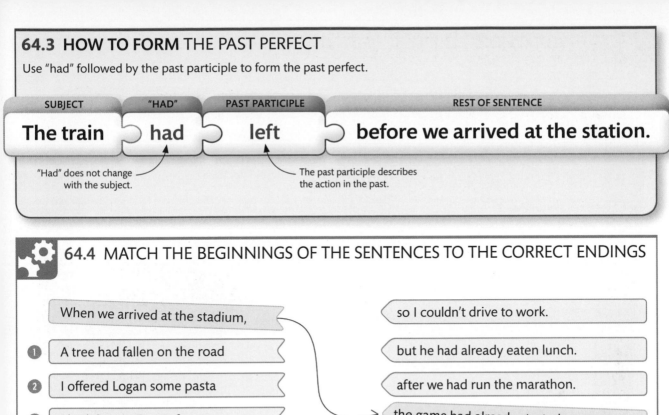

SUBJECT	"HAD"	PAST PARTICIPLE	REST OF SENTENCE
The train	**had**	**left**	**before we arrived at the station.**

"Had" does not change with the subject.

The past participle describes the action in the past.

64.4 MATCH THE BEGINNINGS OF THE SENTENCES TO THE CORRECT ENDINGS

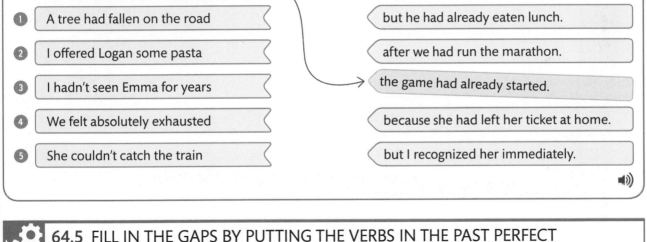

When we arrived at the stadium, → the game had already started.

1. A tree had fallen on the road — so I couldn't drive to work.

2. I offered Logan some pasta — but he had already eaten lunch.

3. I hadn't seen Emma for years — but I recognized her immediately.

4. We felt absolutely exhausted — after we had run the marathon.

5. She couldn't catch the train — because she had left her ticket at home.

64.5 FILL IN THE GAPS BY PUTTING THE VERBS IN THE PAST PERFECT OR PAST SIMPLE

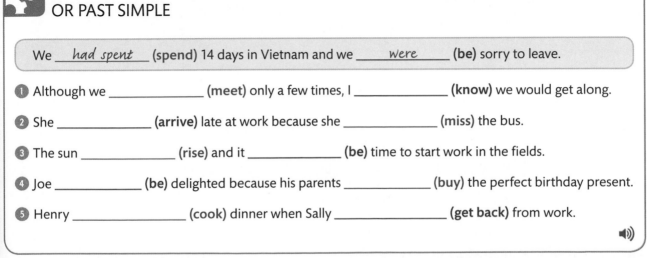

We ___had spent___ (spend) 14 days in Vietnam and we ___were___ (be) sorry to leave.

1. Although we _____ (meet) only a few times, I _____ (know) we would get along.

2. She _____ (arrive) late at work because she _____ (miss) the bus.

3. The sun _____ (rise) and it _____ (be) time to start work in the fields.

4. Joe _____ (be) delighted because his parents _____ (buy) the perfect birthday present.

5. Henry _____ (cook) dinner when Sally _____ (get back) from work.

64.6 READ THE ARTICLE AND WRITE ANSWERS TO THE QUESTIONS AS FULL SENTENCES

DESIGN FOCUS

HOME | ARTISTS | ABOUT | CONTACT

Eva Johanssen
THE LIFE AND CAREER OF THE GREAT CERAMIC ARTIST

When Eva Johanssen was a child, all she wanted to do was draw and paint. Her father, Per, wanted Eva to follow in his footsteps and become an engineer. Eva tried to please her father and worked hard at school, but after she had failed her science exams, Eva's father finally allowed her to study art.

At art school, Eva discovered her lifelong passion: ceramics. She had never worked with clay before she started college. However, once she had made her first pots, she realized how much she loved ceramics. The rest, of course, is history. By the end of the 20th century, Eva had sold her works to every major museum of art.

What did Eva like to do when she was a child?
Eva liked to draw and paint.

❶ What had Per wanted his daughter to be?
_____

❷ How did Eva approach her school work?
_____

❸ What did Per do after Eva had failed her exams?
_____

❹ Where did Eva discover her passion for ceramics?
_____

❺ What hadn't Eva done before starting art school?
_____

❻ When did Eva realize that she loved ceramics?
_____

❼ What had happened by the late 1990s?
_____

64.7 LISTEN TO THE AUDIO AND ANSWER THE QUESTIONS

Tony and Erin are talking about last night's party.

③ Tony will see Jackie again.
True ☐ False ☐ Not given ☐

Tony noticed Jackie right away.
True ☑ False ☐ Not given ☐

④ Erin thought Martin would be at the party.
True ☐ False ☐ Not given ☐

① Jackie was too shy to talk to Tony.
True ☐ False ☐ Not given ☐

⑤ Martin and Jeff don't like each other.
True ☐ False ☐ Not given ☐

② Tony and Jackie were chatting all night.
True ☐ False ☐ Not given ☐

⑥ Martin left the party early.
True ☐ False ☐ Not given ☐

64.8 SAY THE SENTENCES OUT LOUD, FILLING IN THE GAPS BY PUTTING THE VERBS IN THE PAST PERFECT OR PAST SIMPLE

He __had viewed__ (view) the house before he __took__ (take) his wife to see it.

① She _____ (read) a review of the book before she _____ (buy) it.

② After he _____ (finish) watching the movie, he _____ (go) to bed.

③ I _____ (ask) Katy for a ride to work because I _____ (miss) my train.

④ He _____ (study) very hard before he _____ (take) his exams.

⑤ Andy only _____ (resign) once he _____ (find) a new job.

⑥ They _____ (discuss) all the options before they _____ (make) a decision.

64 ✅ CHECKLIST

⚙ Past perfect and past simple ☐   **Aa** Visual arts ☐   🧩 Describing sequences of past events ☐

65 First times

When you talk about the first time something happened, such as visiting a new place, you often use "never" or "ever" with the past perfect or present perfect.

⚙ **New language** "Never" / "ever" with past tenses
Aa Vocabulary Travel adjectives
🧩 **New skill** Describing new experiences

65.1 KEY LANGUAGE PAST PERFECT WITH "NEVER" / "EVER"

Use the past perfect with "never" or "ever" to talk about events in the past that happened for the first time.

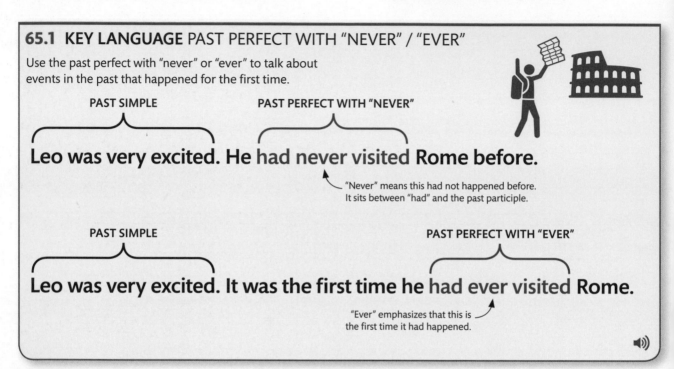

PAST SIMPLE PAST PERFECT WITH "NEVER"

Leo was very excited. He had never visited Rome before.

"Never" means this had not happened before. It sits between "had" and the past participle.

PAST SIMPLE PAST PERFECT WITH "EVER"

Leo was very excited. It was the first time he had ever visited Rome.

"Ever" emphasizes that this is the first time it had happened.

🔊

65.2 CROSS OUT THE INCORRECT WORD IN EACH SENTENCE

Tom had **never** / ~~ever~~ been on a plane before his trip to Madagascar.

1 Last summer was the first time we had **never** / **ever** gone camping. It rained every day!

2 I had **never** / **ever** eaten risotto until I went to Milan. Now I cook it for myself at home.

3 They had **never** / **ever** been overseas before they went to Paris. They thought the flight was exciting!

4 We traveled overnight from Bangkok. It was the first time I had **never** / **ever** slept on a train.

5 I heard you went to Madrid last month. Was that the first time you had **never** / **ever** been there?

6 James had **never** / **ever** been bungee jumping until he tried it in New Zealand last year.

🔊

65.3 KEY LANGUAGE PRESENT PERFECT WITH "NEVER" / "EVER"

Use the present perfect with "never" or "ever" to talk about events that are happening now for the first time.

PRESENT SIMPLE **PRESENT PERFECT WITH "NEVER"**

Nat is very excited. She has never visited Sydney before.

"Never" means that this has not happened before.
It sits between "has" and the past participle.

PRESENT SIMPLE **PRESENT PERFECT WITH "EVER"**

Nat is very excited. It's the first time she has ever visited Sydney.

"Ever" emphasizes that this is
the first time it has happened.

65.4 FILL IN THE GAPS USING "HAVE" IN THE CORRECT TENSE

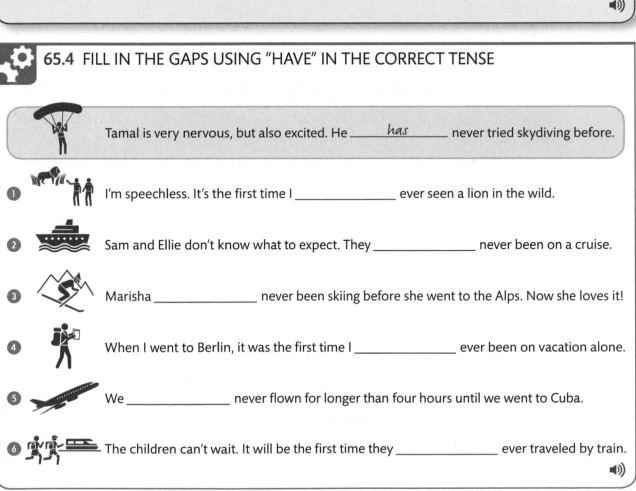

Tamal is very nervous, but also excited. He _____ *has* _____ never tried skydiving before.

① I'm speechless. It's the first time I _____ ever seen a lion in the wild.

② Sam and Ellie don't know what to expect. They _____ never been on a cruise.

③ Marisha _____ never been skiing before she went to the Alps. Now she loves it!

④ When I went to Berlin, it was the first time I _____ ever been on vacation alone.

⑤ We _____ never flown for longer than four hours until we went to Cuba.

⑥ The children can't wait. It will be the first time they _____ ever traveled by train.

Aa 65.5 READ THE PASSAGE AND WRITE THE HIGHLIGHTED WORDS NEXT TO THEIR DEFINITIONS

Lots of space = _spacious_

1 Completely empty = _____

2 Extremely old = _____

3 In poor condition = _____

4 Very pleasant = _____

5 Tall buildings = _____

6 Cozy and relaxing = _____

7 Well liked = _____

8 All in one room = _____

14 TRAVEL GUIDE TO GERMANY

A DAY TOUR OF BERLIN

MORNING
Head to Checkpoint Charlie and see the derelict remains of the Berlin Wall. This is a popular tourist site, so be prepared for crowds. After this, visit the charming Fassbender & Rausch, the world's largest chocolatier. Explore the open-plan shop and have lunch in the comfortable tearoom.

AFTERNOON
Go to the spacious Tiergarten. This park is so large that it can sometimes feel deserted. From here, walk to the Brandenburg Gate. While not ancient (it dates from 1791), this massive stone arch is nonetheless impressive and is the symbol of Berlin.
There aren't too many high-rise buildings in Berlin, but the Berliner Fernsehturm, the tallest building in Germany, has a restaurant at the top with great views of Berlin.

Aa 65.6 FILL IN THE GAPS USING THE WORDS IN THE PANEL

The building was old and _____derelict_____ . It had never been looked after properly.

1 We rented an apartment in Egypt. The rooms were very _____ and airy; we loved it.

2 This bed is so _____ . I don't think I've ever had such a good night's sleep.

3 The famous Parthenon in Athens is such an amazing _____ temple.

4 Newtown is a very trendy place and is _____ with young people. Lots of students live there.

5 When we got to the beach, it was _____ . We were the only people there.

6 There are a lot of _____ buildings in Chicago. The tallest is 110 storeys high.

7 This is such a _____ village. The houses are attractive and the main square is very pleasant.

| ancient | charming | comfortable | derelict | deserted | spacious | high-rise | popular |

65.7 LISTEN TO THE AUDIO AND ANSWER THE QUESTIONS

Xabi is telling his new friend, Elsa, about sights in his home town of Barcelona.

Elsa has never been to Spain before.
True ☐ **False** ☐ **Not given** ☑

1 Lots of people visit the Sagrada Família.
True ☐ **False** ☐ **Not given** ☐

2 Elsa would like to visit the Picasso Museum.
True ☐ **False** ☐ **Not given** ☐

3 Xabi hasn't shown a visitor around his city before.
True ☐ **False** ☐ **Not given** ☐

4 Elsa knows about the Bunkers del Carmel.
True ☐ **False** ☐ **Not given** ☐

5 There is a great view from the Bunkers del Carmel.
True ☐ **False** ☐ **Not given** ☐

6 The bunkers were always in good condition.
True ☐ **False** ☐ **Not given** ☐

65.8 SAY THE SENTENCES OUT LOUD USING "EVER" OR "NEVER," FILLING IN THE GAPS

I didn't know her before. I met her yesterday.

Yesterday was *the first time I had ever met her.*

1 Ben is so excited. It's his first time on a plane.

Ben is so excited. He has _____ _____

2 Until last week Don had never been to Iceland.

Last week was _____ _____

3 Before I went to Japan, I hadn't eaten miso soup.

I _____ _____

4 Until now, Jen has never traveled alone.

It's _____ _____

5 I had never gone sailing before last year.

Last year was _____ _____

---

65 ✓ **CHECKLIST**

⚙ "Never" / "ever" with past tenses ☐ **Aa** Travel adjectives ☐ 🧩 Describing new experiences ☐

66.1 COMMON ENGLISH IDIOMS

She had agreed to make a speech, but at the last minute she got cold feet.

get cold feet
[have a sudden loss of confidence]

I was feeling under the weather for a few days, but I'm better now.

feel under the weather
[feel unwell]

It's obvious that they're head over heels in love with each other.

be head over heels
[be completely or utterly in love with someone]

You're exactly right about Dad. He's so lazy! You've hit the nail on the head.

hit the nail on the head
[to describe exactly what is causing a situation or problem]

I've got so much to do. Do you think you can lend a hand?

lend a hand
[help someone]

I slept terribly last night! I'm really not on the ball today.

be on the ball
[be alert, knowledgeable, or competent]

I heard on the grapevine that Marina got the job.

hear something on the grapevine
[hear information or news via gossip or rumor]

I'm really working against the clock to submit my essay on time.

against the clock
[under time pressure to get something done]

The children won't behave today. They are a pain in the neck!

be a pain in the neck
[be a nuisance]

Aziz told his aunt that he'd keep an eye on her house while she was away.

keep an eye on
[look after or watch carefully]

Peter always helps his grandma with her bags. He **has a heart of gold.**

have a heart of gold
[to be kind and good-natured]

Sandra is a **teacher's pet.** She always arrives early and stays late.

teacher's pet
[someone who seeks and gets approval from a person in a position of authority]

As usual, Paola's reaction to her team losing was **over the top.**

over the top
[an overreaction or a lack of restraint]

My aunt tells great stories, but we **take what she says with a pinch of salt.**

take something with a pinch of salt
[not completely believe something or someone]

I wouldn't take what Derek said seriously. He was just **pulling your leg.**

pull someone's leg
[tease or fool someone]

I have no idea who to vote for. I'm **sitting on the fence.**

sit on the fence
[be unwilling to commit or make a decision]

They **cut corners** to get the project finished, and the quality really suffered.

cut corners
[to do something the easiest or shortest way, at the expense of high standards]

I think I'm going to get into trouble for this, but I'm ready to **face the music.**

face the music
[confront the consequences of your actions]

It's time you **let your hair down.** You have worked so hard!

let your hair down
[let yourself go or relax]

I've done all I can. **The ball is in your court** now.

the ball is in your court
[you are responsible for the next move]

67 Telling a story

The past continuous, past simple, and past perfect are often used together to describe past events in detail. This is especially helpful for telling stories.

🔧 **New language** Narrative tenses
Aa Vocabulary Idioms for storytelling
🧩 **New skill** Using different past tenses

67.1 KEY LANGUAGE NARRATIVE TENSES

The past continuous is used to set the scene. The past simple describes actions in the story. The past perfect is used to talk about things that happened before the beginning of the story.

A crowd of people were celebrating the New Year when one of the young men kneeled down in front of his girlfriend and asked her to marry him. He had planned everything down to the last detail.

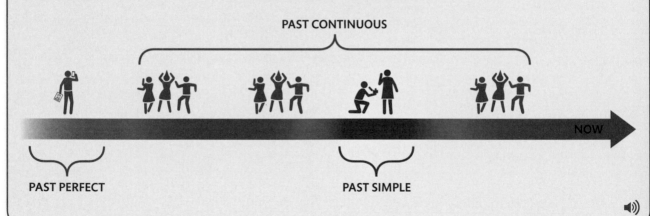

PAST CONTINUOUS

NOW

PAST PERFECT

PAST SIMPLE

🔊

67.2 FILL IN THE GAPS BY PUTTING THE VERBS IN THE CORRECT TENSES

It ___*was raining*___ (rain) heavily, so he ___*rushed*___ (rush) to the train station.

1 Before I _____ (start) the trip, I _____ (plan) which route I would take.

2 Lauren _____ (cross) the road when she _____ (see) the robber inside the bank.

3 I _____ always _____ (want) to visit Brazil, and I finally _____ (go) there last year.

4 Jason _____ (read) a book in the park when a wasp _____ (sting) him.

🔊

67.3 FILL IN THE GAPS USING THE PHRASES IN THE PANEL

It was a stormy night on Station Road. The rain _____*was falling*_____ heavily.

1. Inside her bedroom, Bella _____ hard for an exam.

2. She _____ nervous. The storm outside made it difficult to concentrate.

3. Raindrops _____ gently down the glass. She watched them in silence.

4. She _____ as she watched the raindrops. She began to relax.

5. Fifteen minutes later, the storm ended. Bella _____ so calm.

| breathed deeply | had never felt | ~~was falling~~ | was feeling | was studying | were sliding |

67.4 LISTEN TO THE AUDIO AND ANSWER THE QUESTIONS

Jonah tells Ben how he proposed to his girlfriend.

Ben heard a rumor that Jonah was engaged.
True ☑ **False** ☐

1 Lizzie didn't want to get married.
True ☐ **False** ☐

2 Jonah proposed to Lizzie during their vacation.
True ☐ **False** ☐

3 Jonah wanted his proposal to be unusual.
True ☐ **False** ☐

4 Jonah bought a special plate after he proposed.
True ☐ **False** ☐

5 Jonah almost got too nervous to propose.
True ☐ **False** ☐

6 Ben thinks Lizzie really loves Jonah.
True ☐ **False** ☐

67 ✓ CHECKLIST

⚙ Narrative tenses ☐   **Aa** Idioms for storytelling ☐   🧩 Using different past tenses ☐

68 What happened when?

English uses a number of words and phrases to show the order in which past events occurred. They are often called adverbials of time, and are useful when telling a story.

⚙ **New language** Time adverbs and phrases
Aa Vocabulary Storytelling devices
🧩 **New skill** Putting events in order

68.1 KEY LANGUAGE TIME ADVERBS AND PHRASES

SAME TIME

These phrases show two events happened at the same time. They are often used with descriptions in the past continuous.

"Just as" and "at the very moment" go before the verb they modify.

Just as we were getting on the train, we saw her getting off.

Blake's phone rang at the very moment he was signing the papers.

AFTER

These phrases show one event happened after, or as a result of, another. They are often used with descriptions in the past simple.

Shows something happened after.

He fell backward, and subsequently fell into the tray of paint.

Shows something happened as a result.

Consequently, he made a terrible mess on the floor.

BEFORE

These phrases show one event happened before another. They are often used with descriptions in the past perfect.

Sits before the verb it modifies.

As soon as the babysitter had arrived, they put on their coats.

Sits before the verb it modifies.

She became famous shortly after she had released her first album.

Sits after the verb it modifies.

Mr. Jones had moved to the city not long before I met him.

🔊

68.2 FILL IN THE GAPS USING THE PHRASES IN THE PANEL

_____ *Just as* _____ I was coming out of the café, I saw my friends on the other side of the street.

1. He broke his leg while skiing and _____ had to take three weeks off work.

2. The first guests arrived at 7pm and the others came _____ that.

3. I was about to call her to tell her the good news _____ she called me.

4. _____ it had stopped raining, we went for a walk.

5. They had got married _____ they moved to Wellington in New Zealand.

> not long before   consequently   ~~Just as~~   at the very moment   As soon as   shortly after

68.3 SAY THE SENTENCES OUT LOUD, ADDING IN THE TIME ADVERBS

He was finishing his report. I was finishing mine. (**just as**)

> *He was finishing his report just as I was finishing mine.*

1. Our first child was born. We had bought the house. (**shortly after**)

2. They worked very well together. They went into business together. (**subsequently**)

3. We went to the beach. The weather had improved. (**as soon as**)

4. They had moved to London. She started her new job. (**not long before**)

TRUE STORIES

Bitten by a shark in a supermarket

An ambulance crew was recently called to a local superstore where, not long before, a trainee fish seller had been bitten by a shark.

Fish sellers wear special hygienic boots while at work. Just as the poor trainee was putting on these boots, he lost his balance. He fell backward and subsequently stepped barefoot into a large tray containing a dead, open-mouthed shark. When the trainee stood on the lower jaw of the shark, the upper jaw snapped down on his foot, trapping it completely.

By the time the ambulance arrived, the boy had gone into shock. As soon as he was free, the crew took him to the hospital. Just as they were closing the ambulance doors, the victim's colleagues started clapping and laughing. The trainee is reported to have observed, "I suppose they'll be calling me Jaws, now!"

Who had been bitten by a shark not long before the ambulance crew arrived?

The trainee fish seller had been bitten by a shark.

---

❶ What happened just as the trainee was putting on his boots?

_____

❷ What happened when he stood on the lower jaw of the shark?

_____

❸ Where did the trainee fish seller go as soon as the ambulance crew had freed him?

_____

❹ What did his colleagues do just as the crew were closing the ambulance doors?

_____

68.5 LISTEN TO THE AUDIO AND ANSWER THE QUESTIONS

Gareth tells his friend Maria about a disagreement he had with his neighbors.

Gareth moved into his new house in July.　　True ☐　False ☐　Not given ☑

1 He met his neighbors on the day that he moved in.　　True ☐　False ☐　Not given ☐

2 He was friendly with his neighbors when they first met.　　True ☐　False ☐　Not given ☐

3 The neighbours were both doctors.　　True ☐　False ☐　Not given ☐

4 Jim wanted to tell Gareth how to paint.　　True ☐　False ☐　Not given ☐

5 Gareth spoke to his neighbors last week.　　True ☐　False ☐　Not given ☐

68 ✓ CHECKLIST

⚙ Time adverbs and phrases ☐　　**Aa** Storytelling devices ☐　　🧩 Putting events in order ☐

↻ REVIEW THE ENGLISH YOU HAVE LEARNED IN UNITS 64–68

NEW LANGUAGE	SAMPLE SENTENCE	☑	UNIT
PAST PERFECT AND PAST SIMPLE	Pablo had gone to work when I went to his house.	☐	64.1
PAST PERFECT WITH "NEVER" / "EVER"	He had never visited Rome before. It was the first time he had ever visited Rome.	☐	65.1
PRESENT PERFECT WITH "NEVER" / "EVER"	She has never visited Sydney before. It's the first time she has ever visited Sydney.	☐	65.3
NARRATIVE TENSES: PRESENT CONTINUOUS	A crowd of people were celebrating the New Year...	☐	67.1
NARRATIVE TENSES: PAST SIMPLE	... when one of the men kneeled down in front of his girlfriend and asked her to marry him.	☐	67.1
NARRATIVE TENSES: PAST PERFECT	He had planned everything before, down to the last detail.	☐	67.1
TIME ADVERBS AND PHRASES	Just as we were getting on the bus, we saw her.	☐	68.1

What other people said

We call the words that people say direct speech. If you want to tell someone what another person has said, it is called reported speech.

⚙ **New language** Reported speech
Aa Vocabulary Work and education
🧩 **New skill** Talking about people's lives

69.1 KEY LANGUAGE REPORTED SPEECH

In reported speech, the main verb usually "goes back" a tense. For example, the present simple changes to the past simple.

I feel sick.

Direct speech uses the present simple.

Luke said that he felt sick. I hope he's OK.

Reported speech uses the past simple here.

69.2 FURTHER EXAMPLES REPORTED SPEECH

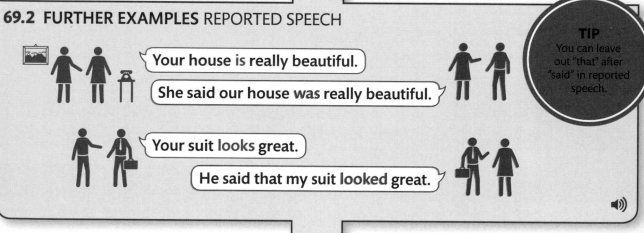

Your house is really beautiful.

She said our house was really beautiful.

Your suit looks great.

He said that my suit looked great.

TIP
You can leave out "that" after "said" in reported speech.

69.3 HOW TO FORM REPORTED SPEECH

The main verb in reported speech is usually "said." The rest of the sentence is usually in the past tense.

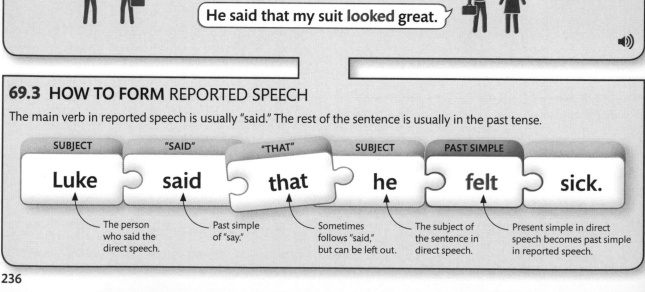

SUBJECT	"SAID"	"THAT"	SUBJECT	PAST SIMPLE	
Luke	**said**	**that**	**he**	**felt**	**sick.**

The person who said the direct speech.

Past simple of "say."

Sometimes follows "said," but can be left out.

The subject of the sentence in direct speech.

Present simple in direct speech becomes past simple in reported speech.

69.4 REWRITE THE SENTENCES USING REPORTED SPEECH

I live in San Diego.   =   He _said that he lived in San Diego._

1 I usually cycle to work.   =   She _____

2 I'm a chef in a busy restaurant.   =   He _____

3 I'm married, and I have two children.   =   She _____

4 My wife is an English teacher.   =   He _____

5 I want to have my own restaurant.   =   She _____

◀))

69.5 LISTEN TO THE AUDIO AND ANSWER THE QUESTIONS

Yesterday, Maya met Alfonso at a college reunion.

What did Alfonso say that he wanted to do next year?
Take a long vacation ☐
Buy a new car ☐
Get a new job ☑

1 What did Alfonso say was good about Roberto's house from his point of view?
It's a bargain ☐
There's room for a studio ☐
It's a beautiful house ☐

2 What did Cara say she wanted to do with the attic?
Turn it into an office ☐
Turn it into a spare room ☐
Turn it into a studio ☐

3 What did Jan say had happened to Maya?
She had sold all her paintings ☐
She had gone to New York ☐
Her exhibition had gone well ☐

4 What did Alfonso say when he heard Maya's news?
He loved her photos ☐
He wanted to buy a photo ☐
Her news was exciting ☐

69.6 KEY LANGUAGE REPORTED SPEECH IN DIFFERENT TENSES

The tense in reported speech is usually one tense
back in time from the tense in direct speech.

I'm working in New York.

⬇

She said she was working in New York.

PRESENT CONTINUOUS

⬇

PAST CONTINUOUS

I've been to China twice.

⬇

He said that he'd been to China twice.

PRESENT PERFECT

⬇

PAST PERFECT

I will call you soon.

⬇

He said he would call them soon.

FUTURE WITH "WILL"

⬇

MODAL VERB "WOULD"

We can speak Japanese.

⬇

They said that they could speak Japanese.

MODAL VERB "CAN"

⬇

MODAL VERB "COULD"

🔊

69.7 KEY LANGUAGE REPORTED SPEECH AND THE PAST SIMPLE

The past simple in direct speech can either stay as the past simple or change
to the past perfect in reported speech. The meaning is the same.

I arrived in Delhi on Saturday.

⬇

He said he arrived in Delhi on Saturday.
He said he'd arrived in Delhi on Saturday.

DIRECT SPEECH WITH PAST SIMPLE

⬇

REPORTED SPEECH WITH PAST SIMPLE OR PAST PERFECT

🔊

69.8 READ THE ARTICLE AND ANSWER THE QUESTIONS IN FULL SENTENCES

TEACHING TODAY

Teaching in Swaziland

Maria Colston, an experienced teacher, takes a working vacation in Africa.

" I'm working in Swaziland, where I've visited five different schools so far. I have already learned so much! It's a great opportunity to be able to watch these talented teachers. They work miracles in their classrooms every day. They don't have the resources we take for granted in my school at home, but they really inspire their students. Next week I'm planning to give a workshop for all the teachers that I've met here. I really hope they'll enjoy it."

> Where did Maria say she was working?
> *Maria said she was working in Swaziland.*

❶ What did Maria say she had visited?

_____

❷ What did Maria say was a great opportunity?

_____

❸ What did Maria say the teachers did every day?

_____

❹ What did Maria say she was planning to do?

_____

❺ What did Maria say she hoped would happen?

_____

69.9 SAY THE SENTENCES OUT LOUD AS REPORTED SPEECH

I'll visit you on Sunday.

She _said that she would_ _visit me on Sunday._

❶ I'm looking for a new job.

He _____

_____

❷ I really enjoyed the party.

You _____

_____

❸ We've just been swimming.

They _____

_____

❹ I can play the piano quite well.

She _____

_____

❺ I've brought some presents for the children.

You _____

_____

❻ I'm going to write a novel.

He _____

_____

---

69 ✓ CHECKLIST

⚙ Reported speech ☐   **Aa** Work and education ☐   🧩 Talking about people's lives ☐

70 Telling things to people

You can use both "say" and "tell" in reported speech. The meaning is the same, but using "tell" allows you to specify who someone was talking to.

⚙️ **New language** Reported speech with "tell"
Aa Vocabulary Collocations with "say" and "tell"
🧩 **New skill** Talking about truth and lies

70.1 KEY LANGUAGE "SAY" AND "TELL" IN REPORTED SPEECH

In reported speech, you can say who someone is talking to when you use "tell" as the main verb. "Tell" must be followed by an object.

I want to learn to drive.

With "say," you do not need an object to show who someone is talking to.

He { **said** / **told me** } **that he wanted to learn to drive.**

In reported speech, you must put an object after "tell" to show who someone is talking to.

🔊

70.2 FURTHER EXAMPLES "SAY" AND "TELL" IN REPORTED SPEECH

She said that she could come to the party.

She told me that she had a very stressful job.

He said he would be late to the meeting.

You can leave out "that" in reported speech with "said."

They told us they were buying a new house.

You can also leave out "that" in reported speech with "told."

🔊

70.3 ⚠️ COMMON MISTAKES "SAY" AND "TELL" IN REPORTED SPEECH

He said that he had a fast car. ✔️

He said me that he had a fast car. ❌
"Said" cannot have an object.

He told me that he had a fast car.

He told that he had a fast car.
"Told" must have an object.

70.4 FILL IN THE GAPS BY ADDING "SAID" OR "TOLD"

She ___said___ she enjoyed meeting people.

1. They _____ us they had a new car.

2. He _____ me he had gotten married.

3. You _____ he was at a birthday party.

4. She _____ she wanted some ice cream.

5. We _____ her the train was delayed.

6. You _____ you would cook tonight.

7. I _____ him I had to work late.

70.5 USE THE CHART TO CREATE 12 CORRECT SENTENCES AND SAY THEM OUT LOUD

He said he was going on safari.

| He / She | said / told | me / us | he was / she was | going on safari. |

70.6 LISTEN TO THE AUDIO AND ANSWER THE QUESTIONS

Grace has been on a date.
She tells her friend Robyn about it.

Grace believed that her date was 30.
True ☐ False ☐ Not given ☑

1. Grace's date told her he hated gardening.
True ☐ False ☐ Not given ☐

2. Grace wanted to have dinner with her date.
True ☐ False ☐ Not given ☐

3. Grace's date said he had a fast car.
True ☐ False ☐ Not given ☐

4. Robyn said Grace's date was telling the truth.
True ☐ False ☐ Not given ☐

5. Grace told Carla her date was too young.
True ☐ False ☐ Not given ☐

70.7 KEY LANGUAGE TIME AND PLACE REFERENCES

If you report speech some time after it was said, you might
need to use different words to talk about times and places.

The time reference is
"yesterday" in direct speech.

I went to work yesterday.

**She said she'd been to
work the day before.**

The time reference is
"the day before" in
reported speech.

APRIL **25**

APRIL **26**

APRIL **27**

Aa 70.8 MATCH THE SENTENCES IN DIRECT SPEECH WITH THEIR EQUIVALENTS IN REPORTED SPEECH

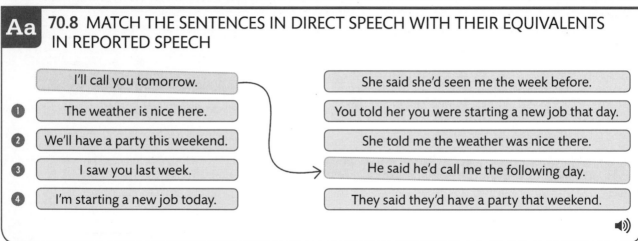

I'll call you tomorrow.

She said she'd seen me the week before.

1 The weather is nice here.

You told her you were starting a new job that day.

2 We'll have a party this weekend.

She told me the weather was nice there.

3 I saw you last week.

He said he'd call me the following day.

4 I'm starting a new job today.

They said they'd have a party that weekend.

70.9 REWRITE THE SENTENCES USING REPORTED SPEECH

I'll finish the report tomorrow.	=	He said _he'd finish the report the following day._

1 I bought a new car yesterday. = She told me _____

2 Regina is leaving the company today. = They said _____

3 There are lots of restaurants here. = She said _____

4 I'm going to a party this weekend. = He told us _____

5 We sold our apartment last week. = They told me _____

242

70.10 READ THE ARTICLE AND MARK THE CORRECT SUMMARY

YOUR RELATIONSHIPS

When is it OK to tell lies?

We know it's wrong to tell lies, but sometimes we don't tell the truth for good reasons. Given the choice of saying something nice but untrue, saying nothing, or telling someone a truth that's hurtful, what do you do?

To avoid conflict, people often say yes when they should say no, or just say anything that comes into their heads as long as it keeps them out of trouble. We also often believe that people are being honest, just because they say so.

We gave 50 people a questionnaire to complete. Of the people we asked, 10 percent said they lie about their age and think people can't tell the difference. Eighty percent think it's OK to tell a "white lie" to avoid hurting someone. As many as 58 percent think it's OK to tell a "story" to hide something they did wrong. Ten percent said they didn't tell lies at all. Do you believe them?

1. We all know it's fine to tell lies, because we often have to. In a tricky situation, the only choices we have are not to say anything at all or say something nice but untrue. ☐

2. Although we know it's wrong to lie, 80 percent of the people interviewed said it's OK to lie in order to be kind to someone. More than 50 percent said it was OK to lie about something they'd done wrong. ☐

3. These days, very few people say yes when they mean no. What's more, over 85 percent of people believe that everyone knows when we are lying about our age. ☐

4. Most people believe that we should always be honest, and not tell lies at all. ☐

Aa 70.11 WRITE THE WORDS FROM THE PANEL IN THE CORRECT GROUPS

COLLOCATIONS WITH "SAY"

something _____

_____ _____

_____ _____

COLLOCATIONS WITH "TELL"

the truth _____

_____ _____

_____ _____

lies	anything	yes	~~something~~	a story	the difference
someone	nothing	a "white lie"	no	~~the truth~~	so

🔊

70 ✓ CHECKLIST

⚙ Reported speech with "tell" ☐   Aa Collocations with "say" and "tell" ☐   🧩 Talking about truth and lies ☐

71 Suggestions and explanations

In reported speech, you can replace "said" with a wide variety of verbs that give people more information about how someone said something.

⚙ **New language** Reporting verbs with "that"
Aa Vocabulary More reporting verbs
🧩 **New skill** Reporting explanations

71.1 KEY LANGUAGE REPORTING VERBS WITH "THAT"

"Say" and "tell" do not give any information about the speaker's manner. You can replace them with other verbs that suggest the speaker's mood or reason for speaking.

I'm not very good at golf.

Neil admitted that he wasn't very good at golf.

Shows reluctance on the part of the speaker.

Reporting verbs with "that" do not take an object.

🔊

71.2 FURTHER EXAMPLES REPORTING VERBS WITH "THAT"

Don't be afraid of the dog. He's just excited to see you.

They **explained that** the dog was barking because he was excited to see me.

Your house is beautiful. It has a nice lawn, too.

Rohit admired our house, and **added that** it had a nice lawn.

🔊

71.3 HOW TO FORM SENTENCES USING REPORTING VERBS WITH "THAT"

SUBJECT	REPORTING VERB (PAST TENSE)	"THAT"	PAST TENSE
Neil	admitted	that	he wasn't very good at golf

Verb introduces reported speech and gives more information about it.

Verb is followed by "that."

Reported speech changes tense as usual.

Aa 71.4 MATCH THE DEFINITIONS TO THE REPORTING VERBS

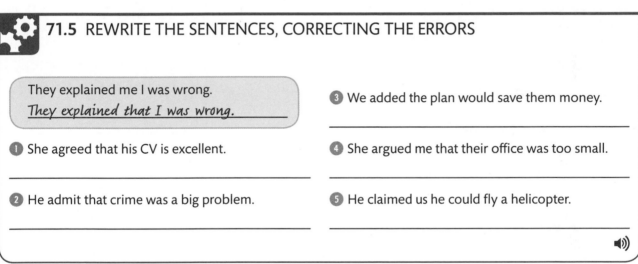

Had the same opinion as someone.	He said he liked his new job, and **added** that his colleagues were friendly.
① Gave reasons to support an idea.	They said the weather was good. I **agreed** that it was beautiful.
② Said something extra.	I **admitted** that I hadn't worked hard enough.
③ Said that something is true without being happy about it.	She **claimed** that she never watched TV, but I don't believe her.
④ Said something that is difficult to believe.	My manager **argued** that we had to cut our costs because profits were down.

71.5 REWRITE THE SENTENCES, CORRECTING THE ERRORS

They explained me I was wrong.
They explained that I was wrong.

① She agreed that his CV is excellent.

_____

② He admit that crime was a big problem.

_____

③ We added the plan would save them money.

_____

④ She argued me that their office was too small.

_____

⑤ He claimed us he could fly a helicopter.

_____

71.6 LISTEN TO THE AUDIO, THEN MARK THE CORRECT ORDER OF THE SUMMARY SENTENCES

Mr. Kelly talks to his personal trainer about his general health and fitness.

Ⓐ The personal trainer claimed that his diet and exercise plan would help Mr. Kelly live longer. ☐

Ⓑ Mr. Kelly admitted that his health and fitness were a real problem. ☑ 1

Ⓒ Mr. Kelly agreed that he should try the personal trainer's plan. ☐

Ⓓ The personal trainer added that his healthy recipes were really delicious. ☐

Ⓔ The personal trainer explained that the diet would help Mr. Kelly lose weight. ☐

71.7 READ THE REPORT AND ANSWER THE QUESTIONS

> The director admitted that profits were down.
> **True** ☐ **False** ☐ **Not given** ☑

1 She explained that the products were low quality.
True ☐ **False** ☐ **Not given** ☐

2 She added that they were selling in new markets.
True ☐ **False** ☐ **Not given** ☐

3 She argued that advertising should double.
True ☐ **False** ☐ **Not given** ☐

4 She claimed that sales would increase every year.
True ☐ **False** ☐ **Not given** ☐

NOTES FOR ANNUAL FINANCIAL MEETING
Noriko Hayashi, Sales Director

• Profits are up again this year by 15 percent, our third annual increase.

• This is because all our products are cheaper to make and better quality since we invested in new machinery.

• We are also now currently selling our products in new markets that have great potential for expansion.

• If we double our advertising efforts, we can increase our sales by 35 percent over two years.

71.8 SAY THE SENTENCES OUT LOUD AS REPORTED SPEECH, FILLING IN THE GAPS AND USING THE VERB IN BRACKETS

> You might not believe me, but I can speak 20 different languages. **(claim)**
>
> He _____*claimed that he could*_____ speak 20 different languages.

1 I don't exercise as regularly as I should. I need to work out more often. **(admit)**

She _____ to work out more often.

2 I have to leave work early today because I have a doctor's appointment. **(explain)**

He _____ leave work early for a doctor's appointment.

3 We have four children, and we also have a dog and two cats. **(add)**

She _____ a dog and two cats.

4 You're right. Mr. Brady is a very important client, and we should meet him again. **(agree)**

He _____ a very important client.

71.9 ⚠ COMMON MISTAKES REPORTED SPEECH WITH "SUGGEST"

"Suggest" is different from other reporting verbs. It is still followed by "that," but the part of the sentence that reports the direct speech uses the infinitive without "to."

I don't feel like cooking. Should we **order** a pizza?

"Suggest" is followed by the infinitive without "to."

Ryan **suggested that we order** a pizza. ✓

Ryan **suggested that we ordered** a pizza. ✗

This is wrong.

71.10 CROSS OUT THE INCORRECT WORDS IN EACH SENTENCE

He **admitted** / ~~suggested~~ that he had stolen a lot of money.

1. They said the party was fun, and **suggested** / **added** that the band was fantastic.

2. She **argued** / **suggested** that they go to the beach this weekend.

3. She **suggested** / **explained** that she had to go home because she was feeling sick.

4. She **agreed** / **claimed** that she was once a famous singer.

5. You said her dress was beautiful. I **agreed** / **suggested** that it was very pretty.

6. He **suggested** / **added** that I start cycling to work because cars cause pollution.

---

71 ✓ CHECKLIST

⚙ Reporting verbs with "that" ☐   **Aa** More reporting verbs ☐   🧩 Reporting explanations ☐

Telling people what to do

Many reporting verbs have to take an object. English often uses these verbs to show that the speaker was giving someone orders or advice.

⚙ **New language** Verbs with object and infinitive
Aa Vocabulary Reporting verbs
🧩 **New skill** Reporting advice and instructions

72.1 KEY LANGUAGE REPORTING VERBS WITH OBJECT AND INFINITIVE

Some reporting verbs are followed by an object and the infinitive. English often uses these verbs to report orders, advice, and instructions.

Remember to buy some milk tonight.

Ellie reminded me to buy some milk tonight.

Reporting verb ⟶   Object ⟶   Infinitive

72.2 FURTHER EXAMPLES REPORTING VERBS WITH OBJECT AND INFINITIVE

You've been very naughty! Go to your room.

I just ordered Aaron to go to his room.

Please could you give me a ride to the station?

Sorry I'm late. Lucia asked me to give her a ride to the station.

Come to the party! You'll have a great time!

We encouraged Gareth to come to the party. I hope he turns up.

72.3 HOW TO FORM REPORTING VERBS WITH OBJECT AND INFINITIVE

SUBJECT	REPORTING VERB (PAST TENSE)	OBJECT	INFINITIVE	
Ellie	**reminded**	**me**	**to buy**	**some milk.**

Object shows who was being spoken to.

The infinitive usually expresses an order, instruction, or piece of advice.

72.4 REWRITE THE SENTENCES, CORRECTING THE ERRORS

He encourage me apply for the job.
He encouraged me to apply for the job.

1 The police ordered to them leave the room.

_____

2 You asked me wash the dishes after dinner.

_____

3 They remembered him to lock the door.

_____

4 My boss asked me go to the meeting.

_____

5 We encouraged to him to join our choir.

_____

6 Didn't I remind to you call your parents?

_____

7 The judge ordered her pay a fine.

_____

72.5 READ THE ARTICLE AND PUT THE SUMMARY SENTENCES IN THE CORRECT ORDER

77 BUSINESS TODAY

TONIA'S STORY

Company director Tonia Lambert tells Business Today the story of her career.

I was bored with managing our local store and I needed a challenge. I went to an employment agency and asked them to help me find a new job. My main contact at the agency, Frances, persuaded me to look at business management jobs. I didn't think I'd be qualified, but she encouraged me to apply anyway, and one company asked me to attend an interview.

Frances was brilliant. She knew the company well and advised me to wear casual business clothes as well as suggesting what kinds of things to say. On the day of the interview, I was so nervous that Frances practically had to order me to keep my appointment! I'm so glad I did. I got the job and loved it. Four years later I decided I wanted to form my own company, but my boss, Amira, asked me to stay and made me a partner!

A Tonia's boss made her a partner because she wanted Tonia to stay at her company. ☐

B Frances encouraged Tonia to think about working in business management. ☐

C Tonia went to an employment agency when she decided to change jobs. 1

D Frances gave advice to Tonia about what to wear for her interview. ☐

E Tonia took Frances' advice and applied for business management posts. ☐

F Frances told Tonia that she had to go to her interview. ☐

G A company invited Tonia to go to a job interview. ☐

72.6 KEY LANGUAGE REPORTING VERBS WITH NEGATIVES

To make a negative sentence with a reporting verb, object, and infinitive, place "not" between the object and infinitive.

You shouldn't sign the contract.

Our lawyer advised me not to sign the contract.

"Not" makes the reported speech negative.

72.7 FURTHER EXAMPLES REPORTING VERBS WITH NEGATIVES

Don't eat any more cake. It's bad for you.

I think I persuaded Evan not to eat any more cake.

Don't go in the water. It's dangerous.

The lifeguard warned me not to go in the water.

72.8 LISTEN TO THE AUDIO AND ANSWER THE QUESTIONS

Zac has been offered a job in New York.
He asks his friend Leah for advice.

Zac's parents are excited about his job offer.
True ☐ **False** ☐ **Not given** ☑

① Zac's parents advised him not to take the job.
True ☐ **False** ☐ **Not given** ☐

② Zac's parents want him to make a quick decision.
True ☐ **False** ☐ **Not given** ☐

③ Zac's boss ordered him to accept the job.
True ☐ **False** ☐ **Not given** ☐

④ Leah encouraged Zac to move to New York.
True ☐ **False** ☐ **Not given** ☐

⑤ Zac's new job would be better paid.
True ☐ **False** ☐ **Not given** ☐

⑥ Leah persuaded Zac not to take the job.
True ☐ **False** ☐ **Not given** ☐

⑦ Zac asked Leah not to tell their friends his news.
True ☐ **False** ☐ **Not given** ☐

72.9 SAY THE SENTENCES OUT LOUD AS REPORTED SPEECH, FILLING IN THE GAPS AND USING THE VERB IN BRACKETS

You must not drive too fast. You might crash the car. **(warn)**

He _____ *warned* _____ me _____ *not to drive* _____ too fast.

1 I won't tolerate such rude behavior! Get out of my office now! **(order)**

She _____ them _____ of her office.

2 Let's go on vacation. You need a break and it will be fun. **(encourage)**

He _____ her _____ on vacation.

3 Please don't leave the company. We'll offer you a promotion if you stay. **(persuade)**

The director _____ me _____ the company.

4 I think you'd be wise to invest in this property. You could make a lot of money from it. **(advise)**

They _____ us _____ in that property.

---

72 ✓ CHECKLIST

⚙ Verbs with object and infinitive ☐   **Aa** Reporting verbs ☐   🧩 Reporting advice and instructions ☐

↻ REVIEW THE ENGLISH YOU HAVE LEARNED IN UNITS 69–72

NEW LANGUAGE	SAMPLE SENTENCE	☑	UNIT
REPORTED SPEECH WITH "SAY"	Luke said that he felt sick.	☐	69.1
REPORTED SPEECH IN DIFFERENT TENSES	She said she was working in New York.	☐	69.6
REPORTED SPEECH WITH "TELL"	He told me that he wanted to learn to drive.	☐	70.1
REPORTING VERBS WITH "THAT"	Neil admitted that he wasn't very good at golf.	☐	71.1
REPORTING VERBS WITH OBJECT AND INFINITIVE	Ellie reminded me to buy some milk tonight.	☐	72.1

73 What other people asked

You can use reported questions to tell someone what someone else has asked. Direct questions and reported questions have different word orders.

⚙ **New language** Reported questions
Aa **Vocabulary** Collocations with "raise"
🧩 **New skill** Reporting direct questions

73.1 KEY LANGUAGE REPORTED QUESTIONS

In reported questions, the tense moves one tense back from the tense in direct questions, and the subject and the verb swap places.

Where are my keys?

Adam asked me where his keys were. Have you seen them?

The subject comes before the verb in reported questions.

The tense in reported questions moves one tense back from the tense in direct questions.

🔊

73.2 FURTHER EXAMPLES REPORTED QUESTIONS

Why can't you come to the party?

He asked me why I couldn't come to the party.

You can include an object to say who was asked the original question.

When will they arrive?

The object of the reporting verb can be omitted.

She asked when they would arrive.

🔊

73.3 HOW TO FORM REPORTED QUESTIONS

SUBJECT	REPORTING VERB	OBJECT	QUESTION WORD	SUBJECT	VERB
Adam	asked	me	where	his keys	were.

The main verb in reported questions is usually "ask."

You can leave out the object.

The subject comes before the verb in reported questions.

The tense moves one tense back from direct speech.

73.4 SAY THE DIRECT QUESTIONS OUT LOUD AS REPORTED QUESTIONS

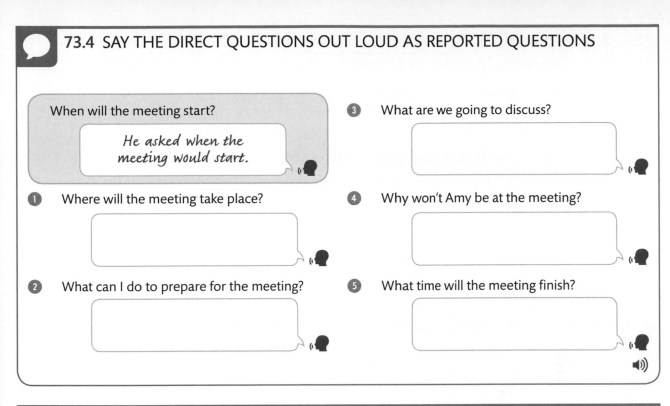

When will the meeting start?

He asked when the meeting would start.

❸ What are we going to discuss?

❶ Where will the meeting take place?

❹ Why won't Amy be at the meeting?

❷ What can I do to prepare for the meeting?

❺ What time will the meeting finish?

73.5 REWRITE THE SENTENCES, PUTTING THE WORDS IN THE CORRECT ORDER

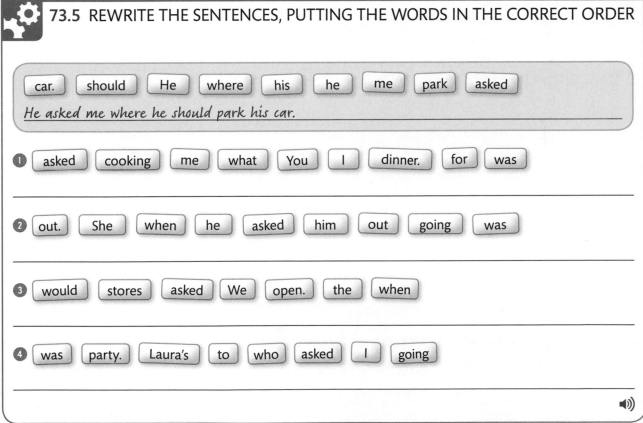

car. | should | He | where | his | he | me | park | asked

He asked me where he should park his car.

❶ asked | cooking | me | what | You | I | dinner. | for | was

❷ out. | She | when | he | asked | him | out | going | was

❸ would | stores | asked | We | open. | the | when

❹ was | party. | Laura's | to | who | asked | I | going

73.6 KEY LANGUAGE REPORTING QUESTIONS WITH "DO"

When a direct question uses the verb "do," leave this out of reported questions.

When does the concert start?

↓

He asked me when the concert started.

Reported questions leave out the auxiliary verb "do."

Use the past form of the verb.

73.7 FURTHER EXAMPLES REPORTING QUESTIONS WITH "DO"

Why do you want to work for us?

They asked me why I wanted to work for them.

Who do you know here?

She asked who I knew there.

73.8 REWRITE THE SENTENCES, CORRECTING THE ERRORS

> You asked me where he did live.
> _You asked me where he lived._

❶ They asked her why does she want the job.

_____

❷ We asked them what day the conference start.

_____

❸ I asked what kind of music did he like.

_____

❹ She asked us when the train did arrived.

_____

❺ You asked me what company do I work for.

_____

73.9 LISTEN TO THE AUDIO AND ANSWER THE QUESTIONS

Sita tells her father about her job interview.

> Sita thought the interview went well.
> **True** ☑ **False** ☐

❶ Sita didn't know why she wanted the job.
True ☐ **False** ☐

❷ The interviewers asked Sita about teamwork.
True ☐ **False** ☐

❸ Sita was asked what salary she expected.
True ☐ **False** ☐

❹ Sita was asked to start the job immediately.
True ☐ **False** ☐

DAILY NEWS

"We must save endangered animals," says leading zoologist

At a special fundraising dinner last night, zoologist and conservationist Mila Barnett gave a speech that first **raised eyebrows**, then **raised the roof**, as celebrity guests rushed to donate money to her cause.

Barnett said she wanted to **raise awareness** of the danger Africa's animals face from poaching and illegal hunting. She **raised fears** that the lion, elephant, and rhino could disappear from the African landscape. She **raised the question** of the fight against poaching. When she asked the audience who would help in her campaign, nearly everyone **raised their hands**.

Barnett is a passionate speaker and has tonight persuaded some very powerful people to **raise money** for this important cause.

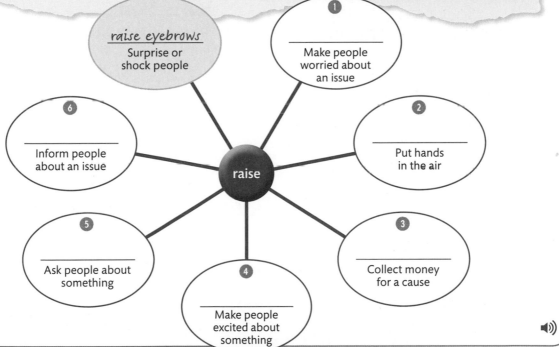

raise eyebrows
Surprise or shock people

1 _____ Make people worried about an issue

2 _____ Put hands in the air

3 _____ Collect money for a cause

4 _____ Make people excited about something

5 _____ Ask people about something

6 _____ Inform people about an issue

raise

Reporting simple questions

Simple questions can be answered with "yes" and "no." English uses "if" and "whether" to report simple questions.

⚙️ **New language** "If" and "whether"
Aa Vocabulary Verb + preposition collocations
🧩 **New skill** Reporting simple questions

74.1 KEY LANGUAGE "IF" AND "WHETHER"

If the answer to a question in direct speech is "yes" or "no," use "if" or "whether" to report the question. "Whether" is more formal than "if."

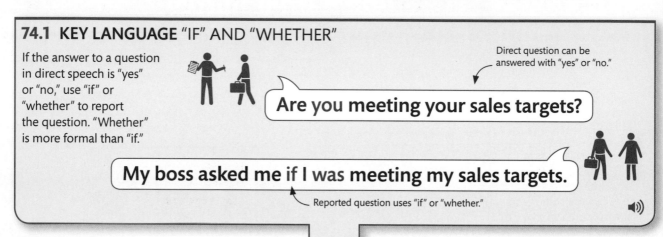

Direct question can be answered with "yes" or "no."

Are you meeting your sales targets?

My boss asked me if I was meeting my sales targets.

Reported question uses "if" or "whether."

74.2 FURTHER EXAMPLES "IF" AND "WHETHER"

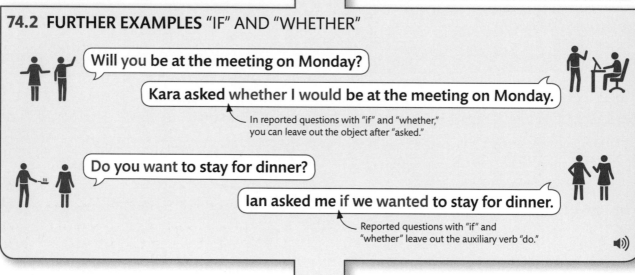

Will you be at the meeting on Monday?

Kara asked whether I would be at the meeting on Monday.

In reported questions with "if" and "whether," you can leave out the object after "asked."

Do you want to stay for dinner?

Ian asked me if we wanted to stay for dinner.

Reported questions with "if" and "whether" leave out the auxiliary verb "do."

74.3 HOW TO FORM REPORTED QUESTIONS WITH "IF" AND "WHETHER"

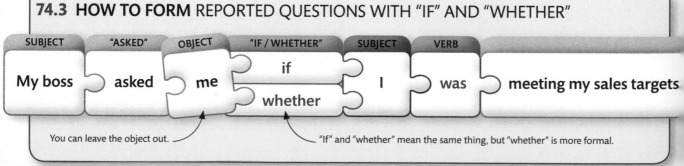

SUBJECT	"ASKED"	OBJECT	"IF / WHETHER"	SUBJECT	VERB	
My boss	asked	me	if / whether	I	was	meeting my sales targets

You can leave the object out.

"If" and "whether" mean the same thing, but "whether" is more formal.

74.4 REWRITE THE DIRECT QUESTIONS AS REPORTED QUESTIONS, FILLING IN THE GAPS

Are you going to be home late?

He asked me ___*if I was going to be home late.*___

1 Have you been waiting long?

She asked us _____

2 Do they have the figures ready?

He asked _____

3 Did you go to the meeting?

She asked us _____

4 Are you working late again?

I asked him _____

5 Do you want a glass of water?

He asked you _____

6 Will you take the early flight?

She asked me _____

7 Did Eva meet you at the airport?

She asked us _____

🔊

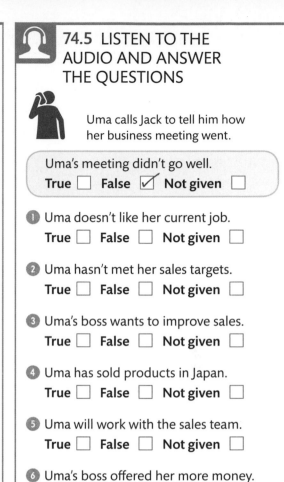

74.5 LISTEN TO THE AUDIO AND ANSWER THE QUESTIONS

Uma calls Jack to tell him how her business meeting went.

Uma's meeting didn't go well.
True ☐ **False** ☐ **Not given** ☑

1 Uma doesn't like her current job.
True ☐ **False** ☐ **Not given** ☐

2 Uma hasn't met her sales targets.
True ☐ **False** ☐ **Not given** ☐

3 Uma's boss wants to improve sales.
True ☐ **False** ☐ **Not given** ☐

4 Uma has sold products in Japan.
True ☐ **False** ☐ **Not given** ☐

5 Uma will work with the sales team.
True ☐ **False** ☐ **Not given** ☐

6 Uma's boss offered her more money.
True ☐ **False** ☐ **Not given** ☐

7 Uma expected to be offered a new job.
True ☐ **False** ☐ **Not given** ☐

74.6 USE THE CHART TO CREATE 8 CORRECT SENTENCES AND SAY THEM OUT LOUD

She asked me if I knew what time it was. 🗣

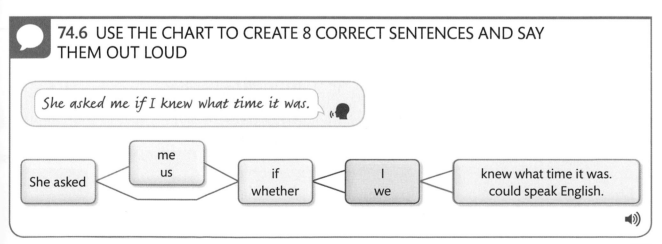

| She asked | me / us | if / whether | I / we | knew what time it was. / could speak English. |

🔊

74.7 KEY LANGUAGE REPORTING QUESTIONS WITH "OR"

You can also use "if" or "whether" to report questions that use "or" in direct speech.

Does Jo want tea or coffee?

Jo, Tom asked me if you wanted tea or coffee.

Verb moves back to past tense.

74.8 FURTHER EXAMPLES REPORTING QUESTIONS WITH "OR"

Do you want to go by car or by train?

She asked whether we wanted to go by car or by train.

Do you prefer books or movies?

Riku asked me if I preferred books or movies.

74.9 MATCH THE PICTURES TO THE CORRECT SENTENCES

He asked me if I played badminton or tennis.

1

We asked if they'd like ice cream or cake.

2

He asked her whether she preferred cycling or walking.

3

She asked if I wanted to cook inside or outside.

4

I asked if I should take flowers or wine to the party.

5

He asked whether they'd rather be rich or famous.

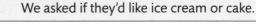

74.10 READ THE ARTICLE AND WRITE ANSWERS TO THE QUESTIONS AS FULL SENTENCES

26 BUSINESS TODAY

"ALL TOO EASY"

In our exclusive report, former businessman Clive Benson, who was sentenced to five years in jail for money laundering, talks to Kamil Hashmi.

"I always dreamed of being seriously rich. I wanted to provide for my family and I made a bad decision. I invested in a company without asking enough questions. Maybe I didn't want to know the answers. It was all too easy.

"The money started to pour into my bank account and everything was great. Then one day, I was arrested and accused of money laundering. I couldn't fight against it, and now I'm in prison.

"I used to sleep in a huge bed and eat in the best restaurants. Now I'm confined to a cell. There's no point in complaining about the situation. Who would I complain to? Now I dream about being with my family again. I hope I can count on them to wait for me and forgive me."

> Why did Clive want to be rich?
> *He wanted to provide for his family.*

❶ What was the bad decision that Clive made?

_____

❷ What started to pour into his bank account?

_____

❸ What was he accused of?

_____

❹ What does he say there's no point in doing?

_____

❺ What does he dream about?

_____

❻ What does he hope his family will do?

_____

Aa 74.11 CROSS OUT THE INCORRECT WORDS IN EACH SENTENCE TO FORM COLLOCATIONS OF VERBS WITH PREPOSITIONS

> I invested money in / ~~on~~ / ~~for~~ my new business.

❶ It's great to know I can count off / in / on you.

❷ I want to provide to / for / on my children.

❸ He always dreamed of / on / for being famous.

❹ The water poured to / into / in the bucket.

❺ They were accused of / on / in stealing a car.

❻ We can't fight of / with / against their decision.

❼ I'll be ready soon. Please wait on / for / to me.

🔊

---

74 ✓ CHECKLIST

⚙ "If" and "whether" ☐   **Aa** Verb + preposition collocations ☐   Reporting simple questions ☐

75 Polite questions

Indirect questions are more polite than direct questions. In spoken English, you might use them to ask people who you don't know very well about practical issues.

⚙ **New language** Indirect questions
Aa **Vocabulary** Practical issues
🧩 **New skill** Asking polite questions

75.1 KEY LANGUAGE INDIRECT QUESTIONS

Indirect questions often start with a polite opening phrase. After the question word, the word order in indirect questions is the same as in positive statements.

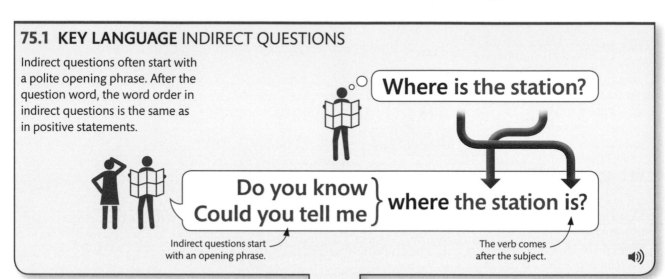

Where is the station?

Do you know } where the station is?
Could you tell me }

Indirect questions start with an opening phrase.

The verb comes after the subject.

75.2 FURTHER EXAMPLES INDIRECT QUESTIONS

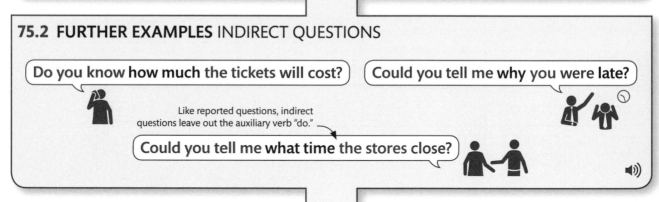

Do you know **how much** the tickets will cost?

Could you tell me **why** you were late?

Like reported questions, indirect questions leave out the auxiliary verb "do."

Could you tell me **what time** the stores close?

75.3 HOW TO FORM INDIRECT QUESTIONS

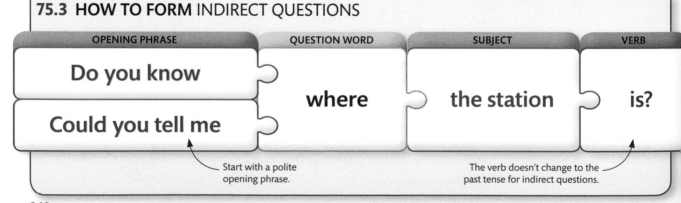

OPENING PHRASE	QUESTION WORD	SUBJECT	VERB
Do you know / Could you tell me	where	the station	is?

Start with a polite opening phrase.

The verb doesn't change to the past tense for indirect questions.

75.4 REWRITE THE INDIRECT QUESTIONS, PUTTING THE WORDS IN THE CORRECT ORDER

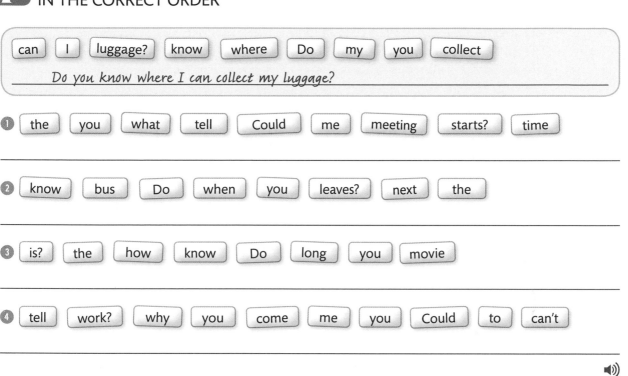

can I luggage? know where Do my you collect

Do you know where I can collect my luggage?

1 the you what tell Could me meeting starts? time

_____

2 know bus Do when you leaves? next the

_____

3 is? the how know Do long you movie

_____

4 tell work? why you come me you Could to can't

_____

75.5 LISTEN TO THE AUDIO, THEN NUMBER THE PICTURES IN THE ORDER THEY ARE DESCRIBED

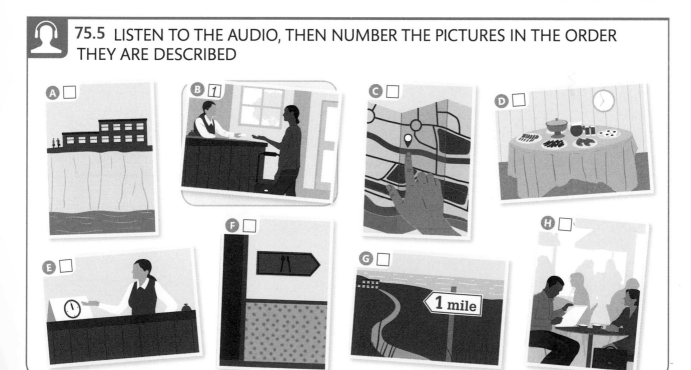

A ☐ B 1 C ☐ D ☐

E ☐ F ☐ G ☐ H ☐

75.6 KEY LANGUAGE INDIRECT SIMPLE QUESTIONS

Like reported simple questions, indirect simple questions use "if" and "whether."

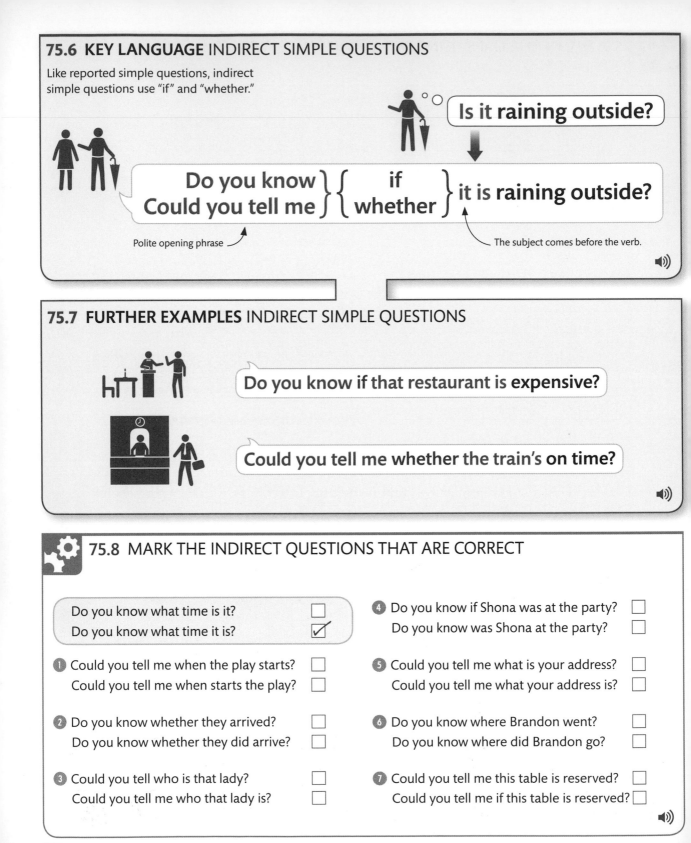

Is it raining outside?

Do you know
Could you tell me

if
whether

it is raining outside?

Polite opening phrase

The subject comes before the verb.

75.7 FURTHER EXAMPLES INDIRECT SIMPLE QUESTIONS

Do you know if that restaurant is **expensive?**

Could you tell me whether the train's **on time?**

75.8 MARK THE INDIRECT QUESTIONS THAT ARE CORRECT

Do you know what time is it? ☐
Do you know what time it is? ☑

1 Could you tell me when the play starts? ☐
Could you tell me when starts the play? ☐

2 Do you know whether they arrived? ☐
Do you know whether they did arrive? ☐

3 Could you tell who is that lady? ☐
Could you tell me who that lady is? ☐

4 Do you know if Shona was at the party? ☐
Do you know was Shona at the party? ☐

5 Could you tell me what is your address? ☐
Could you tell me what your address is? ☐

6 Do you know where Brandon went? ☐
Do you know where did Brandon go? ☐

7 Could you tell me this table is reserved? ☐
Could you tell me if this table is reserved? ☐

75.9 FILL IN THE GAPS USING THE WORDS IN THE PANEL

Could you tell me _____*if this seat is*_____ free?

1 Do you know _____ is delayed?

2 Could you tell me _____ costs?

3 Could you tell me _____ working in sales?

4 Do you know _____ leaves?

5 Could you tell me _____ is served?

when the last bus

how much this jacket

~~if this seat is~~

how long you've been

what time dinner

why the train

75.10 SAY THE SENTENCES OUT LOUD AS INDIRECT QUESTIONS

Does Sada have a driving license?

Do you know if Sada has a driving license?

1 Is our plane going to be delayed?

2 What time will your clients arrive?

3 Will someone meet us at the station?

4 How far is it to the hotel?

5 Do the trains stop running after midnight?

75 ✓ CHECKLIST

⚙ Indirect questions ☐   **Aa** Practical issues ☐   🧩 Asking polite questions ☐

76 Wishes and regrets

English uses the verb "wish" to talk about present and past regrets. The tense of the verb that follows "wish" affects the meaning of the sentence.

⚙ **New language** "Wish" with past tenses
Aa **Vocabulary** Life events
🧩 **New skill** Talking about regrets

76.1 KEY LANGUAGE "WISH" AND PAST SIMPLE

Use "wish" with the past simple, or with the modal verbs "would" and "could," to express regrets and desires about the present.

I wish I **earned** more money.

Use the past simple to talk about the present.

This music is horrible! I wish it **would** stop.

You can also use modal verbs to express wishes about the present.

76.2 FURTHER EXAMPLES "WISH" AND PAST SIMPLE

He wishes he **could** afford a big house.

I wish you **didn't have to** work so hard.

They wish the weather **was** better.

76.3 HOW TO FORM "WISH" AND PAST SIMPLE

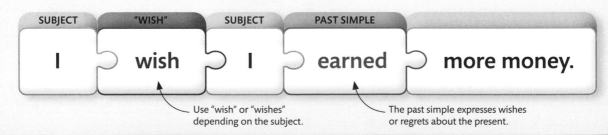

SUBJECT	"WISH"	SUBJECT	PAST SIMPLE	
I	wish	I	earned	more money.

Use "wish" or "wishes" depending on the subject.

The past simple expresses wishes or regrets about the present.

76.4 CROSS OUT THE INCORRECT WORDS IN EACH SENTENCE

 Anna wishes she ~~can buy~~ / could buy / ~~will buy~~ that dress, but it's too expensive.

① I wish I **had** / **have** / **would have** a cat, but my apartment's too small for any pets.

② Bella wishes she **live** / **lives** / **lived** on the coast. She loves the beach.

③ My children are such fussy eaters. I wish they **would eat** / **will eat** / **eat** more vegetables.

④ The phone keeps ringing. I wish someone **answered** / **would answer** / **answers** it.

⑤ I'm sick of this bad weather. I wish it **would stop** / **will stop** / **stopped** raining.

⑥ Joshua can't play any instruments. He wishes he **plays** / **would play** / **could play** the piano.

76.5 USE "I WISH" AND THE PAST SIMPLE TO TALK ABOUT THE SITUATIONS BELOW, SPEAKING OUT LOUD

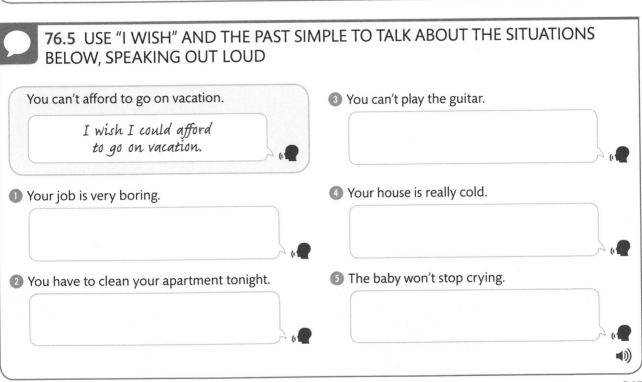

You can't afford to go on vacation.

> *I wish I could afford to go on vacation.*

① Your job is very boring.

② You have to clean your apartment tonight.

③ You can't play the guitar.

④ Your house is really cold.

⑤ The baby won't stop crying.

76.6 KEY LANGUAGE "WISH" AND PAST PERFECT

Use "wish" with the past perfect to express regrets about the past. This construction is used when it is too late for the wish to come true.

I've failed my exams. I wish I had studied harder.

past perfect

76.7 FURTHER EXAMPLES "WISH" AND PAST PERFECT

He's very tired. He wishes he had gone to bed early last night.

My car's useless! I wish I hadn't bought such an old one.

76.8 HOW TO FORM "WISH" AND PAST PERFECT

SUBJECT	"WISH"	SUBJECT	PAST PERFECT	
I	wish	I	had studied	harder.

Use "wish" or "wishes" depending on the subject.

The past perfect expresses regrets about the past.

76.9 LISTEN TO THE AUDIO AND MARK WHETHER THE PICTURES SHOW REGRETS ABOUT THE PRESENT OR THE PAST

A THE PRESENT   B THE PAST

76.10 READ THE LETTER AND COMPLETE THE SENTENCES

Ella wishes _she had stayed at school_ when she was 16.

1 Ella wishes _____ at college.

2 Ella wishes _____ about the great painters.

3 Ella wishes _____ still play the piano.

4 Ella wishes _____ when she was only 20.

5 Ella wishes _____ so far away from her family.

Dear Olive,

I want to tell you about my childhood. I had to drop out of school when I was 16, and I was so disappointed because I really wanted to study art at college. I'd love to know more about the great painters. I also had to give up learning the piano. It's a real shame that I can't play it now.

I married your grandfather when I was 20. Looking back, I think we were too young to get married, but we've been very happy together. It's just sad that we live so far away from our family.

Lots of love, Grandma Ella

---

76 ✓ CHECKLIST

⚙ "Wish" with past tenses ☐   **Aa** Life events ☐   🧩 Talking about regrets ☐

🔄 REVIEW THE ENGLISH YOU HAVE LEARNED IN UNITS 73–76

NEW LANGUAGE	SAMPLE SENTENCE	☑	UNIT
REPORTED QUESTIONS	**Adam** asked me where his keys were. **He** asked me when the concert started.	☐	73.1, 73.6
COLLOCATIONS WITH "RAISE"	**She gave a speech that** raised eyebrows.	☐	73.10
"IF" AND "WHETHER"	**My boss asked** if **I was meeting my targets.** **He asked** whether **I wanted tea or coffee.**	☐	74.1, 74.7
INDIRECT QUESTIONS	Do you know where **the station** is? Could you tell me if it is **raining outside?**	☐	75.1, 75.6
"WISH" AND PAST SIMPLE	I wish I earned **more money.**	☐	76.1
"WISH" AND PAST PERFECT	I wish I had studied **harder.**	☐	76.6

Answers

1.4 🔊
1. She's not very well, **is she**?
2. You're not leaving now, **are you**?
3. Her dress is beautiful, **isn't it**?
4. John's hilarious, **isn't he**?
5. You're tired, **aren't you**?
6. The music is fantastic, **isn't it**?
7. The food isn't healthy, **is it**?

1.5 🔊
1. This venue isn't very nice, **is it**?
2. The weather is perfect, **isn't it**?
3. The food is delicious, **isn't it**?
4. You're dressed nicely, **aren't you**?
5. It's very cold, **isn't it**?

1.6
1. False 2. False 3. True 4. False
5. False 6. True

1.8 🔊
1. Great **to meet you**, too.
2. This **is Tess**.
3. I'm **delighted to meet** you, Mrs. MacIntosh.
4. Hi Cameron. **How are you doing**?
5. May **I introduce** Dev Chandera?

1.9 🔊
1. I'm very well, thank you.
2. I'm delighted to meet you, Ms. Tate.
3. I'm very pleased to meet you, too.
4. Great to meet you.
5. Pete! Great to see you, too!

1.10 🔊
1. Fine, thanks.
2. You, too!
3. I'm delighted to meet you, too.
4. Great to meet you.
5. I'm very well, thank you.
6. I'm very pleased to meet you.
7. Great to meet you.

3.3
Dear Yasmin,
We're having a nice time **on** the island of Tenerife, which is just **off** the African coast. Today we're **in** the city of Santa Cruz. Our hotel is **on** the coast, which is great because I love being **by** the sea.
Love, Hannah

3.4
1. South Africa 2. Off the coast
3. The northwest 4. South of Australia
5. Raj

3.5 🔊 Model Answers
1. I'm Brazilian.
2. I live in Santos.
3. It's in the southeast of Brazil.
4. Yes. I live on the east coast.
5. The capital city of Brazil is Brasília.

3.7 🔊
1. It's in front of the forest.
2. It's diagonally opposite the castle.
3. It's on the coast.
4. It's halfway between the two stores.

3.8
1. Durban is by the Indian Ocean.
2. Durban is on the east coast.
3. Durban is right next to beaches.
4. You can find museums in the city center.
5. Conferences are held at the new conference center.
6. Johannesburg is in the north of South Africa.
7. Cape Town is on the west coast.

4.4 🔊
1. thirty percent 2. zero point seven five / point seven five / nought point seven five
3. an eighth / one eighth 4. eighty-two percent 5. two point nine 6. three and a half

4.5
1. Kamau Mburu's time in the 400m was **43.4** seconds.
2. Kenya holds **50%** of the long-distance medals.
3. Su Chin jumped **2.05** meters in the high jump.
4. The Millennium Stadium was ¾ full.
5. Lorna Davis jumped **7.12** meters in the long jump.
6. John Wood won the 800m by **2.75** seconds.

4.6 🔊
1. Tony Elliot was just thirty centimeters behind Lee.
2. Jessie Cope ran the one hundred meters in nine point six seconds.
3. This was two thirds of a second faster than his last race.
4. Jenny O'Day ran the one hundred meters in ten point two seconds.
5. The US currently holds nineteen percent of the medals.

5.2
1. 17:14 2. 18:55 3. 7:30pm 4. 7:25pm
5. 8:45pm

5.4
1. 06/04/2006 2. 2nd June 2006
3. 09/08/2006 4. 6th May 2006

5.5 🔊 Model Answers
1. At 11:30 in the evening. 2. The 14th of August. 3. The 17th of August.
4. At 11:45 in the morning.

6.3
1. His middle name is William. 2. His house number is 2629. 3. He lives in Portland.
4. His zip code is 97205. 5. His cell phone number is (503) 225-3500.

6.4
1. Chiang Mai 2. Johannesburg
3. Milwaukee 4. Marseilles 5. Pasadena
6. Shanghai 7. Bilbao 8. Winnipeg
9. Vancouver 10. Edinburgh 11. Bangalore

6.5 🔊
1. C-H-I-C-A-G-O
2. M-A-D-A-G-A-S-C-A-R
3. B-E-I-J-I-N-G
4. A-R-K-A-N-S-A-S

6.7

1 029363332 2 1488 3 raj@cuvox.com
4 California 5 90499
6 11 Chatsworth Avenue 7 NW4 1HU

6.9 🔊

Note: Question 3 can be answered in a number of different ways in UK English. See teaching box 6.6.

1 Combe Avenue
2 M-I-N-E-H-E-A-D
3 Zero, seven, seven, zero, zero, nine, zero, zero, seven, four, two
4 Judy two one nine at webmail dot net

07

7.2 🔊

1 overtime 2 full-time 3 intern
4 shift 5 salary 6 part-time
7 annual vacation 8 wage

7.3

1 intern 2 overtime 3 salary
4 full-time 5 part-time

7.5 🔊

1 This is really hard **work**.
2 I can't come as I have to **work** late.
3 It is a difficult **job**, but I love it!
4 It took me years to find a **job** I love.
5 I have a lot of **work** to finish.
6 I really want to **work** in marketing.
7 I have a part-time **job**.
8 Do you get to **work** by car or train?
9 What time do you finish **work**?
10 Tyler wants to leave his **job**.

7.6

1 B 2 F 3 E 4 C 5 A 6 D

7.7 🔊

1 promoted 2 freelance 3 training
4 experience 5 resign 6 unemployed

08

8.2 🔊

1 We **always** spend Christmas together.
2 It **frequently** rains here.
3 She **very often** goes swimming.
4 They **regularly** go to the gym.
5 I **rarely** stay late at work.

8.4 🔊

1 We play tennis once a week.
2 They rarely get home early.
3 She eats breakfast every morning.
4 I hardly ever watch TV.
5 He nearly always cooks dinner.
6 We see the dentist twice a year.

8.5

Just a month to go until our debut gig! We **practice together three times a week**, so that we'll be ready. We **very often go jogging** before band practice. It **sometimes helps us** get ideas for tunes. Rehearsals are going well and we **rarely make mistakes** now. I **have guitar lessons twice a month**, which has really helped. After practice we **nearly always go out** together.

8.8 🔊

1 My house is sometimes too cold.
2 She almost never walks to work.
3 It is very often his fault.
4 They are rarely at home.
5 He usually has coffee with his lunch.
6 My boss is hardly ever angry with me.
7 We often invite friends to our house.

8.9 🔊

1 She **frequently** has lunch with her friends.
2 He **occasionally** meets clients in London.
3 It's **always** great to see you.
4 You're **almost never** late for work.
5 I **usually** read on train trips.

8.10

1 frequently 2 always 3 occasionally
4 rarely 5 hardly ever

8.11

1 False 2 True 3 False 4 True
5 Not given

09

9.4 🔊

1 I don't usually **eat out** in restaurants.
2 She **chills out** on weekends.
3 I **get up** at six in the morning.
4 They **check into** the hotel.
5 He **meets up** with his friends after work.

9.5 🔊

1 turn up 2 grow up 3 come up
4 wake up 5 stay up

9.7 🔊

1 Don't **run away** from me!
2 She **stayed in** last night.
3 We **met up** last Thursday.
4 She**'ll eat out / will eat out** next Saturday.
5 He **turned up** late to work yesterday.

9.8

1 False 2 True 3 True
4 Not given 5 False

9.9 🔊

1 It's nice to **eat out**.
2 I often **meet up** with friends.
3 He doesn't usually **turn up** late.
4 Are you going to **stay in** tonight?
5 She likes to **chill out** after work.

9.10 🔊

1 I usually **chill out** on weekends.
2 We **ate out** last night.
3 She's **working out** at the gym.
4 We're going to **meet up** tomorrow.
5 The bus has **turned up**.

11

11.3

OPINION: **attractive, handsome**
SIZE: **short, small**
SHAPE: **round, straight**
AGE: **young, middle-aged**
COLOR: **blue, blond**

11.4 🔊

1 She has large, round brown eyes.
2 He has beautiful, big blue eyes.
3 He is an attractive middle-aged man.
4 He has a long, curly red beard.
5 He is a short, thin young man.
6 She has attractive, wavy red hair.
7 She has small, round brown eyes.

11.5

1 Ruth 2 Mary 3 Ben 4 Jess 5 Fran

13

13.3 🔊

Note: All answers can also be written in contracted form.

1 They **are buying** pink cotton dresses.
2 I **am wearing** my new leather sandals.

3 He **is trying on** different suits.
4 She **is mending** her yellow polka-dot shirt.

13.4
1 True 2 False 3 False 4 False
5 True 6 False 7 True

13.5 🔊
1 Alice is buying the shirt with pretty buttons.
2 George has five pairs of jeans.
3 Shinko loves wearing high-heeled boots.
4 John prefers plain clothes.
5 Farah is shopping for a party dress.

13.6 🔊
1 He's wearing boots with **laces**.
2 She's wearing a **cardigan** with large **buttons**.
3 He's wearing a jacket with a **zip**.
4 She's wearing a **smart** dress with **high heels**.
5 She's wearing **leather** sandals.

13.7
1 Dominic 2 Dominic 3 Kim 4 Kim
5 Kim 6 Dominic 7 Dominic

15

15.3
1 B 2 C 3 A 4 E 5 D

15.5
Hi Bill,
The landlord is visiting tomorrow so please could you **sweep** the floor, **do** the dishes, **water** the plants, **load** the dishwasher, and **mow** the lawn?
Thanks,
Mandy

15.6 🔊
1 He's **doing** the laundry now.
2 She **waters** the plants every day.
3 Last night, they **walked** the dog.
4 On Sunday, he'll **mow** the lawn.
5 He **did** the dishes last night.

15.8 🔊
1 **I do** the laundry on Tuesdays, but this Tuesday we had visitors so **I'm doing** it today.
2 He normally **goes out** for dinner, but **he's cooking** at home tonight.

3 **I go** to the gym every day after work, but today **I'm having** coffee with a friend instead.
4 **I'm shopping** for clothes on my own today, but usually my friend **comes** with me.

15.9
1 Weekends 2 Now 3 No
4 Have lunch 5 Gita

15.10
1 She usually sings scales and practices her songs.
2 No, she doesn't usually wear elegant clothes at home.
3 She's doing an interview and photo shoot.
4 Kurt and Jack normally help Susie with the chores.
5 Susie doesn't like the noise of the lawn mower.

16

16.3 🔊
1 We'll pick the shopping up.
2 Those people are giving out leaflets.
3 Can you check the menu out?
4 They're filling in that hole in the road.
5 I'm taking those library books back.

16.4 🔊
1 cleaned up 2 try out 3 find out
4 show off 5 sold off

16.6 🔊
1 They're closing it down.
2 She's renting it out.
3 He's cleaning it up.
4 He's showing it off.
5 They tore it down.

16.9
1 B 2 E 3 D 4 A 5 C

16.10
1 Not given 2 True 3 False 4 Not given

16.11
1 unspoiled 2 bustling 3 crowded
4 unsafe 5 friendly 6 vibrant 7 dull

16.12

POSITIVE: **lively, bustling, unspoiled**
NEGATIVE: **polluted, crowded, unsafe**

17

17.3 🔊
1 The mountain is **much** taller than the hill.
2 The church is **slightly** taller than the café.
3 The window is **much** wider than the door.
4 The lighthouse is **a lot** taller than the statue.
5 The castle is **slightly** bigger than the hotel.

17.6 🔊
1 Spain is **much / a lot** warmer than Scotland.
2 Your house is **much more beautiful** than mine.
3 The Nile is **a bit** longer than the Amazon.
4 India is **one of the largest countries** in Asia.
5 The sea is **much / a lot** colder than the pool.
6 This is **easily the most expensive** hotel in town.
7 The tower is **easily / by far** the tallest building here.

17.8
1 Much longer than the Himalayas
2 It's one of the tallest waterfalls
3 The biggest volcano
4 The largest glacier
5 Much bigger than the Atlantic Ocean
6 Shorter than Australia's coastline
7 A lot bigger than Australia

17.9
1 False 2 True 3 False 4 False
5 False 6 True

18

18.3 🔊
1 This movie is really **boring**.
2 That meal was **disgusting**.
3 Your lecture was really **interesting**.
4 I'm really **thrilled** about our trip!
5 The movie was very **exciting**.
6 I always feel **relaxed** after a bath.
7 I'm really **shocked** by the news.

18.4 🔊
1 amazing 2 annoying 3 confused
4 depressing 5 amused

18.5 🔊
1 The yoga class was great. I feel very **relaxed**.
2 It's **annoying** that the show has been postponed.
3 The film was **amazing.** The special effects were very good.
4 I'm really tired, the marathon was **exhausting**.

18.6
1 False 2 True 3 True 4 False

18.10 🔊
1 I **absolutely** hate traveling to the city.
2 I **really** enjoy reading books.
3 I **quite** like swimming.
4 I **really** hate driving to work.

18.11
1 quite like 2 really like 3 absolutely hate 4 really hate

20
20.3 🔊
1 I did behave well as a child.
2 He did take his lunchbox to school.
3 I did enjoy the children's performance.
4 He did give his teacher a birthday card.
5 She did play quietly at Anita's house.

20.5 🔊
1 I **did** tell the babysitter to arrive early.
2 It's true! She **did** say "papa" today!
3 We **did** invite her to the birthday party.
4 I really **did** enjoy the cake Lucy baked.
5 Molly **did** ask if she could play with your toys.

20.6 🔊
1 She did play nicely with her toys.
2 We did ask them to be quiet.
3 I did love that trip to the beach.
4 He did leave the room in a mess.
5 Tommy did enjoy the magic show.
6 Raj really did love playing that game.
7 We did give Lucy's doll back to her.

20.8
1 True 2 False 3 True 4 False 5 True

20.10 🔊
1 He **fed** her in the high chair.
2 Archie **hid** from his sister.
3 Francis **bit** into the pie.

4 Carly **led** her brother to the park.
5 Soolin's toy **sank** in the pond.

20.11
1 Ran after him 2 A fence
3 Joan 4 The fire department

20
22.3 🔊
1 I'm **hopeful** that I will do well in my English exam.
2 You are **unlikely** to pass the exam if you don't work harder.
3 The old science laboratories have been **rebuilt**.
4 I think that worrying about exams is **unhealthy**.
5 I think this plan can be **reorganized** so it works better.
6 Thanks for all your help. You've been absolutely **wonderful**.
7 I had a very **restless** night, as I was worrying about my geography test.

22.4
1 False 2 False 3 True 4 Not given
5 True 6 False 7 True

24
24.2 🔊
1 They **have set off** on the Pilgrim's Way walk to Santiago de Compostela.
2 He **hasn't finished** cycling through Europe.
3 They **have gone** on a cruise to the Caribbean.
4 She **has visited** her family in Cuba every year since 2004.

24.4 🔊
1 Annie went to Kenya last winter.
2 Uma has visited Cuba every year since 2011.
3 I flew to Spain for a vacation last month.
4 Liam has gone on a bus tour of Ireland.
5 Nada studied Tai Chi in China last year.
6 Andrew has gone to Australia.
7 They have reached the North Pole!

24.5
1 No, she's done a road trip every year since 2012.
2 She learned to hang glide.
3 No, she hasn't bought it yet.
4 She's learned to scuba dive.
5 She caught a plane from Madrid.

24.6
1 Steve spent six months in Kenya.
2 His team helped the villagers dig a well.
3 Steve taught English at the local school.
4 He enjoyed learning about traditional dress, music and dance.
5 Steve was taught some simple bead-work designs.
6 Steve is visiting Ethiopia after Kenya.

24.7 🔊 Note: Answers can also be written using the full form without contractions.
1 Amir**'s walked** across the Great Divide in America. 2 They**'ve camped** every year since they were children. 3 We**'ve landed** in Buenos Aires. The vacation begins! 4 Marita**'s gone** to New Zealand on vacation. 5 Simon**'s cycled** from Paris to Berlin.

24.9 🔊
1 **I** ate so much pizza when I was in Italy.
2 **They** received our postcard yesterday.
3 Didn't you **arrive** here on Friday?
4 **Did** you go to Finland this year?
5 **She** found her passport on Tuesday.
6 Did he **write** this travel guide book?
7 **We** taught English in Peru last summer.
8 Did they **cycle** all the way to Spain?
9 **Did** you hike to the top of that mountain?

24.10 🔊
1 Did you visit Peru?
2 Did you finish your packing yet?
3 We had a wonderful time at the beach.
4 I love Spain. Did you go there before?
5 Are you hungry again? Didn't you just eat?
6 I just saw an amazing opera in Rome.

25
25.2 🔊
1 She hasn't been hiking **yet**.
2 I've **already** learned three languages.
3 They've **just** finished canoeing down the river.
4 He's **already** swum in a coral reef.
5 Our flight to Madrid is **still** delayed.

25.3

① Surf ② Take a boat trip ③ Hiking
④ Dolphin ⑤ Kangaroo

25.5

① Ian enjoys snorkeling in the Red Sea.
② Margarita Island is off the coast
of Venezuela.
③ Ian has just been hang gliding
in Interlaken.
④ Yes, Ian has already booked his next trip.
⑤ Ian hopes to see a "big cat" while on safari
in South Africa.
⑥ Ian went skydiving in Hawaii last year.
⑦ You should keep your eyes open
while skydiving.

25.6

① True ② True ③ False ④ True
⑤ False ⑥ True

26

26.4 ◀) Note: All answers can also be written in contracted form.

① They **have been playing** tennis this
morning. Now they're very tired.
② Tom **has been fishing** today. He's caught
lots of fish.
③ We **have been watching** TV all evening.
Now it's time to go to bed.
④ Irina **has been reading** a book in the
park. She says it's really good.
⑤ You **have been cleaning** the apartment
all day. It's time for a break.
⑥ I **have been listening** to music on the
way to work. It helps me relax.

26.5 ◀)

① tiling the kitchen ② making curtains
③ fixing the bathtub ④ putting up shelves
⑤ fitting a carpet

26.8 ◀)

1. I've been tiling the bathroom for
three weeks.
2. I've been tiling the bathroom for two days.
3. I've been painting the walls for three
weeks.
4. I've been painting the walls for two days.
5. She's been tiling the bathroom for
three weeks.
6. She's been tiling the bathroom for
two days.
7. She's been painting the walls for three
weeks.

8. She's been painting the walls for two days.
9. I've been tiling the bathroom since noon.
10. I've been tiling the bathroom since April.
11. I've been painting the walls since noon.
12. I've been painting the walls since April.
13. She's been tiling the bathroom since
noon.
14. She's been tiling the bathroom since
April.
15. She's been painting the walls since noon.
16. She's been painting the walls since April.

26.9 ◀)

① It's been raining **since** Saturday morning. I
hope the weather gets better soon!
② You've been gardening **since** 9 o'clock.
You should take a break.
③ I've been swimming **for** 20 minutes. I'm
quite tired, but I'll keep going.
④ She's been baking **since** 11 o'clock this
morning. We'll have lots of cookies to
eat later.
⑤ He's been tiling the wall **for** three hours. I
think it will be finished today

26.10

① since Monday ② for two days
③ since Saturday ④ for a month
⑤ since January

27

27.4 ◀)

① Has she been training for a race?
② Has he been learning the violin?
③ Have they been playing music together?
④ Has she been taking photos of the city?
⑤ Have you been painting her portrait?

27.5

① False ② True ③ True
④ False ⑤ True

27.6 ◀)

① Your fingers look sore. Have you been
practicing the guitar?
② It looks so neat outside. Has Paula been
mowing the lawn?
③ Your band sounds amazing! Have you
been playing together for long?
④ The house looks really fantastic. Have you
been redecorating it?
⑤ The kitchen's a terrible mess. Have the
twins been baking a cake?

27.9 ◀)

① How long has Melissa been writing her
novel?
② How long have they been painting the
house?
③ How long has Savannah been practicing
the recorder?
④ How long has Alejandro been learning
to drive?

27.10

① At school ② Drums ③ Seven years
④ Three years ⑤ Yes

27.11 ◀)

① How long **have** you **been playing** the
piano?
② How long **have** they **been performing** in
public?
③ How long **has** Ben **been taking** singing
lessons?
④ How long **has** she **been learning** English?

28

28.3 ◀)

① He's been washing the car for half an
hour. There's water all over our driveway.
② Her room looks so neat and tidy. She's put
all her clothes away now.
③ How long have you been walking in the
rain? You're both soaking wet.
④ You've been sunbathing for far too long.
Please go and sit in the shade now.
⑤ Riley has just broken a glass. There are
pieces on the floor, so be careful.
⑥ Has Oliver been eating chocolate all
morning? He won't want any lunch.
⑦ I've just finished a really good book. You
can borrow it now if you like.

28.4

① In progress ② Finished
③ In progress ④ Finished

28.6

① She says it is fascinating to see how
people have decorated their homes.
② She can easily imagine how places might
look.
③ She has been repairing hundreds of little
faults.
④ Sadiq has almost completely rebuilt his
apartment.
⑤ Stella has been calculating how much she
has spent on repairs.

6 She understands how important it is to look after your **property**.

7 She has been painting her living room and tiling the kitchen.

28.7 🔊

Note: All answers can also be written in contracted form.

1 I **have eaten** all the cake. There are only crumbs left.

2 Luca **has** just **caught** a big fish.

3 We **have been walking** in the rain. We're all soaking wet!

4 She **has been cooking** for an hour. The food smells delicious!

28.8

Hi Jacob,
I hear **you've passed** your driving test, and that Uncle George has **bought** you a car. Congratulations! I supposed you've **been driving** around ever since. I'm so jealous. I've always **wanted** to learn to drive. You should visit me soon! I've **been working** too hard recently and I've **realized** that I need a break. Love Alice

29

29.3 🔊

1 It's **impossible** to solve a problem when you don't have all the facts.

2 Her room is so **untidy** that you can't even see the floor.

3 He's very **disorganized**, so I always have to check to confirm our meetings.

4 It's **illegal** to download that movie without paying for it.

29.4 🔊

1 immature   impossible   impatient

2 disorder   disagree   disrespectful

3 unacceptable   unable   unusual

4 irresponsible   irresistible   irrational

29.5 🔊

1 You have made a very **immature** decision.

2 Speeding on the freeway is **irresponsible**.

3 Playing tricks on your colleagues is **unacceptable**.

4 I completely **disagree** with you.

5 Your remarks were very **disrespectful**.

29.7

1 False   **2** True   **3** Not given
4 True   **5** False

29.8 🔊

1 **Unfortunately** there's been an **accident** 2 miles south of us.

2 It's **impossible** to move, and we could be **delayed** for another 2 hours.

3 The highway was already jammed because of the **road works**.

4 The traffic is so bad that the highway is like an **overcrowded** parking lot.

5 People are getting very **impatient**, which I suppose isn't **unusual**.

30

30.3 🔊

1 **The waiter** is just getting us a menu.

2 I enjoy shopping for **shoes**.

3 Jo's back at school now **the vacation** is over.

4 Has he paid you **the money** that he owes you?

5 I like watching **exciting movies**.

30.4

1 New students must do their own cleaning now.

2 Students' parents won't cook meals for them.

3 Students should write down the recipes of dishes that they love.

4 Money can be another problem for students.

5 The student adviser can help students budget.

6 The social life is very exciting at college.

7 The final exams are so important because they could affect a student's future career.

30.6 🔊

1. Do you have your laptop?
2. Have you got your laptop?
3. Do you have your wallet?
4. Have you got your wallet?
5. Do you have your passport?
6. Have you got your passport?

30.7

1 B   **2** D   **3** F   **4** A   **5** E   **6** C

30.8

A   **D**   **G**   **H**   **J**

30.9

1 True   **2** False   **3** False   **4** Not given
5 True   **6** False

32

32.4 🔊

1 I hope the children exhaust **themselves** and sleep tonight.

2 Look at baby Callum trying to feed **himself**. Isn't he smart?

3 I can't find my keys. I hope we haven't locked **ourselves** out.

4 Oh dear. I cut **myself** while I was peeling potatoes.

5 You should take a break. You'll wear **yourself** out.

6 The dishwasher will turn **itself** off when it's finished.

32.5

1 herself   **2** yourself
3 themselves   **4** ourselves

32.6 🔊

1 The baby can pull **herself** up.

2 I'm teaching **them** to swim.

3 You really enjoyed **yourself** tonight.

4 Have you introduced **yourselves** to him?

5 Ouch! That wasp stung **me**.

6 The cake's all gone. I've eaten **it**.

7 The car's dirty. Please wash **it**.

8 Don't tease the cat. You'll scare **her**.

9 The oven will turn **itself** off now.

32.8 🔊

Two pounds of dark chocolate
Two ounces of butter
One tablespoon of instant coffee granules
A quarter of a teaspoon of baking powder
Three fluid ounces of buttermilk
One pint of cream
Two cups of flour
A quarter of a pound of sugar
Three eggs

32.10 🔊

1 I'm so tired this morning. I need a **strong** cup of coffee to wake me up.

2 I'd like some **chilled** fruit juice, please. It's a hot day, and I need a refreshing drink.

3 That curry was too **spicy**. I'll follow a different recipe next time I make it.

4 Remember to buy lots of **fresh** fruit. We're making a fruit salad tonight.

5 The chocolate mousse was too **sweet** for me, but I think the guests will love it.

32.11

1 False   **2** True   **3** False   **4** True
5 False   **6** True

33.3 🔊
1 They use the microwave for **heating** food.
2 We use our juicer to **make** fruit juice.
3 She uses her phone for **texting** her friends.
4 They use this corkscrew to **open** bottles of wine.
5 He uses his laptop for **watching** movies.

33.5 🔊
1 I turned on the heating to warm up the house.
2 You use a refrigerator to keep food fresh.
3 He uses this remote control for turning on the TV.
4 We turned on our sound system to listen to music.
5 I sometimes use my smartphone for taking photos.

33.6
1 True 2 False 3 True
4 False 5 True

33.8 🔊
1 He sometimes **turns** the TV **up** too loud.
2 My laptop has a low battery. I need to **plug** it **in**.
3 You shouldn't **print** emails **out**. It wastes paper.
4 Remember to **shut** the computer **down** after work.

33.9 🔊
1 It's for **charging** your phone.
2 You use it to **dry** your hair.
3 It's for **listening** to music.
4 It's for **opening** cans.
5 You use it to **take** photos.

33.10
1 Turn on the TV 2 The blue button
3 To listen to music 4 The DVD player
5 The TV

35.3 🔊
1 I don't feel like **running** in the park with you now. I'm too tired.
2 I can't stand **working out** in the gym. It's so boring.

3 He likes **watching** basketball, and he plays it on weekends, too.
4 She absolutely loves **diving**, and she's very good at it.

35.4
1 Going faster every time she runs
2 She always makes time for training
3 Whatever the weather is like
4 In an office
5 She wants to train

35.5 🔊
1 Cope with 2 Put off
3 Look forward to 4 Miss
5 Can't stand

35.8 🔊
1 You enjoy **dancing**, don't you?
2 Do you want **to see** the match tonight?
3 He can't stand **watching** soccer.
4 You promised **to play** golf with me.
5 I don't mind **training** with you.

35.9 🔊
1. I enjoy playing tennis.
2. I arranged to play tennis.
3. I miss playing tennis.
4. I decided to play tennis.
5. I enjoy playing basketball.
6. I arranged to play basketball.
7. I miss playing basketball.
8. I decided to play basketball.
9. I enjoy playing squash.
10. I arranged to play squash.
11. I miss playing squash.
12. I decided to play squash.

35.10
1 True 2 False 3 False
4 True 5 False

36.3 🔊
1 **Thomas's catching** the train at 6pm, so he can get to the restaurant by 7pm.
2 Nahid and Eric **are going** to Sally's birthday party next Friday.
3 We **are meeting** Nicole and Yuri at the beach this Saturday.
4 **Sonia's working out** at the gym tomorrow because she's training for a marathon.
5 **Lottie's singing** in a concert this weekend at the city's concert hall.

36.4 🔊
1 **Susan's** playing chess with Kai on Tuesday at 8pm to prepare for the championships.
2 **Vicky's visiting** her grandmother in Finland next week. She's really looking forward to the trip.
3 **Michelle's** going to Roy's surprise birthday party on Friday night. It should be a fun night!
4 **Andrew's having** lunch with Rosi and Maggie on Thursday at 1:30pm at their local café.

36.5
1 Tuesday at noon 2 Jude 3 Thursday
4 Omar's brother 5 Ricky's café

36.7 🔊
1 Take a look 2 Take care of
3 Take a trip 4 Take a picture
5 Take a bow 6 Take time out

36.8
1 B 2 A 3 E 4 C 5 D

36.9 🔊
1 Violet is **taking care of** Stella's dog this weekend.
2 The children are **taking a trip** to the ice rink tomorrow.
3 I'm **taking time off** from work this afternoon because I don't feel well.
5 Connor is planning to **take a look** at the competition entries today.
6 I'm **taking time out** from my schedule to meet friends this weekend.

37.2 🔊
Note: Answers can also use the long form.
1 **Jingjing's going to walk** to work every day, unless it's raining or snowing.
2 **Tilly's going to join** the new pilates class starting at the gym near her house.
3 **Sam's going to learn** judo this year with his friends Shankar and Belinda.
4 **Kadija's going to start** jogging to work and back home from next week.

37.3
1 False 2 True 3 False 4 True

37.5 🔊
1 Carly's going to get better at tennis because she's starting lessons next week.

② Collette's going to win the race as she's in the lead by a long way.
③ Abdel's going to be healthier because he's on a low-sugar diet.
④ Rob's going to be stronger because he's started weight lifting.

37.6
① B **②** A **③** D **④** C **⑤** E

37.9 🔊
① Gary's **certainly** going to run the next marathon to raise money for charity.
② Helena's **definitely** going to improve her fitness level by going to the gym.
③ Ahmed **thinks he's** going to try kick boxing after his judo classes have finished.
④ James **doubts he's** going to stop eating fatty food, but he'll try to eat more fruit.

37.10 🔊
① I think I'm **going** to go jogging, but I might read a book instead.
② They're probably going to **finish** the marathon, but it's a long way to run.
③ She's not going to **play** tennis now, is she? It's raining!
④ You're **definitely going to** look great after working out so much.
⑤ It's too late to **go** out. I think I'm going to go to bed.

37.11 🔊
1. Lucy's probably going to be picked for the baseball team.
2. Lucy's definitely going to be picked for the baseball team.
3. Lucy thinks she's going to be picked for the baseball team.
4. Lucy doubts she's going to be picked for the baseball team.
5. Lucy's probably going to eat healthier food.
6. Lucy's definitely going to eat healthier food.
7. Lucy thinks she's going to eat healthier food.
8. Lucy doubts she's going to eat healthier food.

39

39.2 🔊
① Have a rest, and **I'll** cook a warm stew for us to eat tonight.
② **I'll** take the dog for a walk after it stops raining, I promise!
③ Amelia and Jill **are going to** buy dresses tomorow to wear to Tom's birthday party.

④ **You'll** be cold playing football today. It was snowing this morning!

39.3
① Decision **②** Prediction
③ Promise **④** Offer

39.4
① Carla will make soup and a beef casserole.
② Carla will pick Kevin up after his guitar lesson.
③ Yes, Stacey will go to Carla's to eat this evening.
④ Carla will pick Stacey up at 5:30pm after her favorite TV show.

39.7 🔊
① I'll **definitely** be at the airport by 7pm so I have enough time to catch the plane.
② You'll **certainly** look handsome in your new suit. It's a really nice color and cut.
③ I **doubt** you'll win the race because you've not been training very hard.
④ I **hope** I'll pass my geography exam tomorrow. I'm very nervous about it.

39.8
① True **②** False **③** True **④** True **⑤** False

39.9
① certainly **②** know
③ probably **④** hope

40

40.3 🔊
① I can't find my purse. I **might have left** it on the metro.
② Don't disturb him. He **might be sleeping**.
③ I **might go** out later if it stops raining.
④ I don't know where we are. We **might have taken** the wrong turn.
⑤ I **might be wrong**, but I think the answer is A.
⑥ When we're in Venice, I **might ask** him to marry me.
⑦ Show everyone her photograph. Someone **might have seen** her.
⑧ Cameron **might be** stuck in traffic. He should be here by now.

40.4
① might be **②** might have got **③** might fall
④ might have lost **⑤** might have been
⑥ might go **⑦** might take

40.6 🔊
① Georgia **might've** walked around the lake.
② They **might not've** reached the valley yet.
③ We **might've** left the supplies at the tent.
④ Horace **might not've** climbed the mountain.

40.7 🔊
① Dad might've bought me a new compass.
② They might not've crossed the river yet.
③ Jonah might've pitched the tent by now.
④ I can't find my map. I might not've packed it.
⑤ Don might've hiked over the mountain already.

40.8
① False **②** True **③** False **④** True

42

42.4 🔊
① You mustn't eat too much sugar.
② Everyone must wear a helmet.
③ You must not run while your leg is healing.
④ I don't have to take vitamins.
⑤ He has to lose weight.

42.5
① No, she doesn't have to see the surgeon again.
② She must eat before taking her medication.
③ No, she mustn't go back to work for 14 days.
④ No, she doesn't have to do any special exercises.
⑤ She has to call Dr. Turner immediately.

43

43.3 🔊
① Carla felt so sick last weekend that she **couldn't** go back to work until Wednesday.
② Bastian **might not** be able to come over as he's allergic to most pets, and I have three dogs.
③ Your wrist **can't** be broken as you're able to lean on it without much pain.
④ I recommend you go to the hospital. Your stomach pain **could** be appendicitis.

43.4
❶ Not given ❷ False ❸ True ❹ False
❺ True

43.5 ◀))
❶ It **can't** be broken.
❷ He **might not** go to work today.
❸ You **might** have a cold.
❹ I **couldn't** get out of bed!

43.6 ◀))
❶ I can't find my doctor's letter, so it might be lost.
❷ My hay fever could be getting worse because my eyes are itchy and sore.
❸ Marco's arm could be infected because it's red and swollen.
❹ I think my dad has a cold because he can't stop sneezing.
❺ Jackie had a skiing accident and might need an operation on her knee.
❻ If you don't feel any better soon, you might need to go to the doctor.
❼ That can't be Ailsa skating over there because her ankle's broken.
❽ We're stuck in traffic so we might be late for the appointment.

43.7 ◀))
❶ Majeed **can't** be feeling very sick. He's playing soccer tonight.
❷ I'm starting to get a lot of headaches. My sister said I **might** need glasses.
❸ My shoulders ache. It **could** be because I work all day at a desk.
❹ Your stomach ache **might not** be serious. It might just be something you ate.
❺ The reason you've got a pain in your foot **could** be because your shoes are too small.

43.8
❶ Tonsillitis ❷ Backache
❸ Because he hadn't eaten much
❹ His tonsils aren't swollen
❺ Go back to work

44

44.3 ◀))
❶ I'm afraid I don't know.
❷ Yes, when I've finished my coffee.
❸ Yes, that sounds perfect Ms. Eliker.
❹ I'm sorry, but I have meetings all day.

44.4 ◀))
❶ **I'm sorry**, but I've sold out.
❷ **Of course.** Enjoy it.
❸ No, you **can't**. I need it.
❹ Yes, you **may**.
❺ **I'm afraid** he's busy.
❻ Yes, **please**.

45

45.2 ◀))
❶ I don't **get along with** my sister.
❷ We've **run out of** milk.
❸ I won't **put up with** his loud music.
❹ Are you **looking forward to** the concert?
❺ He **looks down on** everyone.
❻ You **came up with** a great plan.

45.3
❶ True ❷ False ❸ True ❹ False ❺ True

45.5 ◀))
❶ Turn the radio down. I can't **put up with** that noise.
❷ Our department works well because we **get along with** each other.
❸ Dad **came up with** a great idea for Madison's birthday.
❹ Don't **look down on** your staff. They're just as important as you!

45.6 ◀))
❶ Alexa is **looking forward to** her vacation.
❷ Trevor **gets along with** Pam.
❸ Michelle always **comes up with** good ideas.
❹ Gavin **looks down on** us.
❺ I can't **put up with** his behavior any longer!

46

46.2 ◀))
❶ We haven't met, have we?
❷ You walked the dog, didn't you?
❸ She cycles to work, doesn't she?
❹ This book is amazing, isn't it?

46.3 ◀))
❶ Ben has gone to China, **hasn't he**?
❷ That was a good concert, **wasn't it**?
❸ You're not upset, **are you**?
❹ She doesn't like cheese, **does she**?

❺ You went to work today, **didn't you**?
❻ They haven't eaten yet, **have they**?
❼ Luis speaks English, **doesn't he**?
❽ Zoe is working late, **isn't she**?

46.4 ◀))
Note: All answers can also use a negative statement and a positive question tag.
❶ Renata worked in sales, didn't she?
❷ You were listening to me, weren't you?
❸ He knows the answer, doesn't he?
❹ The phone's ringing, isn't it?
❺ Will was at the party, wasn't he?
❻ That was a good book, wasn't it?
❼ Liam has done the dishes, hasn't he?

46.7 ◀))
❶ You wouldn't go alone, **would you**?
❷ He shouldn't eat so much, **should he**?
❸ We would love to go to your party, **wouldn't we**?
❹ You could help me, **couldn't you**?
❺ She could stay with you, **couldn't she**?
❻ We should save some money, **shouldn't we**?
❼ You wouldn't tell her, **would you**?
❽ She shouldn't work so hard, **should she**?
❾ You would like a snack, **wouldn't you**?

46.8
❶ False ❷ True ❸ True ❹ False

46.9 ◀))
❶ He would enjoy this book, **wouldn't he**?
❷ He wouldn't let me try, **would he**?
❸ They should buy the house, **shouldn't they**?
❹ It isn't too cold here, **is it**?
❺ She did tell you, **didn't she**?

48

48.4 ◀))
❶ If you throw a ball up, it falls down again.
❷ If you mix blue and yellow paint, you make green paint.
❸ When you freeze water, it turns to ice.
❹ If you put sugar in water, it dissolves.
❺ If you set fire to paper, it burns.
❻ If you don't water plants, they die.
❼ When you boil water, you produce steam.

48.5
❶ False ❷ Not given ❸ True
❹ False ❺ Not given

48.6
1 B 2 F 3 E 4 A 5 D 6 C

48.7 ◄))
1 If you **drop** a ball, it **bounces**.
2 If you **mix** red and blue, you **get** purple.
3 When you **put** salt in water, it **dissolves**.
4 If you **boil** water, it **becomes** steam.
5 When you **strike** a match, it **burns**.

48.9 ◄))
1 If you mix red and yellow, you get orange.
2 You produce steam when you boil water.
3 Wood doesn't burn if there is no oxygen.
4 When the sun sets, it gets dark.

48.10 ◄))
1 Ice melts when you heat it.
2 If you kick a ball, it moves.
3 Plants grow if you water them.
4 When the sun rises, it gets light.

49

49.4 ◄))
1 The liquid **is heated** for several minutes until it starts to boil.
2 The plant cells **are observed** using a state-of-the-art microscope.
3 Static electricity **is generated** when you rub a balloon against your hair.
4 The chemicals **are added** slowly to the water to start the reaction.
5 The temperature of the salt water **is taken** using a thermometer.
6 Two beakers **are filled** almost to the top with a mixture of oil and water.

49.5 ◄)) Note: Negative answers can also be written in contracted form.
1 The liquid is not removed from the heat.
2 The liquid is left to cool in a glass jar.
3 Crystals are observed forming in the jar.
4 The size of the crystals is measured.
5 Oil is not poured into the water.
6 The water is boiled to make steam.
7 Salt is dissolved in the water.
8 The oil and water are not mixed together.
9 The results of the experiment are recorded.

49.6 ◄))
1 The water **is removed** from the heat once it has boiled.
2 The chemicals **are poured** into a test tube to start the reaction.

3 When the substance **is mixed** with water, it changes color.
4 The reaction between the chemicals and the water **is observed**.
5 The mixture **is cooled** for approximately one hour until it sets.
6 The water **is stirred** for five minutes until all the salt dissolves.
7 The two substances **are placed** in a test tube together.
8 The results **are estimated** before the experiment takes place.

49.7
1 A 2 B 3 A 4 A 5 B

49.8
1 Newspapers
2 Results of their research
3 They design an experiment
4 Analyzing the results
5 Review the results

50

50.4 ◄)) Note: All answers can also be written in contracted form.
1 If I **eat** healthily, I **will lose** weight.
2 We **will dance** if the band **plays** good music.
3 If we **go** shopping, I **will buy** you something nice.
4 I **will build** the cupboard if you **read** the instructions.

50.5
1 True 2 True 3 False 4 False 5 True

50.6 ◄))
1 If he looks for it, he'll find it.
2 I'll cook dinner if she's hungry.
3 Will they fix it if it's broken?
4 If I see him, I'll tell him to call you.

50.9 ◄))
1 You'll damage the floor unless you cover it.
2 Unless you go to bed, you'll be tired tomorrow.
3 He'll get annoyed unless you speak politely.
4 The cat won't run away unless she's frightened.
5 She'll arrive on time unless her train is delayed.
6 Unless you attach it securely, it will break.
7 We'll do the job unless it's too difficult.

50.10
1 The screws might be too tight.
2 You can finish the process by hand.
3 You must check that all the pieces are in the right place.
4 Check that the doors fit before you tighten the hinges.
5 They will stick and look uneven.

51

51.4 ◄))
1 Open the window if you need some fresh air.
2 If you get too cold, turn on the heating.
3 If you see Malik, tell him I tried to call him.
4 Remember to lock the door if you go out this afternoon.

51.5 ◄))
1 **If you** don't like your job, look for a new one.
2 If you like those **shoes, buy** them.
3 Help yourself if you **want** some more food.
4 If you need to talk to someone, call me.
5 Take a break **if** you feel stressed.

51.6
1 True 2 False 3 False
4 False 5 True

51.7
1 Ask your colleagues to help you
2 Plan your day carefully
3 Read a book
4 Get rid of some of them
5 Buy a smaller one

51.8 ◄))
1 possessions 2 your surroundings
3 to downsize 4 to delegate tasks
5 constantly

51.9 ◄))
Note: All answers can also start with the imperative.
1 If you're stressed at work, go for a walk during your lunch break.
2 If you're always checking your emails, turn off your smartphone.
3 If you like that car, buy it.
4 If you're lonely, visit me this weekend.

52.4 🔊
Note: All answers can also be written in contracted form.
1 We **will sing** "Happy Birthday" as soon as she **comes** in.
2 When I **finish** fixing the car, I **will drive** you to the station.
3 As soon as she **gets** to the beach, she **will go** swimming.
4 I **will call** him when I **arrive** at the hotel.
5 As soon as I **find** my keys, I **will lock** the door.

52.5
1 False 2 True 3 False
4 Not given 5 False

52.7
1 C 2 D 3 B 4 E 5 A

52.8 🔊
1 When I've saved enough money, I'll buy a car.
2 When you've had a rest, you'll feel better.
3 We'll meet up as soon as I finish work.
4 I'll go out when the weather's better.
5 When the paint dries, they'll put up pictures.

52.9 🔊
1 They'll buy new furniture when they've finished redecorating.
2 When we've built a fire, we'll cook some food.
3 We'll go and sit outside when the sun comes out.
4 She'll look for a job as soon as she finishes college.
5 When we go to New York, we'll visit the Statue of Liberty.
6 As soon as I get paid, I'll buy that expensive dress.

53.4 🔊
Note: All answers can also be written in contracted form.
1 If my job **was** better paid, I **would buy** my own apartment.
2 We **would employ** many more staff if we **had** more office space.

3 If they **raised** enough money, they **would start** their own business.
4 We **would increase** our profits if we **advertised** on national TV.

53.5
1 True 2 False 3 False
4 True 5 True 6 False

53.6 🔊
1 If he sold his apartment, he'd buy a villa in Spain.
2 If she invested her money wisely, she'd be very rich.
3 If he took his work seriously, he'd be offered a promotion.
4 If we modernized the factory, we'd increase productivity.

53.8 🔊
1 Do your research 2 Do your paperwork
3 Do your job 4 Make a mistake
5 Make an appointment
6 Make an exception
7 Make suggestions

53.9 🔊
1 I think I've **made** the right decision.
2 Levi can help you **do** the paperwork.
3 I enjoy **doing** business with new clients.
4 If you worked harder, you'd **do** a better job.
5 Selma always **makes** great suggestions.
6 I need to **make** an important call.
7 Have you **done** your research properly?
8 Can you **make** an exception for me?
9 I've **made** an appointment to see Mr. Cox.

53.10 🔊
1 He **makes** mistakes all the time.
2 It was great to **do** business with you.
3 Can I **make** a suggestion?
4 I'm afraid we can't **make** an exception.
5 You've **done** a great job this week.
6 It's important to **do** your research.
7 I hate **doing** the paperwork.

55.3 🔊
1 If I were you, I'd apply for a promotion.
2 I'd invest some of my money if I were you.
3 If I were you, I wouldn't buy that car.
4 I'd take a long vacation if I were you.
5 If I were you, I'd start my own company.

55.4 🔊
1 I'd call a doctor if I were you.
2 If I were you, I'd study harder.
3 I wouldn't go out if I were you.
4 If I were you, I'd join a choir.
5 If I were you, I wouldn't tell him.

55.5 🔊
1 If I were you, I'd change the tire.
2 If I were you, I'd take the promotion.
3 If I were you, I wouldn't go outside.
4 If I were you, I'd go to the party.

55.6
1 Happy 2 Talking to large groups of people 3 Won prizes 4 Call in sick

55.8 🔊
1 Have you tried discussing the idea with your colleagues and seeing what they think of it?
2 How about meeting our new clients for dinner at a nice restaurant?
3 What about planning a marketing strategy with your team before you present it to your boss?
4 Have you thought of investing in property and buying some apartments to rent out?

55.9 🔊
1. How about talking to your colleagues?
2. What about talking to your colleagues?
3. Have you tried talking to your colleagues?
4. Have you thought of talking to your colleagues?
5. How about talking to your boss?
6. What about talking to your boss?
7. Have you tried talking to your boss?
8. Have you thought of talking to your boss?
9. How about hiring extra staff?
10. What about hiring extra staff?
11. Have you tried hiring extra staff?
12. Have you thought of hiring extra staff?

55.10
1 True 2 Not given 3 False
4 True 5 False 6 Not given

56

56.2 🔊
1 If I got a big bonus at work, I would give half the money to charity.
2 If Karin got a job in Italy, she would have to sell her house and move.
3 If they don't hire more staff, their employees will be overworked.
4 If I get an interview, I will buy a new suit.

56.3 🔊
1 If I were you, I'd stop eating so much junk food and join a gym.
2 If he was a better listener, he'd realize that I'm not happy in my job.
3 If I feel lonely or bored, I'll video call my brother in New Zealand.
4 If we were very rich, we'd go on a round-the-world trip.
5 If they have time to spare before the train leaves, they'll go shopping.

56.4
1 False 2 True 3 True
4 False 5 False

56.6 🔊
1 Give some help 2 Held discussions
3 Hold off on 4 Set a precedent
5 Set limits

56.7 🔊
1 I've never really given **much thought to** working overseas, but I wouldn't mind.
2 I'm sorry, I can't give you extra time off. It would set **a precedent**.
3 Let's think about what we want to achieve this year and set **some goals**.
4 I think we should hold **a meeting** with our supplier to talk about prices.
5 Janice, please could you give **some help to** Hakim? It's his first day today.
6 Let's hold **off on** making big decisions until we have all the facts.
7 We've **set** limits on the number of new people we can hire this year.
8 This year, we need to give **priority** to boosting sales in all our markets.

56.8 🔊
1. He gave priority to the biggest client.
2. They gave priority to the biggest client.
3. He set limits on the new budget.
4. They set limits on the new budget.
5. He held a meeting last Wednesday.
6. They held a meeting last Wednesday.

57

57.3 🔊
1 I want to find a job that is near my home.
2 They work with people who are interesting and unusual.
3 It is important to eat good food that is fresh and healthy.
4 You should get daily exercise that raises your heart rate.
5 Stella has married a man who is generous and friendly.

57.4
1 True 2 True 3 False 4 True
5 False

57.5 🔊
1 cheerful 2 caring 3 confident
4 efficient 5 reliable 6 outgoing
7 fun-loving 8 good sense of humor

57.6
1 C 2 D 3 E 4 B 5 A 6 F

57.7 🔊
1 It's important to have a good boss who is confident and reliable.
2 It's good to have interesting work that is challenging.
3 We are looking for a new secretary who is calm and efficient.
4 I'm working on a project that is new and exciting.

58

58.4 🔊
1 My friend, **who's really funny**, is a comic actor and also a director.
2 Our neighbors, **who are very friendly people**, invited us for a barbecue lunch.
3 Our cat, **who's black and white**, has been missing for three days.
4 The action film, **which has won lots of awards**, is on at our local movie theater.

58.5 🔊
1 My brother, who is very talented, is an opera singer.
2 My house, which is very old, is located in a quiet street in Ringwood.
3 The teacher, who is very outgoing, loves soccer.
4 This fashion magazine, which is very expensive, is extremely boring.
5 My dog, who is very energetic, likes to go running in the park.

58.6
1 B 2 A 3 E 4 F 5 C 6 D

58.7 🔊
1. My mother, who is kind, is a doctor.
2. My mother, who is kind, is beautiful.
3. My mother, who is kind, is wonderful.
4. My mother, who is cheerful, is a doctor.
5. My mother, who is cheerful, is beautiful.
6. My mother, who is cheerful, is wonderful.
7. Amanda, who is kind, is a doctor.
8. Amanda, who is kind, is beautiful.
9. Amanda, who is kind, is wonderful.
10. Amanda, who is cheerful, is a doctor.
11. Amanda, who is cheerful, is beautiful.
12. Amanda, who is cheerful, is wonderful.
13. His house, which is near the city, is beautiful.
14. His house, which is near the city, is wonderful.
15. The beach, which is near the city, is beautiful.
16. The beach, which is near the city, is wonderful.

59

59.4 🔊
1 They **were singing** in the choir last night. It was a very good concert.
2 You **were talking** on the phone at lunchtime today. I didn't want to interrupt your call.
3 Sorry I didn't answer the phone. I **was eating** my dinner when you called.
4 She **was driving** down my road earlier today. I waved, but she didn't see me.
5 He **was doing** his homework when his friend arrived. So he still has lots to do.
6 Ethan **was picking** apples outside this morning. They look absolutely delicious!

59.5
1 C 2 F 3 A 4 B 5 G 6 D
7 E 8 H

59.6

At 10:30, Mr. Black **was gardening** when he saw a man get into a car. The man **was wearing** jeans and a black t-shirt. At 10:37, Mrs. Gomez **was walking** back from the stores. Ten minutes later, she saw the same man in a car. He **was driving** very fast. Mr. Chandra **was washing** his car at 10:30. At 10:38, he also saw the same man. The suspect **was walking** up and down the road, and **looking** at all the houses. Mr. Chandra saw him again at 10:45. This time, he **was leaving** the house next door, and **carrying** a big, heavy-looking bag.

59.7 ◀))

1. You **were vacuuming** the living room.
2. She **was working** outside.
3. They **were washing** the car.
4. We **were walking** home.
5. He **was looking** at houses.

59.8 ◀))

1. make an effort　2. make sense of
3. have a plan　4. take time
5. have a discussion　6. have the chance
7. take a view　8. take advantage
9. make a discovery　10. make progress

59.9 ◀))

1. This project will **take time**, but I must get it right.
2. Thanks for helping me **make sense of** my homework.
3. It's good to **have a discussion** to solve problems.
4. Let's meet up next week if we **have the chance**.
5. You must not let people **take advantage** of you.

61

61.2

1. They were shopping and chatting.
2. They were skateboarding along the sidewalk.
3. She was watching the alleyway between two stores.
4. They were waiting for someone to appear.
5. He was carrying a large bag.

61.3 ◀))

1. Colorful　2. Peaceful　3. Picturesque
4. Rural　5. Open　6. Magical

61.4

1. False　2. False　3. Not given　4. True

61.5

Today we were **walking** in the country. The mountains were looking **magnificent** against the blue sky. There were **colorful** flowers everywhere, and the children were **picking** bunches of them to take home. We stopped for coffee in a **picturesque** little village and we sat in the sunshine while the children played in the playground. It was a really **magical** day.

62

62.3

1. Past simple　2. Past simple
3. Past continuous　4. Past continuous

62.4 ◀))

1. When I **entered** the forest, a monkey **was swinging** through the trees.
2. The next day, Chloe **was reading** a book when Russell **walked** into the café.
3. Kelly and Dean **were surfing** when Dean **fell** off his board.
4. We **saw** some baby turtles while we **were jogging** along the beach.

62.5

1. False　2. False　3. True
4. Not given　5. False

62.6 ◀))

1. bustling　2. bizarre　3. ancient
4. intricate　5. intact　6. exotic　7. touristy

62.7 ◀))

1. She **was surfing** when she **fell** off her board.
2. I **was reading** the menu when the waiter **arrived**.
3. It **started** to rain while they **were dancing** outside.
4. I **was diving** when I **saw** a shark.
5. He **found** a starfish while he **was lying** in the sun.

62.8 ◀))

1. Felipe **was taking** a long bath when someone **knocked** on his door.
2. Karen **met** her old friend Madeleine while she **was traveling** in Australia.
3. Christopher **was cooking** dinner when his party guests **arrived** early.

4. We **learned** to speak Thai while we **were staying** in Bangkok.
5. I **was writing** a report when my boss **asked** me to come to her office.

62.9

Hi Emily,
Paul and I are having a great time in Marrakesh. Today we were **walking** in the old part of the city when we saw an old man. Actually, he looked **ancient**! He was **carrying** a large, heavy basket, so I offered to carry it for him. The old man was **smiling** at me but I **felt** nervous, so I gave the basket to Paul. Suddenly we arrived in a **bustling** square with market stalls and people everywhere. I looked for the old man. He was sitting with the basket open. He was **playing** the flute and out of the basket came two enormous snakes. I'd never seen anything like it in my life: it was **bizarre**. They were moving to the music he was playing. It was **fascinating** to watch, but I didn't offer to carry his basket again.
Love Hania

63

63.4 ◀))

1. Several buildings **were destroyed** after a powerful earthquake.
2. The factory **was demolished** because it was unsafe.
3. Many homes **were flooded** after the river burst its banks.
4. The explorer **was rescued** after she got lost in the mountains.
5. The beaches **were covered** in oil this morning.
6. My train **was delayed** because a tree fell onto the line.

63.5 ◀))

1. The factory was destroyed.
2. The oil was spilled into the ocean.
3. The lake was polluted.
4. The animals were hurt.
5. Many people's homes were damaged.

63.7

1. Lake Bander was turned red.
2. The chemicals were carried into the lake by last night's rain.
3. Thousands of fish were killed.
4. Local farmers' crops were destroyed.

⑤ The Bander area was declared a disaster area.
⑥ John Hawkins' business was ruined.

63.8
① True **②** False **③** False **④** Not given
⑤ True **⑥** Not given **⑦** True

64

64.4 🔊
① A tree had fallen on the road so I couldn't drive to work.
② I offered Logan some pasta but he had already eaten lunch.
③ I hadn't seen Emma for years but I recognized her immediately.
④ We felt absolutely exhausted after we had run the marathon.
⑤ She couldn't catch the train because she had left her ticket at home.

64.5 🔊
Note: All answers can also be written in contracted form.
① Although we **had met** only a few times, I **knew** we would get along.
② She **arrived** late at work because she **had missed** the bus.
③ The sun **had risen** and it **was** time to start work in the fields.
④ Joe **was** delighted because his parents **had bought** the perfect birthday present.
⑤ Henry **had cooked** dinner when Sally **got back** from work.

64.6
① Per wanted his daughter to be an engineer.
② Eva worked hard at school.
③ Per allowed Eva to study art.
④ Eva discovered her passion for ceramics at art school.
⑤ Eva hadn't worked with clay.
⑥ Eva realized that she loved ceramics once she had made her first pots.
⑦ Eva had sold her works to every major museum of art.

64.7
① False **②** True **③** Not given
④ False **⑤** True **⑥** Not given

64.8 🔊 Note: All answers can also be written in contracted form.
① She **had read** a review of the book before she **bought** it.
② After he **had finished** watching the movie, he **went** to bed.
③ I **asked** Katy for a ride to work because I **had missed** my train.
④ He **had studied** very hard before he **took** his exams.
⑤ Andy only **resigned** once he **had found** a new job.
⑥ They **had discussed** all the options before they **made** a decision.

65

65.2 🔊
① Last summer was the first time we had **ever** gone camping. It rained every day!
② I had **never** eaten risotto until I went to Milan. Now I cook it for myself at home.
③ They had **never** been overseas before they went to Paris. They thought the flight was exciting!
④ We traveled overnight from Bangkok. It was the first time I had **ever** slept on a train.
⑤ I heard you went to Madrid last month. Was that the first time you had **ever** been there?
⑥ James had **never** been bungee jumping until he tried it in New Zealand last year.

65.4 🔊
① I'm speechless. It's the first time I **have** ever seen a lion in the wild.
② Sam and Ellie don't know what to expect. They **have** never been on a cruise.
③ Marisha **had** never been skiing before she went to the Alps. Now she loves it!
④ When I went to Berlin, it was the first time I **had** ever been on vacation alone.
⑤ We **had** never flown for longer than four hours until we went to Cuba.
⑥ The children can't wait. It will be the first time they **have** ever traveled by train.

65.5 🔊
① deserted **②** ancient **③** derelict
④ charming **⑤** high-rise buildings
⑥ comfortable **⑦** popular **⑧** open-plan

65.6 🔊
① We rented an apartment in Egypt. The rooms were very **spacious** and airy; we loved it.

② This bed is so **comfortable**. I don't think I've ever had such a good night's sleep.
③ The famous Parthenon in Athens is such an amazing **ancient** temple.
④ Newtown is a very trendy place and is **popular** with young people. Lots of students live there.
⑤ When we got to the beach, it was **deserted**. We were the only people there.
⑥ There are a lot of **high-rise** buildings in Chicago. The tallest is 110 storeys high.
⑦ This is such a **charming** village. The houses are attractive and the main square is very pleasant.

65.7
① True **②** True **③** Not given **④** False
⑤ True **⑥** False

65.8 🔊
① Ben is so excited. He has **never been on a plane before.**
② Last week was **the first time Don had ever been to Iceland.**
③ I **had never eaten miso soup before I went to Japan.**
④ It's **the first time Jen has ever traveled alone.**
⑤ Last year was **the first time I had ever gone sailing**.

67

67.2 🔊
Note: All answers can also be written in contracted form.
① Before I **started** the trip, I **had planned** which route I would take.
② Lauren **was crossing** the road when she **saw** the robber inside the bank.
③ I **had** always **wanted** to visit Brazil, and I finally **went** there last year.
④ Jason **was reading** a book in the park when a wasp **stung** him.

67.3 🔊
① Inside her bedroom, Bella **was studying** hard for an exam.
② She **was feeling** nervous. The storm outside made it difficult to concentrate.
③ Raindrops **were sliding** gently down the glass. She watched them in silence.
④ She **breathed deeply** as she watched the raindrops. She began to relax.
⑤ Fifteen minutes later, the storm ended. Bella **had never felt** so calm.

67.4
1 False **2** False **3** True **4** False
5 True **6** True

68

68.2 🔊
1 He broke his leg while skiing and **consequently** had to take three weeks off work.
2 The first guests arrived at 7pm and the others came **shortly after** that.
3 I was about to call her to tell her the good news **at the very moment** she called me.
4 **As soon as** it had stopped raining, we went for a walk.
5 They had got married **not long before** they moved to Wellington in New Zealand.

68.3 🔊
1 Our first child was born shortly after we had bought the house.
2 They worked very well together, and subsequently they went into business together.
3 We went to the beach as soon as the weather had improved.
4 They had moved to London not long before she started her new job.

68.4
1 The trainee lost his balance and fell backward.
2 The upper jaw snapped down on his foot.
3 He was put in the ambulance to be taken to hospital.
4 His colleagues started clapping and laughing.

68.5
1 False **2** True **3** Not given **4** True
5 False

69

69.4 🔊
Note: All answers can also omit "that."
1 She said that she usually cycled to work.
2 He said that he was a chef in a busy restaurant.
3 She said that she was married, and that she had two children.

4 He said that his wife was an English teacher.
5 She said that she wanted to have her own restaurant.

69.5
1 There's room for a studio
2 Turn it into an office
3 Her exhibition had gone well
4 Her news was exciting

69.8
Note: All answers can also omit "that."
1 Maria said that she had visited five different schools.
2 Maria said that it was a great opportunity to watch talented teachers.
3 Maria said that the teachers worked miracles every day.
4 Maria said that she was planning to give a workshop.
5 Maria said that she hoped the teachers would enjoy her workshop.

69.9 🔊
Note: All answers can also omit "that" and be written in contracted form.
1 He said that he was looking for a new job.
2 You said that you really enjoyed / had really enjoyed the party.
3 They said that they had just been swimming.
4 She said that she could play the piano quite well.
5 You said that you brought / had brought some presents for the children.
6 He said that he was going to write a novel.

70

70.4 🔊
1 They **told** us they had a new car.
2 He **told** me he had gotten married.
3 You **said** he was at a birthday party.
4 She **said** she wanted some ice cream.
5 We **told** her the train was delayed.
6 You **said** you would cook tonight.
7 I **told** him I had to work late.

70.5 🔊
1. He said he was going on safari.
2. He said she was going on safari.
3. He told me he was going on safari.
4. He told me she was going on safari.
5. He told us he was going on safari.
6. He told us she was going on safari.

7. She said he was going on safari.
8. She said she was going on safari.
9. She told me he was going on safari.
10. She told me she was going on safari.
11. She told us he was going on safari.
12. She told us she was going on safari.

70.6
1 False **2** Not given **3** True
4 False **5** True

70.8 🔊
1 She told me the weather was nice there.
2 They said they'd have a party that weekend.
3 She said she'd seen me the week before.
4 You told her you were starting a new job that day.

70.9 🔊
Note: All answers can also include "that" after "said," or after the object pronoun following "told." Answers with the past perfect can also use the long form.
1 She told me **she bought / she'd bought a new car the day before**.
2 They said Regina **was leaving the company that day**.
3 She said **there were lots of restaurants there**.
4 He told us **he was going to a party that weekend**.
5 They told me **they sold / they'd sold their apartment the week before**.

70.10

70.11 🔊
COLLOCATIONS WITH "SAY":
say anything, say yes, say something, say nothing, say no, say so
COLLOCATIONS WITH "TELL":
tell lies, tell a story, tell the difference, tell someone, tell a "white lie", tell the truth

71

71.4 🔊
1 My manager **argued** that we had to cut our costs because profits were down.
2 He said he liked his new job, and **added** that his colleagues were friendly.
3 I **admitted** that I hadn't worked hard enough.

282

4 She **claimed** that she never watched TV, but I don't believe her.

71.5 🔊
1 She agreed that his CV **was** excellent.
2 He **admitted** that crime was a big problem.
3 We added **that** the plan would save them money.
4 She **argued that** their office was too small.
5 He claimed **that** he could fly a helicopter.

71.6
1 B **2** E **3** D **4** A **5** C

71.7
1 False **2** True **3** True **4** Not given

71.8 🔊
1 She **admitted that she needed** to work out more often.
2 He **explained that he had to** leave work early for a doctor's appointment.
3 She **added that they had** a dog and two cats.
4 He **agreed that Mr. Brady was** a very important client.

71.10 🔊
1 They said the party was fun, and **added** that the band was fantastic.
2 She **suggested** that they go to the beach this weekend.
3 She **explained** that she had to go home because she was feeling sick.
4 She **claimed** that she was once a famous singer.
5 You said her dress was beautiful. I **agreed** that it was very pretty.
6 He **suggested** that I start cycling to work because cars cause pollution.

72

72.4 🔊
1 The police ordered **them to** leave the room.
2 You asked me **to** wash the dishes after dinner.
3 They **reminded** him to lock the door.
4 My boss asked me **to** go to the meeting.
5 We **encouraged him** to join our choir.
6 Didn't I remind **you to** call your parents?
7 The judge ordered her **to** pay a fine.

72.5
1 C **2** B **3** E **4** G **5** D **6** F **7** A

72.8
1 True **2** False **3** False **4** True
5 Not given **6** False **7** True

72.9 🔊
1 She **ordered** them **to get out** of her office.
2 He **encouraged** her **to go** on vacation.
3 The director **persuaded** me **not to leave** the company.
4 They **advised** us **to invest** in that property.

73

73.4 🔊
Note: All answers can also include an object pronoun, such as "me", after "asked."
1 He asked where the meeting would take place.
2 He asked what he could do to prepare for the meeting.
3 He asked what we were going to discuss.
4 He asked why Amy wouldn't be at the meeting.
5 He asked what time the meeting would finish.

73.5 🔊
1 You asked me what I was cooking for dinner.
2 She asked him when he was going out.
3 We asked when the stores would open.
4 I asked who was going to Laura's party.

73.8 🔊
1 They asked her why **she wanted** the job.
2 We asked them what day the conference **started**.
3 I asked what kind of music **he liked**.
4 She asked us when the train **arrived / had arrived**.
5 You asked me what company **I worked** for.

73.9
1 False **2** True **3** True **4** False

73.10 🔊
1 raise fears **2** raise hands
3 raise money **4** raise the roof
5 raise the question **6** raise awareness

74

74.4 🔊
Note: You can replace "if" with "whether" in all answers.
1 She asked us **if we had been waiting long**.
2 He asked **if they had the figures ready**.
3 She asked us **if we went / had gone to the meeting**.
4 I asked him **if he was working late again**.
5 He asked you **if you wanted a glass of water**.
6 She asked me **if I would take the early flight**.
7 She asked us **if Eva met / had met us at the airport**.

74.5
1 Not given **2** False **3** True
4 Not given **5** True **6** Not given
7 False

74.6 🔊
1. She asked me if I knew what time it was.
2. She asked us if we knew what time it was.
3. She asked me whether I knew what time it was.
4. She asked us whether we knew what time it was.
5. She asked me if I could speak English.
6. She asked us if we could speak English.
7. She asked me whether I could speak English.
8. She asked us whether we could speak English.

74.9 🔊
1 He asked me if I played badminton or tennis.
2 I asked if I should take flowers or wine to the party.
3 He asked whether they'd rather be rich or famous.
4 We asked if they'd like ice cream or cake.
5 She asked if I wanted to cook inside or outside.

74.10
1 He invested in a company without asking enough questions.
2 Money started to pour into his bank account.
3 He was accused of money laundering.
4 He says there's no point in complaining about the situation.

283

5 He dreams about being with his family again.

6 He hopes they will wait for him and forgive him.

74.11 🔊

1 It's great to know I can count **on** you.

2 I want to provide **for** my children.

3 He always dreamed **of** being famous.

4 The water poured **into** the bucket.

5 They were accused **of** stealing a car.

6 We can't fight **against** their decision.

7 I'll be ready soon. Please wait **for** me.

75

75.4 🔊

1 Could you tell me what time the meeting starts?

2 Do you know when the next bus leaves?

3 Do you know how long the movie is?

4 Could you tell me why you can't come to work?

75.5

1 B **2** D **3** F **4** C **5** A **6** G
7 H **8** E

75.8 🔊

1 Could you tell me when the play starts?

2 Do you know whether they arrived?

3 Could you tell me who that lady is?

4 Do you know if Shona was at the party?

5 Could you tell me what your address is?

6 Do you know where Brandon went?

7 Could you tell me if this table is reserved?

75.9 🔊

1 Do you know **why the train** is delayed?

2 Could you tell me **how much this jacket** costs?

3 Could you tell me **how long you've been** working in sales?

4 Do you know **when the last bus** leaves?

5 Could you tell me **what time dinner** is served?

75.10 🔊

Note: You can replace "Do you know" with "Could you tell me," and "if" with "whether." You can also use contractions.

1 Do you know if our plane is going to be delayed?

2 Do you know what time your clients will arrive?

3 Do you know if someone will meet us at the station?

4 Do you know how far it is to the hotel?

5 Do you know if the trains stop running after midnight?

76

76.4 🔊

1 I wish I **had** a cat, but my apartment's too small for any pets.

2 Bella wishes she **lived** on the coast. She loves the beach.

3 My children are such fussy eaters. I wish they **would eat** more vegetables.

4 The phone keeps ringing. I wish someone **would answer** it.

5 I'm sick of this bad weather. I wish it **would stop** raining.

6 Joshua can't play any instruments. He wishes he **could play** the piano.

76.5 🔊

1 I wish my job wasn't so boring.

2 I wish I didn't have to clean my apartment tonight.

3 I wish I could play the guitar.

4 I wish my house wasn't so cold.

5 I wish the baby would stop crying.

76.9

1 B **2** A **3** A **4** B

76.10

1 Ella wishes **she had studied art** at college.

2 Ella wishes **she knew more** about the great painters.

3 Ella wishes **she could** still play the piano.

4 Ella wishes **she hadn't gotten / got married** when she was only 20.

5 Ella wishes **she didn't live so far away** from her family.

Index

All entries are indexed by unit number.
Main entries are highlighted in **bold**.

Acknowledgments

The publisher would like to thank:
Jo Kent, Trish Burrow, and Emma Watkins
for additional text; Thomas Booth, Helen
Fanthorpe, Helen Leech, Carrie Lewis, and Vicky
Richards for editorial assistance; Stephen Bere,
Sarah Hilder, Amy Child, and Fiona Macdonald
for additional design work; Peter Chrisp for fact
checking; Penny Hands, Amanda Learmonth,
and Carrie Lewis for proofreading; Elizabeth
Wise for indexing; Tatiana Boyko, Rory Farrell,
Clare Joyce, and Viola Wang for additional
illustrations; Liz Hammond for editing audio

scripts and managing audio recordings; Hannah
Bowen and Scarlett O'Hara for compiling audio
scripts; Heather Hughes, Tommy Callan, Tom
Morse, Gillian Reid, and Sonia Charbonnier
for creative technical support. Sachin Gupta,
Shipra Jain, Vishal Bhatia, Tushar Kansal, Kartik
Gera, Anita Yadav, Jaileen Kaur, Manish Upreti,
Nehal Verma, Nisha Shaw, and Ankita Yadav for
technical assistance.

**DK would like to thank the following for their
kind permission to use their photographs:**
39 **Alamy**: MBI (bottom right). 218 **Fotolia**:
Malbert (bottom center). 234 **Dreamstime.com**:
Carol Buchanan / Cbpix (center right).
255 **Fotolia**: Sergey Khachatryan (center right).
259 **Dorling Kindersley, Courtesy of American
Police Hall of Fame and Museum**: Steven
Greaves (top center).
All other images are copyright DK.
For more information, please visit
www.dkimages.com.

DISCARD